Jouissance

SUNY series, Insinuations: Philosophy, Psychoanalysis, Literature

Charles Shepherdson, editor

Jouissance

A LACANIAN CONCEPT

NÉSTOR A. BRAUNSTEIN

TRANSLATED BY

SILVIA ROSMAN

Translation of El goce: un concepto lacaniano (Siglo XXI Editores, 2006)

Published by State University of New York Press, Albany

For information, contact State University of New York Press, Albany, NY
www.sunypress.edu

Library of Congress Cataloging-in-Publication Data

Names: Braunstein, Néstor A., author.
Title: Jouissance : a Lacanian concept / Néstor A. Braunstein ; Silvia Rosman,
    translator.
Other titles: Goce. English
Description: Albany : State University of New York Press, [2020] | Series:
    SUNY series, insinuations: philosophy, psychoanalysis, literature |
    Includes bibliographical references and index.
Identifiers: LCCN 2019032143 | ISBN 9781438479033 (hardcover : alk. paper) |
    ISBN 9781438479040 (pbk. : alk. paper) | ISBN 9781438479057 (ebook)
Subjects: LCSH: Joy—Psychological aspects. | Psychoanalysis. | Psychoanalysis and
    philosophy. | Lacan, Jacques, 1901–1981.
Classification: LCC BF175.5.J69 B7313 2020 | DDC 150.19/5—dc23
LC record available at https://lccn.loc.gov/2019032143

10 9 8 7 6 5 4 3 2 1

Contents

Translator's Note   ix

Abbreviations   xi

Introduction: Translating *Jouissance*   1
   Silvia Rosman

Part I. Theory

Chapter 1. *Jouissance*: From Lacan to Freud   13
   In the Beginning . . .   13
   Jouissance in Freud   20
   A Return to Freudian Beginnings   32
   Beyond Pleasure   39

Chapter 2. Jouissology, Logic of *Jouissance*   49
   Between *Jouissance* and Language   49
   Jouissance Is (Not) the Satisfaction of a Drive   52
   Speech: Diaphragm of *Jouissance*   59
   The Thing and Object @   67
   Castration and the Name-of-the-Father   73
   The Barriers to *Jouissance*   85
   The "Causation of the Subject" or Beyond *Angst*   92

Chapter 3. *Jouissance* and Sexuality   101
   Equivocations of Sexuality   101
   Jouissance of Being, Phallic *Jouissance* and *Jouissance* of
      the Other   109
   Castration as Cause   119
   The Three *Jouissance*(s) and the Mobius Strip   126
   Freud (Lacan) or Foucault   131

Chapter 4. Deciphering *Jouissance*   145
   Jouissance Is Ciphered   145
   Letter 52   150
   Psychoanalysis in Proust's Way: *Jouissance* and Time   160

Part II. The Clinic

Chapter 5. *Jouissance* and Hysteria   175
   The Psychoanalyst and the Hysteric   175
   In Function of *Jouissance*   182
   Hysteria and *Savoir*   190

Chapter 6. Perversion, Disavowal of *Jouissance*   197
   The "Positive" Side of Neurosis?   197
   The Perverse Phantasm: *Savoirjouir*   202
   Perversion and Feminine *Jouissance*   210

Chapter 7. @-diction of *Jouissance*   217
   Psychosis Is Not Chosen   217
   Psychosis and Discourse   222
   Drug @-diction   227

Chapter 8. *Jouissance* and Ethics in Psychoanalytic Experience   235
   A *Langagière* Practice   235
   Pro(*pulsions*) and Their Vicissitudes   238
   The Duty of Desire   243
   The Act and Guilt   247
   The Immunological Analogy   252

Letter to His Father   257
Give Up on Desire?   261
For Three *Jouissance*(s), Three Superegos   266
On Love in Psychoanalysis   269

Notes   275

Index   285

Translator's Note

Where English translations are available, works are cited according to the page number of the translation. Where no English translation is listed in Abbreviations, the translations are my own. Untranslatable Lacanian concepts and neologisms are explained fully in the body of the text.

I would like to thank Néstor Braunstein for his enthusiasm, suggestions and clarifications throughout the translation process, as well as for generously providing me with his later writings, conferences and other texts. I would also like to thank Adriana Passini and Gabriel Riera for their invaluable comments on the manuscript. Much appreciation goes to the anonymous reviewer and to Charles Shepherdson, the series editor, who supported this project from the start and was key to its fruition.

Abbreviations

AE   J. Lacan, *Autres écrits* (Paris: Seuil, 2001).

BGE   F. Nietzsche, *Beyond Good and Evil. Prelude to a Philosophy of the Future*. Edited by R. Hortsmann and J. Norman (Cambridge: Cambridge University Press, 2002).

E1   J. Lacan, *Écrits* (Paris: Seuil, 1966).

E   J. Lacan, *Écrits*. Translated by B. Fink (New York: Norton, 2006).

F   *The Complete Letters of Sigmund Freud to Wilhelm Fleiss 1887-1904*. Edited by J. Masson (Cambridge, MA: Harvard University Press, 1995).

FL   N.A. Braunstein, *Freudiano y lacaniano* (Buenos Aires: Manantial, 1994).

HS1   M. Foucault, *The History of Sexuality*, Vol. 1: An Introduction. Translated by R. Hurley (New York: Pantheon, 1978).

HS2   M. Foucault, *The History of Sexuality*, Vol. 2: The Use of Pleasure. Translated by R. Hurley (New York: Pantheon, 1985).

HS3   M. Foucault, *The History of Sexuality*, Vol. 3: The Care of the Self. Translated by R. Hurley (New York: Pantheon, 1986).

CF   N.A. Braunstein, *Por el camino de Freud* (Mexico: Sigo XXI, 2001).

CR1   J. Lacan, "Comptes rendus d'enseignement 1964-1968." *Ornicar?* 29 (Avril–Juin 1984).

EP   D. Eribon, *Échapper à la psychanalyse* (Paris: Léo Scheer, 2005).

LI   N.A. Braunstein, *El lenguaje y el inconsciente freudiano* (Mexico: Siglo XXI, 1982).

M   J. Lacan, "La Place de la Psychanalyse Dans la Medicine" (Conférence et débat du Collège de Médecine à La Salpetrière: Cahiers du Collège de Médecine 1966).

N   J. Lacan, "The Neurotic's Individual Myth." Translated by M. Evans. *The Psychoanalytic Quarterly*, 48(3): 2017: 405–425.

NP   E. Porge, *Les noms-du-Père chez Jacques Lacan. Ponctuations et problématique* (Ramonville: Érès, 1997).

PC   J. Derrida, *The Postcard: From Socrates to Freud and Beyond*. Translated by A. Bass (Chicago: University of Chicago, 1987).

PP   G.W.F. Hegel, *The Philosophical Propaedeutic*. Edited by M. George and A. Vincent (Oxford: Basil Blackwell, 1986).

QT   T. Dean, "Lacan and Queer Theory." *The Cambridge Companion to Lacan*. Edited by J.M. Rabaté (Cambridge: Cambridge University Press, 2003).

R   *La re-flexión de los conceptos de Freud en la obra de Lacan*. Edited by N. Braunstein (Mexico: Siglo XXI, 1984).

RTP   M. Proust, *Remembrance of Things Past*, Vol. 3. Translated by A. Mayor (New York: Vintage, 1982).

S I   J. Lacan, The Seminar of Jacques Lacan, Book I: *Freud's Papers on Technique, 1953–54*. Edited by J-A. Miller. Translated by J. Forrester (New York: Norton, 1988).

S II   J. Lacan, The Seminar of Jacques Lacan, Book II: *The Ego in Freud's Theory and in the Technique of Psychoanalysis, 1954–55*. Edited by J-A. Miller. Translated by S. Tomaselli (New York: Norton, 1988).

S V   J. Lacan, The Seminar of Jacques Lacan, Book V: *Formations of the Unconscious*. Edited by J-A. Miller. Translated by R. Grigg (UK: Polity Press, 2017).

S VII   J. Lacan, The Seminar of Jacques Lacan, Book VII: *The Ethics of Psychoanalysis, 1959–60*. Edited by J-A. Miller. Translated by D. Porter (New York: Norton, 1992).

S VIII J. Lacan, Le Seminaire, livre VIII: *Le transfert*. Texte établi par J-A. Miller (Paris: Seuil, 1991).

S X   J. Lacan, The Seminar of Jacques Lacan, Book X: *Anxiety*. Edited by J-A. Miller. Translated by A. Price (UK: Polity Press, 2014).

S XI   J. Lacan, The Seminar of Jacques Lacan, Book XI: *The Four Fundamental Concepts of Psychoanalysis*. Edited by J-A. Miller. Translated by A. Sheridan (New York: Norton, 1978).

S XIV   J. Lacan, Le Seminaire, Livre XIV: *La logique du fantasme* (Paris: Association Lacanienne International, 2004).

S XVI   J. Lacan, Le Seminaire, Livre XVI. *D'un autre a l'autre*. Texte établi par J-A. Miller (Paris: Seuil, 2006).

S XVIII J. Lacan, Le Seminaire, Livre XVIII. *D'un discours qui ne serait pas du semblant*. Texte établi par J-A. Miller (Paris: Seuil, 2006).

S XX   J. Lacan, The Seminar of Jacques Lacan, Book XX: *On Feminine Sexuality. The Limits of Love and Knowledge. Encore* 1972–1973. Edited by J-A. Miller. Translated by B. Fink (New York: Norton, 1999).

S XXI   J. Lacan, Le Seminaire, Livre XXI: *Les non-dupes errant*. Unpublished.

S XXII   J. Lacan, Le Seminaire, Livre XXII: *R.S.I.* Unpublished.

S XXIII J. Lacan, The Seminar of Jacques Lacan. Book XXIII: *The Sinthome*. Edited by J-A. Miller. Translated by A. Price (Cambridge: Polity Press, 2016).

SE   S. Freud, *The Standard Edition of the Complete Psychological Works*. Edited and translated by James Strachey (London: The Hogarth Press, 1953). Volume numbers are given parenthetically.

SF   D. Halperin, *San Foucault* (Córdoba, Argentina: *Cuadernos del Litoral* [Edelp], 2000).

SM   J. Allouch, *Le sexe du maître* (Paris: Exils, 2001).

T   J. Lacan, "Television." Translated by D. Hollier, R. Krauss, and A. Michelson. In *Television: A Challenge to the Psychoanalytic Establishment*. Edited by Joan Copjec (New York: Norton, 1990).

TG   S. Ferenczi, *Thallasa. A Theory of Genitality*. Translated by H. Bunker (New York: The Psychoanalytic Quarterly, 1938).

TR   J. Lacan, "La troisiéme." *La Cause Freudienne* 73(3): 2011: 11–33.

Y   J. Lacan, "Yale University, Kanzer Seminar." Translated by J. Stone. *Scilicet* 6/7 (1975): 7–31.

Introduction

Translating *Jouissance*

Silvia Rosman

To translate the spirit is so enormous and phantasmal an intent that
it may well be innocuous; to translate the letter, a requirement so
extravagant that there is no risk of its ever being attempted.[1]

—Jorge Luis Borges

Beginning in the 1950s the International Psychoanalytical Association
(IPA) waged a battle against Lacan's teachings and analytic technique that
resulted in his removal from the sanctioned list of teaching analysts. At a
1963 conference in London, Lacan sought to make his case one last time.
It is the year of Seminar X on *angst* (anxiety) when he presents the outlines
of what he later called "his only invention": object *a*, a nonphenomeno-
logical, nonspecular "object" that points to the subject's cause of desire.
Speaking in English, Lacan struggles to translate the word *reste*, the crucial
remainder for reading object *a* in relation to desire. He asks his audience
for help with the translation and the response is silence. The decision had
been made.[2] The next day, Lacan interrupts his planned seminar on the
names-of-the-Father after one class and announces he will not continue it
in the future. Lacan thus leaves a hole in the trajectory of his teaching. His
"excommunication," as he called the decision made by the IPA, becomes
the introduction to Seminar XI: *The Four Fundamental Concepts of Psychoanalysis*. The scene of the London conference marks the impossibility

1

of translation, or translation as impossibility. It is the confrontation with a void: what cannot be said and therefore remains a secret, although not without leaving a rest. Object *a* points to what is lost in the sphere of signification, but also to what founds the desiring subject. Perhaps for this reason that same year Lacan establishes the *École Freudienne de Paris*.[3]

More than a decade later, during his 1975 Seminar RSI, a trip to London again confirms the difficult relations between English and psychoanalysis:

> It is completely true that not even the English, no, I would not say English psychoanalysts since I only know one who is English, and he is probably Scottish! *Lalangue*, I think it is the English *lalangue* that is the obstacle. This is not very promising, because the English language is on its way to becoming universal; I want to say it is marking the way. I can't say that people don't get angry when they translate me. Those who read me, from time to time, must be aware of the difficulties, to translate me into English *lalangue*. In any case, one must recognize things as they are: I am not, I am not the first to note English *lalangue*'s resistance to the unconscious.[4] (S XXII, February 11, 1975)

These are certainly ominous words to introduce the English translation of Néstor Braunstein's *Jouissance: A Lacanian Concept*. Perhaps with Lacan's pronouncement in mind, Braunstein also issues a warning in chapter 1 regarding the translation of *jouissance*: "Never enjoyment!"[5] Innovative rest, impossible sense, effects of signification: a translation exposes the disparities and gaps across and between languages in a never-ending movement of mis-naming and missing the mark: the unconscious at work. It is an interpretation and transference of sense that, as in psychoanalysis, is not exempt of desire and *jouissance*. Like the analytic act, a translation confronts the impossible, as Lacan shows in 1963, a hole that language cannot represent and can only be said between the lines. Lack is structural, loss is inevitable: for the *parlêtre*,[6] the destiny of the analyst (expelled as object *a* at the end of analysis) and, as Lacan muses regarding (the) English, even for the survival of psychoanalysis.

Néstor Braunstein is an Argentine-born psychoanalyst, doctor, psychiatrist, professor, and scholar who works and teaches in Latin America (Mexico) and Europe. He is a leading figure in the field of psychoanalysis with a long list of publications that also include studies in philosophy, literature, and art. He is the first to have published a comprehensive study of *jouissance*, originally appearing in Spanish in 1990 as *Goce*. This edition was followed by a French translation in 1994, with a revised and expanded French version in 2005. A new revised Spanish translation was published in 2006, which is the edition on which we base the present volume. A Portuguese translation came soon after (2007).[7] Although more than twenty years have passed since the original publication, Braunstein presents a concept that in some sectors of contemporary psychoanalysis has become a sort of transcendental signifier. Its discursive presence in other disciplines, such as philosophy, political theory, art history, gender studies, and literary studies is also noteworthy. Yet while most studies of *jouissance* in English frame it within broader political and cultural discussions, Braunstein's book focuses on Freudian and Lacanian theory and the psychoanalytic clinic, making it an indispensable reference point in any serious consideration of this concept.[8]

Whether inscribed within the context of capitalist or neoliberal logic and its imperative to "enjoy," as a critique of all forms of hetero-norma-tivity, a liberating force in a positive reading of biopolitics, the point of inflection in the ethics of psychoanalysis, or articulated in the knot of the sinthome, *jouissance* is either the diagnosis, response, or solution for a wide range of contemporary discontents. Why does *jouissance* occupy such a central place in contemporary psychoanalytic discourse? What is *jouissance* the name for?

The rise in neuroscience, mental health systems, behavioral therapies, and pharmacological solutions question the efficacy of the *langagière*[9] practice of psychoanalysis and the dimension of speech as event. Lacan noted: "The symptom is first of all the silence in the supposed speaking subject" (S XI, 11). If psychoanalytic practice lends an ear to that silence so it may speak, contemporary approaches to the discontent in culture often exclude the symptom and, therefore, the singularity of the subject of the unconscious (the case by case) in favor of generalized solutions able to produce satisfied, fulfilled subjects in accordance to societal ideals.

In *Why Psychoanalysis?* E. Roudinesco defends psychoanalysis from contemporary claims "seeking to reduce thought to a neuron or to equate desire with a chemical secretion," due to the rise of medicalization and neuroscience.[10] The relation between scientific knowledge and psychoanalysis, which privileges *savoir* (unknown knowledge) deciphered by forms of the unconscious, is what for Roudinesco provokes the "great quarrel" that emerges with the Freudian discovery: "It is neither hereditary, nor cerebral, nor automatic, nor neural, nor cognitive, nor metaphysical, nor symbolic and so on. But then what is its nature, and why is it the point at issue for bitter polemics?"[11]

The quest for total rationalization negates the notion of the split subject of the unconscious in its relation to knowledge; its unfolding evades apprehension. Freud articulates the divisions within the psychic apparatus as the ego, superego, and Id. Lacan speaks of a subject of the enunciation and the subject of the statement and later conceives the subject in relation to three registers (symbolic, imaginary, and real). The subject of the unconscious is a *parlêtre* and language inscribes lack in being (*manque à être*), making the axis of existence inaccessible to the subject. The subject is expropriated from his intimacy. That is why Lacan speaks of "extimacy," of an outside that is inside. As subjects of the unconscious, we are exposed to a cipher of destiny that is not knowable in a general, positive, or anticipated manner. Unconscious *savoir* is always *aprés-coup*, after the fact, not immediately knowable. Language is not simply a tool at one's disposal, but rather precedes the *parlêtre* while being exterior to it. The subject is thus constitutively split, signaling an impossible unity with the Thing (Freudian *Das Ding*, the lost [incestuous] object of desire, the Mother), which "suffers" from the fact that language manifests itself in the world. As Braunstein notes, there is an incompatibility between *jouissance* and the Law: "the Law of language . . . orders to desire and renounce *jouissance*" (chapter 2).

Throughout the book Braunstein contends that *jouissance* and language are co-terminus. This affirmation outlines the parameters of the book's trajectory:

> I am tempted to begin with a gnomic formula: *Im Anfang war der Genuss* (In the beginning was *jouissance*), which is clearly different from the beginning of the Gospel of St. John: *Im Anfang war das Wort* (In the beginning was the word), but it would be a false opposition. One cannot say which came first, whether *jouissance* or the word. They both delimit and overlap in a way that the experience of psychoanalysis shows to be inextricable. (chapter 1)

The epistemological suppositions are thus laid out from "the beginning," starting with the book's title: *jouissance* is a Lacanian concept. Although not explicitly developed in the book, the concept is not considered here in the restricted, classical sense of an apprehension that delimits and captures meaning. Instead, it is read topologically as a "limit concept," which Braunstein demonstrates in chapter 3 in relation to the three *jouissance*(s), "localized" on the borders of the Mobius strip that signal their "littoral union and disunion.[12]

Topology allows thinking the unconscious sayings of analysis in the relations instantiated by a cut, making a re-positioning both for the subject and the analyst possible. The cut (interpretation, scansion) intervenes in the temporality of analytic discourse, producing synchronic effects on the signifiers in diachronic unconscious repetition. As Lacan notes in "Subversion of the Subject and Dialectic of Desire" (1960), the cut makes it so the analysts' pursuit not be in vain, "it verifies the structure of the subject as a discontinuity in the real" (E, 6, my translation). The object *a*, the phantasm, castration, and the phallus can also be written topologically on the edge of those borders where language inscribes the effects of *jouissance* on the body. For this reason, throughout the book Braunstein discusses the torus, the Mobius strip, the Borromean knot, as well as graphs and Eulerian circles.

The spirit of this way of understanding a Lacanian concept seems to be confirmed by Braunstein in a recent conference titled "Jouissology" (2017). He recounts that at the presentation of the second edition of *Jouissance: A Lacanian Concept* in Mexico in 2006 someone in the audience asked the author how he would define *jouissance*. Braunstein realized at that point that the book did not contain such a definition (from *de-finere*: to delimit), although its more than three hundred pages were dedicated to this concept.[13]

With Freud and Lacan, Braunstein reads the concept of *jouissance* vis a vis other key figures in the field of psychoanalysis (J. Allouch, J-A. Miller, C. Soler) and philosophy (M. Foucault, J. Derrida). Literary texts (Proust, Kafka, Bataille, Fitzgerald) and queer theory are also mobilized to further explore the implications of these interpretations. The reader will find spirited engagement not devoid of polemic, meant to re-enliven unexamined truisms, sedimented (mis)readings, and ideological distortions. There is also a purposefully creative stance or "style," given that Braunstein approaches Lacan as an open text (following Lacan's edict to "do as I do, but do not imitate me"), always with the intention of clarifying certain points in the theory or in response to criticisms from other disciplines, such as philosophy or gender studies.

Although too many to discuss at length here, the reader encounters conceptualizations, terms, and neologisms not present in either Freud's or Lacan's own texts. Such is the case of object @, written with the "at" sign, that for Braunstein avoids the ambiguities of *a* in the Lacanian algebra (chapter 1) and "jouissology," contrasted to Bataille's erotology in order to "specify" *jouissance*—here the three *jouissance*(s), much like Lacan does with object *a* (chapter 3). The author also supplements the forms of *jouissance* established in Lacan's Borromean knot in Seminar XX (phallic *jouissance* JΦ, *jouissance of the Other* JA) with *jouissance* of being: bodily, linked to the Thing, prior to castration and phallic signification, which he differentiates from the *jouissance* of the Other (sex): also linked to the body, ineffable although emerging from castration; feminine *jouissance* (explained in chapter 3 in part to respond to critics deeming psychoanalysis "phallocentric"). Braunstein's explanation of the differences between *jouissance* of the Other and feminine *jouissance* is especially important, clarifying and contrasting a *jouissance* linked to the order of the Law and the phallus to feminine *jouissance* that, although ineffable, should not be confused with the Thing and impossible signification. This distinction serves to dispel criticisms made by certain proponents within gender studies that comment on Lacanian texts and often make gender and sexuation synonymous.

Lacanian psychoanalysis is fraught with misunderstandings, some due to a decontextualization of Lacan's teaching, in which certain parts are read independently from other seminars or prior developments. These are then repeated in a common-sensical manner in commentaries or scholarly works. Such is the case of "do not give up on desire" that, although never said by Lacan, has been raised to the status of an aphorism. Braunstein provides a lengthy review of what Lacan *did* say about desire in chapter 8. Another example comes from Seminar VII, *The Ethics of Psychoanalysis*. In session XVI, titled "The Death Drive," the editor J-A. Miller subtitles one of the sections "*Jouissance*, the satisfaction of a drive," where the grammatical construction affirms that drive satisfaction is possible, as well as making the drives and *jouissance* homologous.

Braunstein takes a two-step approach in his critique of this syntagm. In chapter 2, he notes that to posit the satisfaction of the drives is contrary to Freud's formulations, as evidenced even in the early "Drives and their Vicissitudes" (1915): only necessity can be satisfied, but the drives are a constant force that cannot bring the process to a conclusion. This is especially evident after Freud develops the second topic and the publication of *Beyond the Pleasure Principle* (1920), where he develops the death drive more clearly. Freud outlines a system that cannot be closed off completely, but rather is continually open due to the constant force of repetition (the compulsion to repeat, dreams of traumatic neuroses, and the playful *fort-da* are summoned as evidence). It is a movement that opens to close, leaving a gap that re-launches the movement anew each and every time.

As for Lacan, the only drive that could be totally satisfied is the death drive, in the return to an inanimate pure *jouissance* (the Thing). But repression makes it so this satisfaction is only possible at the price of its death, resulting in a historicizing memorable movement that seeks to re-find the lost object by always missing the mark.[14] Lacan notes the drive's trajectory implies non-reciprocity and torsion in the return (S XI). Total *jouissance* is impossible because there is always a deviation from the source. The result is the gap or lack that inscribes the subject of the unconscious in the signifying chain through the invoking call of the Other.

The subject's inscription in language requires a renunciation of *jouissance*, while producing a rest (object *a*) that makes *jouissance* ek-sist. Therefore, while there is no total satisfaction of the drive and *jouissance* is an interdiction for the *parlêtre*, it can be said "between the lines" (*inter-dit*), at the margins or borders around which the object *a* turns, the void of the Thing. What accounts for the misreading in the subtitle of Seminar VII—what is gained in formulating *jouissance* as the satisfaction of a drive? To what conception of the body, the subject, and ethics does this reading respond? Or, if we consider the resistances to psychoanalysis mentioned above, what social imperatives does this reading presuppose?

The clinic informs the theoretical discussions in this book, and Braunstein devotes three chapters to a rich, detailed reading of neurosis, perversion, and psychosis in their relation to speech and *jouissance*. The author studies the triad as being either before, after, and instead of speech in each of the three "structures." Psychoanalysts today question whether the notion of "clinical structure" remains a viable and pertinent one for the clinic. The debate responds to three main concerns regarding "clinical structure": (1) its terminology harks back to a medical (psychiatric) conception of psychoanalysis which considers the cure in terms of pathologies; (2) the notion belonged to a "structuralist" Lacan and was later abandoned in favor of topology and nodal logic; and (3) it defies the very premise of psychoanalysis as a practice of the singular "case by case" in favor of a classificatory system.[15]

In a recent conference[16] Braunstein weighs in on these discussions by noting his preference for the expression "subject position" or the relation between subject and analyst under transference, instead of a theory of "clinical structures," which is not found in Lacan's own seminars or written texts.[17] Although Braunstein notes in this same conference that he made use of "clinical structures" until some five years ago, in 2006 (the publication of the second edition of *Jouissance*) Braunstein had already posed these same concerns when he questions the "misnamed clinical structures" (chapter 2) and when discussing *jouissance* in psychosis, which he shows to be markedly different to how *jouissance* is filtered by speech in *parlêtres*: "not necessarily neurotic, psychotic or perverse (is that possible?)" (chapter 7). Posed as a question in 2006, Braunstein clarifies in his recent conference that the rejection of a psychopathological taxonomy goes hand in hand with the incompatibility between psychoanalysis and medicine, the political maneuver to make psychoanalysis compatible with university discourse and a moralizing normativity.

Jouissance: A Lacanian Concept closes by foregrounding the ethical dimension of psychoanalysis and the position of the analyst. Neither a therapeutic strategy for assuring well-being, a technique for procuring limitless *jouissance*, nor the promise of absolute knowledge:

> In psychoanalysis it is not a question of the laws, but the Law, which prohibits *jouissance* (of the Thing) in the real, displaces it to the field of the *semblant*, and orders it be reached through other discursive means. *Jouissance* thus becomes a *semblant* and occupies the place of agent in a new analytic discourse: inverse, an inversion, the reverse of the master's discourse. The Law orders desire while making the (absolute) object of desire, the Thing, unreachable. Led to desire in vain, circling the object @ as cause of desire, and only under the appearances of the *semblant* of an impossible *jouissance*, the Law elevates *jouissance* to the place of the Thing. This is how men and women inscribe themselves as historical beings by making themselves a name (the meaning of the "proper" name, the signifier given at birth) and record their path toward *jouissance*, by passing through desire. (chapter 8)

R.S.I: as Lacan notes in Seminar XXII, *jouissance* is imbricated in the knot of the three registers (real, symbolic, imaginary) for every *parlêtre*. It cannot be considered autonomously, pretending to forego the symbolic and foreclosing castration. Lacan reiterates this idea in *Talking to Brick Walls*:

> What differentiates the discourse of capitalism is *Verwerfung*, the fact of rejecting, outside all the fields of the symbolic. This brings with it the consequence I have already said it has. What does it reject? Well, castration. Any order, any discourse that aligns itself with capitalism, sweeps to one side what we simply call, my fine friends, the things of love. Do you see that? It's no small thing![18]

Castration is not submission to the law of the Father, but a pathway toward becoming a desiring subject: "Castration means that jouissance must be refused so that it can be reached on the inverted ladder (*l'échelle renversée*) of the Law of desire" (E, 827). In Lacan's presentation at St. Anne in 1972, "the things of love" refer to a-love (*a-mur*), a love of object *a*, which surrounds the void of the Thing and is the cause of desire. The capitalist discourse is here shown to be the opposite of the analyst's discourse that Lacan had presented in Seminar XVII: *The Other Side of Psychoanalysis*. While the former is another form of the discourse of the master, in the latter the analyst takes the place of object *a* and by so doing reverses the position of domination previously occupied by the master. In the analyst's discourse, the subject has access to the cause of desire as unconscious *savoir*. This is the ethical position of psychoanalysis.

PART I

THEORY

Chapter 1

Jouissance

From Lacan to Freud

In the Beginning . . .

I am tempted to begin with a gnomic formula: *Im Anfang war der Genuss* (In the beginning was *jouissance*), which is clearly different from the beginning of the Gospel of St. John: *Im Anfang war das Wort* (In the beginning was the word), but it would be a false opposition. One cannot say which came first, whether *jouissance* or the word. They both delimit and overlap in a way that the experience of psychoanalysis shows to be inextricable. There is only *jouissance* for the being who speaks and because he speaks. As we will see, words make *jouissance* possible even as they restrict and denaturalize it. It is clear that the formula *Im Anfang war der Genuss* would have pleased the later Lacan, but for Goethe and his Faust it was impossible to imagine going from the word to force, to meaning, and finally to the act. *In the beginning was the act*, an act that is, by force, also the effect of the word and has a relation to *jouissance*.

An alternative is to look for a seemingly acceptable synonym that would render it ambiguous and write: *Im Anfang war die Freude* (In the beginning was joy), an aphorism that emphasizes the blessed and jubilant aspect of *jouissance*. But by doing so I would be confusing *jouissance* with its commonplace unspecified meaning, so different from the sense we give the central concept of *jouissance* in contemporary psychoanalysis. When it comes to psychoanalysis, another formula presents itself: *Im Anfang war die Freud* (In the beginning was Freud) and, once pronounced, we must look for the *Genuss*, the *jouissance* in Freud, for whom *jouissance* was never more than a common word in language, not a theoretical concept.

13

To be precise with the psychoanalytic sense of the term, it is convenient to differentiate *jouissance* from the common dictionary meaning that is only its shadow. But to differentiate them is no easy task; the two meanings imperceptibly pass from opposition to proximity. The common meaning makes *jouissance* and pleasure synonymous; the psychoanalytic meaning confronts them, making *jouissance* now an excess intolerable to pleasure, now a manifestation of the body closer to extreme tension, to pain and suffering. And one must choose: either the one or the other.

Yet here I am about to link together discourse and *jouissance*, an impossible task since *jouissance*, being of the body and in the body, is ineffable, while at the same time, only in speech can it be referred to and circumscribed. *Jouissance* slips away from discourse, but that ineffable object is the very substance that is spoken throughout an analysis. As I attempt to show, since its inception the real object in the discourse of psychoanalysis has been *jouissance*.

Jouissance in Spanish is an imperative, a command, or an injunction that cannot be confused with its more archaic predecessor in the language (*gozo*, joy). Due to its ineffability, it cannot be said in the present indicative of the first-person singular else it dissolves, like the unpronounceable name of God. *Goce* in Spanish, *der Genuss* in German, *la jouissance* in French. Never enjoyment. The translators into English delight in finding a more appropriate word. Keenly aware of the impossibility of naming it, as well as to the origin of the Lacanian concept, many psychoanalysts writing in English simply opt for the French term *jouissance*.

Goce and *jouissance*, from the Latin verb *gaudere* (to be glad, to rejoice) (*sich freuen, Freude*, Freud!) reveal some surprises when their definitions are broken down. According to the *Dictionary of the Spanish Royal Academy*, these are:

> *Jouir* (verb) 1. To have and possess some thing, such as dignity, primogeniture or income 2. To have pleasure, complacency and happiness of some thing 3. To know a woman carnally; 4. To feel pleasure, experience pleasant emotions.

It is interesting that the objective dimension of the first definition prevails over the subjective dimension of the second and fourth: *jouissance* is something one has rather than something one feels. The third definition is also surprising. By not excluding that "another" woman could carnally know "one," the academician gives proof of an involuntary nonchalance.

Given that women can only be treated one by one, his use of the indefinite article "a" is further proof of an embarrassment not exempt from a certain Lacanianism. A semantic sexism puts its unconfessed stamp on this definition: *jouir*, yes, in the carnal knowledge of a woman. It seems inconceivable that a man could be the object of *jouir*. As for women, it could only be the case of "knowing" another (woman). There is no reciprocity in *jouissance*. The psychoanalyst must reflect on the academic's meaningful words here.

The Spanish *gozar*, which comes from the Latin *gaudere*, has an unrecognized legacy in the verb *joder* (to fuck), a term that had to wait until 1984 and the thirtieth edition of the *Dictionary of the Spanish Royal Academy* to be given its due, although with an arbitrary etymology: from the Latin *futuere* (to fornicate), from which the French term *foutre* derives. The verb *joder* had to wait centuries to be included in the dictionary and could only do so preceded by an uncanny warning: "Sounds rude or nasty" (is there a relation here, even in contrast, with the Lacanian affirmation of psychoanalysis as an "ethics of saying well" [*une étique du bien-dire*]?). It is a verb that does not have much to complain of, since once admitted it erupts with four definitions linked to the Latin *gaudere* and its associated *gozar* and *jouir*. In brief, these four definitions are (1) to fornicate; (2) to bother, to hinder; (3) to ruin, to waste; (4) interjection that denotes surprise or incredulity.[1]

The semantic proximity between *gozar* and *joder* leads us to add the verb "to play," especially when considering the phonological similarity in French between *jouir* and *jouer* (to play). However, our philological research indicates that words such as to play and jewel (*joya*, from the old French *joie* [joy]) are not derived from *gaudere* but from *jocus* (a joke), closer to the Freudian *Witz*. We can also consider that the Spanish *jugar* (to play) is linked to *conjugar* (to conjugate), the work done with a verb, but the conjugation is not play, but rather a subjugation, the subjection of the verb to the torment of a common yoke (the Latin *jugum*). To play and conjugate also refer to the study of the antithetical meaning of words, some primitive, others derivative: the paralinguistics that interested Freud (SE XI, 153–161). Such are the semantic and etymological differences needed to introduce the term *jouissance* that psychoanalysis infuses with another spirit and vigor.

In psychoanalysis, *jouissance* comes in through the door of conventional meaning. That is how it appears sometimes in Freud's writings, as well as in Lacan's early texts: synonymous of great joy, extreme pleasure, jubilation, ecstasy. It would be idle and pedestrian to trace all the instances when Freud uses the term *Genuss*, but it would do well to recall, independent of the terms used, when *jouissance*, the Lacanian one, is recognized by Freud in his clinical work. In this regard, one must mention the "voluptuous" expression Freud finds in the Rat Man, when the latter recalls the account of torture: an intense pleasure that reaches the height of an evocative horror previously unknown to the patient. Or the joy Freud perceives on his grandson's face, when obstinately playing with an object, the famous spool, in the same way that the child is "played" by the alternate presence and absence of the mother: a game of the to and fro of being, affirmed when the child's image appears and disappears from the frame of the mirror. Or the infinite voluptuous *jouissance* that President Schreber experiences before a mirror when he notices his slow transformation into a feminine body.

As could not be otherwise, the term *jouissance* also appears in Lacan in the conventional sense until a certain moment that can be pinpointed with chronological rigor. Prior to that point we find *jouissance* to be the equivalent of joy, the joy before the mirror when recognizing the unified image of the ego, the *moi* (*aha Erlebnis*). Later, *jouissance* arrives with the advent of the symbol (*fort-da*) that allows for a first level of autonomy in relation to life's constraints. There are other references to *jouissance* in the first years of Lacan's teaching, which centers primarily on desire: the relation of desire with the Other's desire and the recognition of reciprocal, dialectical, intersubjective desires—a desire that has transcended the limits of necessity and can make itself known only by alienating itself in the signifier, in the Other, as the site of the code and the Law.

It is not that desire is denaturalized by alienation for having to express itself through language as demand; it is not that desire falls under the yoke of the signifier and the letter transforms or diverts it. No, it is that desire only becomes desire because it is mediated by the symbolic order that constitutes it as such. The signifier is that redemptive curse without which no subject, desire, or world would exist. That is the pivotal point of Lacan's teaching for some time, at least until the end of the 1950s. The key concepts at that time were desire, alienation, and the signifier. His discourse revolves around the vicissitudes of desire: its refraction into an articulated demand, the desire for recognition and the recognition of desire, the access to reality that depends on the impositions made on the subject by the Other (the world, the symbolic order that produces imaginary effects, the regulation of the satisfaction of necessity, and the conformity to the conditions of that satisfaction). These are the inescapable consequences of conceiving analytic practice as a revolving wheel of words and recognizing the function of the word in the field of language.

Not a few of Lacan's disciples and readers adhered to this less pathological than pathetic assessment of the concepts. There were not many, if any, who noticed the shake-up that took place on a day now long past when Lacan announced that the originality of the condition of man's desire was implicated in a different dimension, in a pole opposite to desire, which is *jouissance*. Nothing was noticed immediately, but slowly it became evident that the new concept reconsidered the status of psychoanalysis and required a second return to Freud, beyond the dialectic of desire in the subversion of the subject, whether the subject of science or of philosophy.

Lacan's surprising advance of *jouissance* to a central place in analytic reflection, contraposing it to the "other pole" that is desire was not arbitrary. For this reason, it is necessary that the concept of *jouissance* be doubly differentiated, on the one hand from desire, on the other from what appears as its synonym, pleasure. To define *jouissance* as a concept is to distinguish its diacritical, differential value and, in that double articulation, its difference from pleasure and desire.

Whence *jouissance*? Why does Lacan resort to the term *jouissance* and make it a central concept? He does not draw it from the dictionary, where it is confused with pleasure, nor does he find it in Freud's works, where it is linked to joy and voluptuousness, even if masochistic. *Jouissance* reaches Lacan through an unexpected path: the law. Lacan draws from Hegel's philosophy of right; it is there that *genuss*, *jouissance* appears as something "subjective," "particular," impossible to share, inaccessible to understanding, opposed to the desire that results from the reciprocal recognition of two consciousness and is "objective," "universal," subject to the law. The opposition between *jouissance* and desire, key to Lacan, has Hegelian roots. Lacan reads Freud with a knife sharpened on a Hegelian stone.

This point has not been made sufficiently, even when Lacan clarified it in the first few classes of Seminar XX. The conceptual borrowing from the theory of right (prohibitions) and the moral law (responsibilities) could be extensively developed with an abundance of quotes. I will simply refer the reader to Hegel's *Philosophical Propaedeutic* of 1810 (PP, 36–39). It is when the dialectician takes sides against *jouissance*, which is "accidental," and pronounces himself in favor of forgetting oneself in order to be guided to what is "essential" in human work: what refers to or interests mankind.

From this remote origin one can see that to consider *jouissance* as particular is already an ethical question. Psychoanalysis cannot be indifferent to the opposition that confronts the body of *jouissance* with desire, regulated by the signifier and the law. Philosophy and the law, in synthesis, the discourse of the master, privilege the dimension of desire. In the above-mentioned text, Hegel states: "If I say that a thing pleases me, or I appeal to my pleasure, I only express the relation of the thing to me and thereby ignore the relation I have to others as a rational being" (PP, 37). *Jouissance* in the discourse of the law refers to the notion of usufruct, the enjoyment of a thing inasmuch as it is an object of appropriation. Legal discourse conceals that appropriation is also an expropriation given that something is "mine" insofar as there are others for whom what is "mine" is alien. One can only legitimately enjoy what one possesses and in order to do so fully it is necessary for the other to relinquish his claim to that object.

Here theories of the law and of psychoanalysis meet and converge. Both posit the fundamental question regarding the foremost property of each subject, his body, as well as its relation to the body of the other, regulated by a certain discourse or social link. This question has been present in the sale and possession of the other's body in slavery, feudalism, and capitalism. It is also a psychoanalytic problem regarding the object of demand, be it an oral or excremental object. The key is *jouissance*, the usufruct, the property of the object, the dispute regarding *jouissance* of the same and the same *jouissance* as object of dispute, the appropriation or expropriation of *jouissance* in relation to the Other. Is a body *mine* or is it dedicated to the *jouissance* of the Other—the Other of the signifier and the law that deprive me of this property—that can only be mine when I am able to tear it away from its ambition or whim? The Law here shows its essence: the regulation of the restrictions imposed on the *jouissance* of bodies—in other words, the social contract. What is it lawful to do and what are the limits in regard to one's own body and that of others? As one can see, this is an issue regarding the barriers to *jouissance*: legality and liberties.

It is not only the Law. The field of medicine is also a source of inspiration for the Lacanian concept of *jouissance*. On March 5, 1958, in a seminar dedicated to the *Formations of the Unconscious*, Lacan proposes the above-mentioned bipolarity of *jouissance* and desire (S V). Many years later in a 1966 conference on "Psychoanalysis and Medicine," Lacan recalls the banal experience of the doctor who notes time and again that, under the appearance of a demand for treatment and without mitigating circumstances, the illness persists and defies the technical skills at his disposal. The body is not only the material substance (*res extensa*) preached by Descartes in contrast to the mental substance (*res cogitans*). It "is made for *jouissance*, a *jouissance* of itself" (*un corps est quelque chose qui est fait pour jouir, jouir de soi même*) (M, 761–774). *Jouissance*, he states, is most evident and hidden in the relation between *savoir*, science and technology, regarding the suffering flesh-made body, handled and placed in the doctor's hands. It is there for all to see: *jouissance* is the purloined letter the ignorant police prefect cannot find in the body of the patient after photographing, x-raying, calibrating, and diagramming it at a molecular level. *Jouissance* is the living part of a substance that makes itself heard as it tears away from the subject, questioning the knowledge that attempts to control it.

The field of medicine is born (one must remember Canguilhem's lesson) as a reflection on illness and the painful suffering of bodies.[2] The concern for health and physiology are secondary to the interest in pathology. Medicine defines its goal as the accomplishment of a state of well-being, adaptation, and balance. It is not difficult to recognize the initial Freudian ideal (medical, for sure) of the pleasure principle here: the least tension, constancy and balance. The classical medical definition of health is "the silence of the organs." Silence here is ignorance, the indifference toward the body and its parts in the bustle of life. To "enjoy good health" can be to renounce the experience of *jouissance* in favor of the experience of pleasure: what distances and alienates the subject from the life of his body, inasmuch as it is someone's property (his own) and he is therefore able to appropriate it. In the above-mentioned conference, Lacan states,

> What I call *jouissance* in the sense that the body experiences it, is always of the order of tension, forcing, expenditure, even of exploit. Undoubtedly, there is *jouissance* at the point where pain appears, and we know that it is only at that point that such a dimension of the organism can be experienced, which would otherwise remain veiled. (M, 770)

To "enjoy good health" can be the opposite of *jouissance* of the body as lived experience. Medicine is thus divided between pleasure and *jouissance* and generally accepts the demand made uncritically: to put a barrier to *jouissance*, ignoring it as a corporal dimension of subjectivity. One can refer to this relation between medicine and *jouissance*: the link between the doctor's not wanting to know and the discourse of the master, or it can be ignored. I prefer to make reference to it, leaving the detailed study to others.[3] They will not be the first, but perhaps the most insightful. At the end of his 1966 conference, Lacan defined his goal: to continue and keep Freud's discovery alive by himself becoming a "doctor's missionary." By drawing attention to the *jouissance* of a body "beyond the pleasure principle," Lacan radically took on his mission, opposing it to the universal goal of productivity. Knowledge resists the notion of *jouissance* of the body, an idea that can be posed only since "Freud's discovery," in the subjective sense of what Freud discovered, and also in the objective sense: what Lacan discovered when he discovered Freud. This discovery *of* Freud's has an unequivocal name: the unconscious. The question still needs to be posed: why is it only since Freud that *jouissance* and the body can be articulated? To answer this question, we must "return to Freud" for a second time.

Jouissance in Freud

Therefore, *Im Anfang war Freud*. In the beginning was Freud, influenced by the official discourse of medicine, adhering to a mechanical and physiological conception of the nervous system as a reflex apparatus that received and discharged excitations. The organism, as Freud first conceived it, was regulated by afferent and efferent nervous pathways that sought to avoid tension and pain and produce states of distension and calm: a reduced level of tension subjectively felt as pleasure. For Freud the doctor and neurologist, at the scene more than the author of the discovery of the unconscious, the neuroses were morbid states that took the form of suffering and occurred when the apparatus could not discharge the increase in energy that perturbed it. Let us recall, schematically, that Freud recognizes the different organizations of the apparatus: the phi system (φ) that receives the excitations and accounts for the changes produced in its environment, a psi system (ψ) to maintain a balance between the charge and discharge of tension, and an omega system (ω) to register the events as memorized experience and offer a direct access to reality (SE I, 283–397). In this first metapsychological presentation of 1895, the ego forms part of the ψ system and occupies a decisive place in the defensive mechanisms at the service of the pleasure-unpleasure principle. This apparatus presents the first version of the origin and function of the unconscious.

The patient who suffers from neurosis is a child who has passively lived a seduction perpetrated by an adult; sexuality first appears in the Other. That child has registered (in ω) the eruption of the external sexual real. The memory is a trace that cannot be integrated in the system of representations (or "neurons") that is the system of the ego (ψ) because its presence provokes an increase in tension that cannot find a pathway for discharge. In other words, the traumatic memory is a foreign body in relation to the ego that threatens the system as a whole. For the pleasure principle, which aspires to a balance of energy, this memory cannot be assimilated or accommodated and is thus separated from the recognized system of representations. In this way, memory becomes trauma, a wound and weapon that cannot be tolerated, the pain and suffering of an irreconcilable memory for the ego. The neural system apparatus (or the subject, if we wish to anticipate Lacan) distances itself from the memory in horror. But instead of making the recollection of the trauma disappear, the distancing and repression makes it eternal: impossible to metabolize and digest, the memory remains fixed in the psychic structure, like a cyst. It cannot be bypassed through rational avoidance or forgetting.

The paradox is evident: the pleasure principle has determined the ostracism and exile of the traumatic memory. In order to protect itself from displeasure, the apparatus decrees ignorance of the presence of a lascivious Other and its desire that affects the body of the child, a defenseless abused object of *jouissance*. However, when split as a repressed nucleus of representation irreconcilable with the ego, this psychic outcast, transformed into unconscious memory, is conserved forever and made indestructible. It attracts and links subsequent experiences and returns repeatedly in what will later be called "formations of the unconscious," the symptom being what makes the most racket. Lacan points out insistently that the repressed only exists in its return and that repression is the same as the return of the repressed. The economic pleasure principle engendered the onerous and anti-economic persistence of what is intolerable, yet returns and wounds. The subject of the unconscious experiences itself in the suffering of this recurrent memory that situates him as an object for the Other's lust.

The ego has produced the paradoxical effect of imprisoning the dangerous enemy that, if left free, can be the cause of unpredictable reactions. In order to keep it in prison, it must defend itself constantly from a possible escape that can occur when the defenses are weakened. The ego is thus subjugated to what it sought to subjugate, a slave to the enslaved. The traumatizing agent is no longer the Other, but rather the memory of the seduction that now always attacks from the inside, from its prison. There is no possible escape. The system generated what it will defend itself from now on. What was external is now intimate, an inaccessible and threatening interior.

This first theory of the etiology of the neuroses is the native soil from which psychoanalysis will never entirely break away, including its theory of *jouissance*. Seduction: the child's body is a defenseless thing that can be abused—the object demanded for and by the Other. Seduction is present from the start, beginning with the child's care: the ways in which its needs are administered, the regulation and subjection of the child's body to the unconscious demands and desires of the Other. There is a reason for which there is no reason, an irresoluble enigma. Who can define the place the child occupies as object in the Other's phantasm, especially the maternal Other as subject? Who can know since birth what he represents in the desire of the Other? Se-duction vectorizes, attracts, and alienates the child's desire toward the desire of that Other that leads it toward him (se-duces); it puts up defenses and issues prohibitions that both constitute the object of an eventual *jouissance* as well as surround it with barbed wire.[4] To desire is to desire what is prohibited. This original, essential, and nonanecdotal seduction localizes *jouissance* in the body while preparing it for immediate censure. *Jouissance* becomes unacceptable, unbearable, unspeakable, and impossible to be said in articulate discourse. In other words, it is subject to castration, making sexuality sexual, channeled through the roads that Freud baptized with the name of a certain unlucky king of Thebes with bad memory.

It seemed we were following Freud's steps but, without distancing ourselves from his formulations, have deviated regarding their consequences. The psychic apparatus examined thus far is not governed by a sovereign principle, pleasure-unpleasure, but rather by two opposing principles. Schematically, one could say that on one hand is the classic pleasure principle, regulating and homeostatic (if we dare use a word that Freud did not use or perhaps even know); on the other hand, there is a principle that is beyond, let us call it *jouissance* for now, *jouissance* of the body, that commands the incessant return of untamed excitations: a constant force that unbalances, sexualizes, and makes for a desiring subject, not simply a reflex mechanism. Isn't it reasonable to imagine in this way, via *jouissance*, the Acheron of the indelible epigraph of *The Interpretation of Dreams* (*Traumedutung*), the burning bush where the inveterate shadows that disturb the slumber of the living dwell? *Flectere si nequeo superas, Acheronte movebo* (SE IV, 1).

The *infans'* flesh is an object of the Other's *jouissance*, desire and phantasm, from the beginning. He represents his place for the Other, an object of its *jouissance*, desire and fantasy. Inevitably, he must constitute himself as a subject by passing through the Other's signifiers, seductive as well as "inter-dicter" of *jouissance*. Due to the intervention of the word, *jouissance* is thus confined to a silenced body, the body of drives, as well as to the compulsive search for an always-failed re-encounter with the object. I am referring to the Freudian *Wunsch* resulting from the experience of satisfaction or, in other words, the subject and unconscious desire.

The speaking subject Lacan introduces in psychoanalysis is produced as an articulating function, a hinge between two Others: the Other of the symbolic system, language and the Law on the one hand, and the *real* Other, which is the body of *jouissance*, unable to find a place in symbolic exchange, "appearing" between the lines of a concealed and supposed text.

Freud's first theory of trauma shows an incoming excessive overload of excitations, a *jouissance* impossible to control, that presents itself beyond the place of the Other, a muffled system of representations (Freud) or signifiers (Lacan). *Jouissance*: ineffable and illegal, traumatic, an excess (*trop-matisme* for C. Soler), which is a hole (*trou-matisme*) in the symbolic, according to Lacan's expression (S XXI, February 19, 1974).[5] This hole marks the place of the impossible real. *Jouissance* thus comes to be the most exterior Other within oneself, a remembrance of the One that had to be renounced in order to enter the world of exchange and reciprocity: the inaccessible *topos* for the subject who houses it and which must be cautiously exiled, given that it is an exterior Other-made interior. Lacan addresses the position of "intimate exterior" (akin to what Freud called Id [*Es*] and Lacan *ça*) when he speaks of *extimité* (S VII). It is without a doubt the obscure nucleus of being (*Kern unseres Wesen*). It is not a question of words or of the unconscious; neither is it alien to language since it is through language (as excluded) that it can be circumscribed. It is the word, a letter, a writing to be deciphered. The deciphering of *jouissance* will require a separate discussion in chapter 4.

Speaking of his 1967 seminar *The Logic of the Phantasm*, Lacan states that *jouissance*, the nucleus of our being, is the "only avowable (*avouable*) ontic [consideration] for us" (AE, 327): the sub-stance of analysis. But *jouissance* cannot be addressed if not by its loss, the erosion of *jouissance* produced in the body by what comes from the Other and leaves its mark.

The Other does not find its correspondence in any psychological subjectivity but only in the scars left on the skin and mucous membrane: stalks attached to the orifices, ulceration and usury, scarification and effrontery; injury and injunction; penetration and castration. This is just paraphrasis.

Freudian trauma explained the psychoneuroses of defense; now we can say that it is a defense when faced with an increase of *jouissance*. The defense is a neutralization of a memory lived in a pleasant or unpleasant manner. If the experience was of pleasure, the defenses and controls must be erected in the subject: the symptomatic configuration, centered on a reactive formation, results in the obsessional neurosis of someone who distances himself from his *jouissance*. If the experience was unpleasant, according to Freud, the danger is represented as coming from a seductive and abusive Other; the defenses are disgust and the somatic conversion proper to hysteria, when faced with a *jouissance* attributed to the Other. The two modes of relation with the desire of the Other that characterize, distinguish, and oppose obsessional neurosis and hysteria are modes of separation. The subject alienates him- or herself from *jouissance*, which is then displaced and relocated in the body as a symptom.

In neurosis, the Id (*ça*, Es, the body) speaks; the banished *jouissance* returns with a vengeance; it demands an interlocutor; addresses a lack in *savoir* so that its inscriptions can be deciphered by the only means possible: the word. That is the Freudian doctrine, the established and oft-repeated Freudian formula for the symptom: a "substitute for sexual satisfaction."

From the beginning, the theory of the psychoanalytic cure is founded on the possibility of enabling the path of speech toward the sexual *jouissance* that is encapsulated and sequestered, not accessible to the subject. In Freud, and at first also in Lacan, the objective is the inclusion of the repressed in the context of an ample and coherent discourse. The analytic practice should allow the inclusion of *jouissance* in the subject's history, integrating it to a *savoir* that can be someone's *savoir*, set to acquire meaning and, for that same reason, set for misunderstanding and the incommensurable. *Wo Es war soll Ich werden*. It is impossible to say it more succinctly.

This position of the symptom as encapsulated *jouissance* is paradigmatic and valid for all the formations of the unconscious. The unconscious consists of (it is nothing other than) the activity of the primary processes in charge of operating a first decipherment, transposition, *Entstellung* (distortion) of the movement of the drives and to configure them as fulfillments of desire. Condensation and displacement, the operations performed on the signifying substance, are paths from that primal writing to speech, processes of transformation of *jouissance* into speech, *jouissance* of the body into speech about *jouissance*. The primary processes smuggle *jouissance* by contraband. Because it is said, *jouissance* is evoked, missed, displaced onto the field of what has been lost to the other pole, which is desire.

The unconscious exists only insofar as it is heard. Only if what is said encounters a good listener, someone who does not drown it out in a tidal wave of meaning, can recover its enigmatic condition and enable a possible *jouissance* of decipherment. In this way, the unconscious depends on the formation of the analyst. *Jouissance*, previously supposed, is thus the effect and product of the punctuation or interpretative act that produces the good luck (*bonheur*) of a gay science.

Lacan knocks down Freud's theory of dreams and their interpretation beginning with his radio conferences of June 1970, in which the unconscious processes are related to *jouissance* (AE). Later, in Seminar XX, he clarifies his terms by noting that while the unconscious is structured like a language, it is no less certain the unconscious depends on *jouissance* and is an apparatus that converts *jouissance* into discourse (S XX, 51). I do not think it is wrong to find the sense of the classic Freudian maxim here: "the dream is the fulfillment of desire." The fulfillment of desire (*Erfüllung*) is a "filling up" and, therefore, its disappearance as desire, lack in being, or split subject. That is why one can say that the dream is a hallucination of *jouissance* and also a defense against it (in short, it is a compromise formation) because it runs up against what is impossible to represent and say. It is well known that the process of interpreting the dream encounters a limit in its contact with the bare satisfaction of desire that it must represent. That is the moment of awakening and *angst* (*angoisse*). *Angst* is the affect that interposes itself between desire and *jouissance*, between the subject and the Thing.

It is also known that the interpretation of a dream leads to an enigma that cannot be interpreted: the point at which the dream takes root in what is not knowable, an inaccessible place that is forever in the shadows. Freud recognizes and names this point the "navel" of the dream—the dream being the navel of all formations of the unconscious (SE V, 525). These can be understood as efflorescence, fungi that grow from the mycelium beyond the possibilities of saying: S (Å). The words needed are lacking, those able to symbolize what these very words produce as impossible, real, *jouissance*.

It would be worthwhile to reread *The Interpretation of Dreams* in light of these insights, showing the relation between the *Entstellung* (distorsion) performed by the work of the dream as a first decipherment of *jouissance* and the interpretative work of the analyst. Following that route we reach the *Traumdeutung*'s chapter 7 and find Freud's conception of the psychic apparatus as a machine that converts *jouissance* into the discourse that evokes it: the only way it can be approached. This is the reason the dream is the royal road that leads to . . . the impossible: deciphered and made unrecognizable by the work of the unconscious.

The unconscious, weaving dreams in its loom, allows for the continuation of sleep. It is the guardian of sleep. If the dream is a compromise formation at the service of the pleasure principle, it is due to its two-sided nature. It deciphers *jouissance*, puts it into words, guarding all the while that the amount does not exceed certain safe limits, trying to place the flow of oneiric representations at the center of the safety barrier where airplanes must fly in order not to be perturbed by an encounter with other flying objects. We should recall that while preparing his Rome discourse and at a conference on the imaginary, the real, and the symbolic, presented on July 6, 1953, Lacan maintained that dreaming in *The Traumdeutung* showed the symbol as imaginary, while to interpret the dream symbolized the image. It could well be this way, but only at the cost of ignoring the rest, the signifier of the *unsayable* stumbled upon when symbolizing the image, (S𝒜), and the *unrepresentable* when presenting the symbol as imaginary. What is left out? The nonspecular object @ that, as cause of desire (*plus de jouir*), is precisely the mycelium on which the mushroom of the dream rises as discourse and also discourse as dream, the place and support for a first decipherment of *jouissance*.[6] This is how we read, along with Lacan, Freud's fungal metaphor: the dream, mushroom of *jouissance*. A displacement? Yes, to displace, to transpose, that is the work of the unconscious. A hell (*sacré*) of a displacement. And Lacan's? *Entstellung*, a re-flection on Freud, beginning with *jouissance*: a second return. We will have to return as well.

By considering discourse as a dream, *The Psychopathology of Everyday Life* illustrates the presence of this ciphering and deciphering of *jouissance*. The dislocated subject: subverted by the emergence of an unexpected *savoir* (lapsus, slip) or by the lack of a signifier that produces perturbing associations (the forgetting of proper names, the unforgettable Signorelli) or by an action that misses the mark of the hypocrisy of the ego. The subject is thus dislocated and embarrassed. The tension or uneasiness of the body acknowledges the *jouissance* that has filtered out from the gaps in the intentional use of words, which had consisted in keeping it divided and unknown. The subject of the *lapsus* is the embarrassed (*embarras*) subject who manifests his embarrassment at not knowing who he is because the extimate Other has spoken. Truth traps the lie in the equivocation and at that moment the ego reveals itself as unknowing function: a protection against any excess. The word, normally, has the mission of impeding that these escapes (routine and psychopathological) repeat themselves. Mission impossible.

It is well known that in 1905 Freud worked on two tables. On one he wrote *Jokes and Their Relation to the Unconscious*, while on the other, *Three Essays on the Theory of Sexuality* (SE VII, VIII). Has anyone pointed out that the two works are one? Freudian scholars still wish to know which of the two was finished or published first without realizing the closeness between the two pillars, which are the body of the symbolic and the symbolic of the body. The joke and sexuality, the knot between the word and *jouissance*, are revealed in both texts. On the side of *Witz* (the joke), affect, joy, the jocund explosion of laughter, the excitement of the joke either remembered or heard, laughter as an object of exchange, the demand implicit in telling a joke ("Give me your laughter"), the shaking of the body caused by a surprising and unlikely word foreign to that discourse. All of these are the expressions of sexuality that slide and slip on the pavement of the signifier. The body is the effect made on the flesh by the word that inhabits it: the body constituted by the exchanges and reciprocal responses to demands. The 1905 thesis is that sexuality has a genealogy, which is the dialectic of demand and desire between the subject and the Other. The subject is the articulating function between the body and the Other, the body as Other and the Other as body. Affect is an effect of the incorporation of structure and the incorporation of the subject to the structure. That is the joke.

The word takes body, the body takes the floor (speaks). *Jouissance* is deciphered in laughter beyond meaning. If an explanation kills off the joke, it is because it transports it from non-sense, where there is *jouissance*, to sense, where its existence is pleasure. *Jouissance* disconcerts; pleasure concerts, calms, and harmonizes. It is up to psychoanalysts to learn the lesson and decide in what direction they will point their intervention: to the sense that produces pleasure or to *jouissance* that reveals being?

Sexuality: endogenous or exogenous? The drive: natural or the effect of exchanges? *Jouissance*: emanating from the subject or the Other? The bilateral, dyadic, contrasting topologies err, necessarily. The realm of the Mobius strip and its disconcerting continuity here is absolute. Sexuality does not affect the body from inside the body or outside the perverse *jouissance* of the Other; it is rather a littoral union-disunion of the subject and the Other. If we draw the subject and the Other as two Eulerian circles, we have to be careful not to do so with two closed strokes,

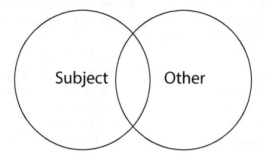

but rather with a stroke as continuous as the edge of the Mobius strip,

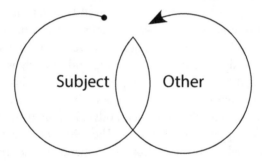

where a minimum discontinuity imposed on the starting position of the vector is nothing more than the necessary artifice for an intuitive representation, since no discontinuity can be traced on the real between one and an Other sexuality. Sexuality, drive, *jouissance*. The One and the Other. From an outside which is inside and from an inside which is outside. And the brain? It is the hinge that straddles two realities: the body and world presented through language.

The pleasure principle thus reveals its essence, containing and restraining *jouissance* through an intermediary, the ego. Its function does not depend on the Law. It is a barrier that Lacan calls "almost natural" and operates much like a fuse in an electrical system (E, 695). The Law (with a capital L) is added secondarily and makes of this almost natural barrier a barred subject. Pleasure is a built-in device, incorporated from the start, a function of vital order, incoherent but indispensable. At a logically later moment, an external prohibition is added; it is beyond objection: the Law. Lacan writes "law of pleasure" and "Law of desire." One must note the use of the lower- and uppercase letters: the former refers to the natural order, and the latter to the symbolic. The law of pleasure is the "organic" basis of the Law.

Jouissance is prohibited to those who speak. The Law is based on this prohibition; it is an Other, second interdiction—the one Freud finds both in his theory and in the clinic: the decisive, irreducible, and heteroclite castration complex, the prohibition of *jouissance* that carries a mark and a sacrifice befalling the phallus, the symbol of that prohibition. The Law makes the law of pleasure enter the symbolic order, the Law of desire.

A review of Freud's works from the perspective of a return and re-signification of the concept of *jouissance* serves as a preface to the Lacanian theory of *jouissance*. As is well known, the castration complex is the culmination of Freud's theory of sexuality. In fact, the three essays of 1905 were not completed until 1923. In "The Infantile Genital Organization," Freud advances the decisive additions that will be made to the three essays in 1924: the re-writing of a psychoanalytic psychopathology in "Inhibition, Symptom and Anxiety" (1926) and a new theory of perversions in "Fetishism" (1927), the true end to the *Three Essays on the Theory of Sexuality* (SE XIX, XXI).

We will return to the relation between *jouissance* and castration further on. It is fundamental in the Lacanian clinic, as well as the pivot that articulates the direction of the treatment. Our interest, for the moment, is to show that Freud's theory of sexuality must be understood beginning with the castration complex and to note the relation between the two laws: the law of pleasure and the Law of castration or desire. The latter is embodied or incorporated in the subject through what Freud discovered even before the castration complex: the Oedipal complex. It is embodied because it makes a body of flesh, dislodging *jouissance* from the flesh: barring, prohibiting, displacing it, as promise. The subject must renounce *jouissance* in exchange for the promise of an other *jouissance* proper to those subjects of the Law. Through the means indicated by Freud (a masculine castration anxiety and a feminine penis envy), justly challenged by Lacan, the subject is led first to a localization of *jouissance* in a part of the body and second to the inability to access that localized *jouissance* without first passing through the demand made to the Other, the Other sex (sex as Other), in the field of love. Original *jouissance*, of the Thing, and before the Law, is a prohibited and doomed *jouissance* that must be rejected and substituted by the promise of phallic *jouissance*, which is subsequent to the acceptance of castration. "You are only allowed to look for what you have already lost." Phallic *jouissance* is possible once the subject is inscribed in the symbolic order as subject to the Law, to speech (the laws of language). By means of the symbolic, sexual *jouissance* becomes a permitted *jouissance*. The Freudian Oedipal complex thus finds its place as the hinge straddling two different *jouissance*(s). The Law, which allows for a separation from the *jouissance* of the mother and puts the name-of-the-Father in its place, commands desire. Desire finds its possible fulfillment through the detours of love. As affect, love is charged with compensating the inexistence of the sexual relation and re-introducing the previously renounced *jouissance*. This topic is developed in chapter 8.

In Freud's works, the *Three Essays on the Theory of Sexuality* find their logical continuity in his texts on the psychology of love, which are also three, as well as in his most transcendent work on love, paradoxically titled "On Narcissism: An Introduction" (SE XI). As a clinician of the amorous history of his subjects, Freud finds dissociative tendencies in the sexual life of men, leading them to divide tenderness and sensuality in themselves and to split the love object into the mother and the prostitute, thus assuring dissatisfaction and making them flee incessantly from one to the other. For this reason, in "On the Universal Tendency to Debasement in the Sphere of Love" (1912), Freud noted there is something implicit in the sexual drive that conspires against its total satisfaction. Finally, in his third article on love, "The Taboo of Virginity" (1918), Freud is able to distinguish the inhibiting characteristic of *jouissance*, which the phantasm of the *jouissance* of the Other (of women in this case) has in sexual life. With clarity, Freud posits that desire is engendered reciprocally (although the formula that desire is the desire of the Other is not his), while the *jouissance* of the one and the other (sex) are established on a convergent plane of opposition and concurrence (SE XI).

Love is never a promise of beatitude and complementarity for Freud. This is clear when one reads "On Narcissism: An Introduction." Through love the subject attempts to recover the state of absolute joy that was supposedly at his disposal when he was "His Majesty, the Baby" and was commissioned to fulfill what the mOther lacked. The first stage of the Oedipus complex is an identification with the phallus more than "primary narcissism," as it is called in Freud's text: "The child shall fulfill those wishful dreams of the parents which they never carried out" (SE XIV, 91). To do so, he depends on love for himself, a reflection of the love that the Other provides. The investment without limits that he receives from his own specular image is the model, the ideal ego that will be lost only to attempt to be re-found through obedience to the dictates of the Other, which constitutes the ego ideal. The idealized love for oneself passes through the love relation with an other that is chosen according to a narcissistic model. The other, the so-called object choice by attachment or anaclitic (*Anlehnung*), is only a variation of the narcissistic choice, inasmuch as the figures of love objects, the nurturing mother or protective father, are the necessary supports for the narcissistic ego. The other four forms for the object choice of love (which is not, surely, the object of desire) that Freud distinguishes are clearly narcissistic. From *jouissance* to desire; from desire to love—love, for its part, befalling an object that displaces one's image. No, there's nothing to be done, the sexual relation does not exist.

Beginning with *The Project for a Scientific Psychology* (*Entwurf*) of 1895, the ego is first protection and deflection from charges of tension; its purpose is to make them innocuous and thus limit sexual tension, *jouissance*, arising in the organism when it is oriented toward the original and mythical experience of satisfaction. The function of the ego is regulated by the pleasure principle; it tends toward an equilibrium of the charges (homeostasis) and to avoiding displeasure, the least effort. Its objective is to serve the organism economically as a whole by putting limits to the tension that the organism generates. For Lacan, *jouissance* is of no use ("La Jouissance se définit comme ce qui ne sert à rien" [S XX, 10]). In Freud, not only is it useless, it also threatens and rejects the unpleasure-pleasure principle. If we go back to *Three Essays on the Theory of Sexuality*, the Freudian model of *jouissance* we find is in the *Vorlust* (forepleasure) that Freud opposes to the final pleasure of orgasmic discharge. Of that previous pleasure that arises from the erogenous zones, Freud says it is an aimless effect without end that does not contribute (before puberty) to the continuation of the sexual process (SE VII). For this reason, Freud distinguished between the sexual excitation of sexual satisfaction that eliminates all tension and serves, by *la petite morte* (orgasm), as an anticipation of what will later be the Nirvana Principle, the state impervious to any new incitement. This is why, with good reason, the section Freud dedicates to forepleasure is titled "The *Problem* of Sexual Excitation" (my emphasis). This "problem" (for whom?) is the clearest foreshadowing of the Lacanian concept of *jouissance* that takes shape in Freud even before the subversive concepts formulated in *Beyond the Pleasure Principle* in 1920.

The misunderstandings that arose regarding the Freudian thesis that moved sexuality to a central place in the constitution and architecture of the subject are well known. They purported to establish structures of a theoretical nature that advocated sexual liberation, confusing the orgasm with mental health and even with happiness. They made psychoanalysis the new gospel of genital normativity. What was left out was what anyone could have noticed in Freud's works: few, relative, ambiguous and scant reassurance regarding copulation and the orgasm, as well as skepticism regarding love as a gateway to happiness. Now we can understand this in light of the theory of *jouissance* because pleasure appears in relation to *jouissance* as a short circuit, a sudden cut that puts limits on the body being experienced as a body. It is the pleasure of so-called "sexual satisfaction" that interrupts the increase in tension, the model being the release of seminal fluid in the male orgasm, which harbors deception in its discharge.

For Freud and Lacan, psychoanalysis is incompatible with illusions that dream of overcoming the subjective division through an amorous encounter that physically and spiritually sutures the subject to the object, the exile with the homeland, and the desiring subject with the Thing. Lacan's scandalous aphorism "the sexual relation does not exist" is constructed on this fact and confirmed in the experience of analysis. The sexual relation does not exist as *rapport*, a relation established by logic, and it does not exist as a re-apportioning of what one has lost in the beginning of life as the effect of the sectioning, the sex-ioning, or the re-sectioning of *jouissance* called castration.

A Return to Freudian Beginnings

Let us return to the beginning: *Die Anfänge* of psychoanalysis, *The Project for a Scientific Psychology* of 1895 (originally *Psychology for Neurologists*), the unavoidable cornerstone of Freud's later metapsychological developments. To return to the beginning is to return to that mythical and absolute starting point in the experience of satisfaction that is the *fiat-lux* of existence. Before there was chaos, so absolute that it could not be called chaos: unnamed and un-representable, the void in the dark maternal womb where one could not presume anything to be found or missing.

The point of departure for the subject, the birth of the psyche, is conceived as the experience of the absolute helplessness of an organism with needs, unable to alleviate or fulfill the internal excitation without the production of an alteration in the external world able to provide the object of satisfaction, thus allowing for a specific and pacifying action. The organism's incapacity to survive on its own sentences it to death. Only the Other is able to save him, from which its "obscure authority" derives. The premise is that someone, "an experienced person is drawn to the child's state" (SE I, 318). For this to occur, it is necessary that the Other be available and that its attention be on the alert to the child's screams: "In this way this path of discharge acquires a secondary function of the highest importance, that of communication, and the initial helplessness of human beings is the primal source of all moral motives" (SE I, 318).

The helpful person's specific actions allow for the experience of satisfaction that, from the perspective of the organism, makes survival possible and, from the perspective of psychic life, is marked by the stamp of an invariable North in the compass of desire. Desire (*Wunsch*) is a subjective movement of constant re-activation of the memory of this fundamental experience. All its subsequent fortunes and misfortunes will be compared to the supposed Paradise of that experience of satisfaction, which is nothing more than a retroactive fiction. Outlining in the third person his speculations on the experience of satisfaction, Freud then jumps to the first-person singular: "I do not doubt that in the first instance this wishful activation will produce the same thing as a perception—namely a hallucination. If reflex action is thereupon introduced, disappointment cannot fail to occur" (SE I, 319).

The experience of satisfaction-desire-reactivation of the past as hallucination and comparison of what there is with what there was ("reflex action"), disappointment. Ever present. What is not lacking is the lack when comparing what we have with the mythical, magical, fantastic, paradisiacal, perfect experience of what we had and lost. What cannot be lacking is the disappointment. It is what is present at the beginning . . . of the psyche and psychoanalysis.

So it goes. The perception of things does not coincide with the fundamental memory ("the wished for mnemic image")—not completely, "at least partly" (SE I, 330). A part of the complex of representations ("a perceptual complex"), an "ingredient," remains identical, while a second ingredient varies. The object of perception falls apart: it satisfies desire and does not satisfy it. "Language creates for this falling apart the term *judgment*" (SE I, 373). In this way, the constant ingredient is the thing in the world (*Das Ding*) and the inconstant element its activity or property, its "predicate."

Not only the moral motives but also all thought, "judgment," emerges from the decisive mark of the Other in the future subject, the initial representation of the Thing that condemns the subject to live in disappointment. There would be no disappointment if there were no previous deception. For a being in this world there are only disparities, dissimilarities, missed encounters, deviations, dis-courses. The coincidence between what is looked for and what is found puts limits on the act of thinking; the organism discharges and empties itself out. The discordance, on the contrary, impels the work of thinking in order to discern, in the present perception, the distance with respect to the representation of the absent *das Ding*. If a fortunate encounter with the object occurs, there is no possibility of thought. The sections that are in discordance are what produce "thought interest" (SE I, 337).

One lives because of the Other, the neighbor (*Nebenmensch*). But the latter is not only savior, he is also the "[subject's] first satisfying object and further his first hostile object, as well as his sole helping power. For this reason it is in relation to a fellow human-being that a human being learns to cognize . . . Thus the complex of the fellow human-being falls apart into two components, of which one makes an impression by its constant structure and stays together as a *thing*, while the other can be *understood* by the activity of memory—that is, can be traced back to information from the [subject's] own body" (SE I, 331). Perhaps I should apologize for this brief review of the early Freud, but it is best to proceed with its development. My intent is to contextualize the origins of *das Ding*, the Freudian Thing, to then delve into the twists and turns of Lacanian *jouissance*.

In the beginning . . . *Im Anfang war das Ding*, but when there is the Thing, there is no subject to judge its existence and attributes. After the Thing is lost (inasmuch as *jouissance* is on the side of the Thing and desire on the side of the Other), after the insurmountable disparity with the object is established, there can be a subject, as a trace of the Thing (E, 723). The lost object is the cause of the subject: the one who is no longer the One, but rather one who counts, thinks, and has ethical motives, the subject of the unconscious ($), beyond psychology. The subject cannot subsist without that Other whom he calls, at first, with his screams and later with his articulated word.

Das Ding is what remains in the subject as a trace of what can no longer be. The "discharge" is now prohibited; the subject from now on must live with disappointment; he will have to think, discern, and establish the difference between all things and *the* Thing: the absolute object, intangible dominatrix of the psyche.

Freud did not linger at this point of departure; ten days later (from September 25 to October 5, 1895), he tackled its consequences. That is, the movement from this myth of origins to "the normal psychic processes," which are made possible by "speech associations" that allow for "conscious, observing thought." Why? Because "the *indications of speech-discharge* . . . put thought-processes on the level with perceptual processes, lend them reality and *make memory of them possible*" (SE I, 336). For Freud, the thought processes clearly do not have an "objective reality" in themselves but are made possible by the linguistic signs that equate thought and perception, thus making them memorable, historical (signs = *Zeichen*). We will return to Freud's terminology in chapter 4, dedicated to the decipherment of *jouissance*.

The objective reality of thought proceeds from linguistic facilitations (*Bahnungen*). The decipherment, the transference of being through the filter of language, does not begin in language itself, in the learning process or the imitation of a word, but rather in the experience of pain, in contact with

> objects—perceptions—that make one scream, because they arouse pain; and it turns out as an immensely important fact that this association of a sound . . . with a perceptual image . . . emphasizes that object as a hostile one and serves to direct attention to the perceptual [image]. When otherwise, owing to pain, one has received no good indication of the quality of the object, the *information of one's own scream* serves to characterize the object. Thus this association is a means of making memories that arouse unpleasure conscious and objects of attention: the first class of conscious memories has been created. Not much is now needed in order to invent speech. . . . Thus we have found that it is characteristic of the process of *cognitive* thought that during it attention is from the first directed to the indications of thought-discharge, to the indications of speech. (SE I, 366–367)

What remains of *das Ding* for a subject in the making? Nothing: neither the representation nor the memory, only the naked scream of its absence. The foundation of being lies in this difference between possible representations and the Thing that has disappeared forever, leaving a mark of a missed encounter and discordance in the experiences of reality. This reality depends on and is nothing more than the Other of language that has to traverse the disappointments and establish differences. Alienation is the mandatory result. The in-corporation of being in language is the reason for a definitive and irreversible exile from the Thing. In his seminar on the ethics of psychoanalysis, Lacan's definition of The Thing is "that which in the real suffers from the signifier" (*Ce qui du réel pâtit du signifant*) (S VII, 125). Just as one would say that someone "suffers from a cough," or that he "suffers from a symptom." We will return to this definition.

Speech is the trail flowing behind the ship, the furrow that cannot reach the plow that causes it, but it is impossible to know about the ship or the plow if not for the traces left in their path. The earth and the sea, the body, in a word, carry the inscription of the irrecoverable. Speech is imprinted on flesh and makes of that flesh a body, symbolized in the exchange with the Other. To speak, think, and traverse the signifiers of the Law: such are the effects that the lost object takes as Cause (*Ding*). We are all castaways rescued from the *jouissance* lost on the way to language. The effect is judgment, the *langagière* distinction of the plurality and variety of objects in the world. The subject is born and enters a reality that is consensual and shared due to its exile from the Thing, that Thing that creates silence or chaos as what came before. The homeland is an effect of exile and nostalgia.

Lacan thus constitutes *jouissance* on the basis of a Freudian "myth-psychology." In the beginning was *jouissance*, but one knows nothing about that *jouissance* except that it is lost. Because it is lost and because *jouissance* is the real, the impossible, it is sought through the creative paths of repetition. Speech, originating from the Other, is the *pharmakon*, medicine and poison, an ambivalent instrument that separates and restores, stamping it with a minus, a loss which is the insurmountable difference between the signifier and the referent, between words and things (D, 35). The *jouissance* of the Thing is lost; from now on *jouissance* is only possible by traversing the field of words. But it will be an *other jouissance*: failed and evocative, nostalgic.

We continue with Freud and with him take the irreversible plunge, from the *Amfangen* to the *Jenseits*, from the beginnings to beyond the pleasure principle, treading on ground fertile with the implications of the discovery of the unconscious and its modes for approaching *jouissance*: by displacing and putting it into words. At this point we can perhaps propose a new aphorism: *the unconscious is a work whose raw material is jouissance and whose product is discourse.* The unconscious would be nothing without the theory of sex and vice versa. The same can be said of psychoanalysis; nothing would remain were it not standing on those two feet: the unconscious (that we know is Lacan's, not Freud's) and sexuality that, as a theory, accounts for the emptying out of *jouissance* from the body and its movement toward a signifying articulation. The result is the subject and the object cause of its desire. I will come back to these topics in the next chapter.

At first Freud had difficulty in recognizing the perturbing source that storms the apparatus from the inside and does not aspire to fantasy or withdrawal. Naturalism later led him to conceive it as "energy" and give it the name *libido*, a word from the Latin that only reaches its full meaning when one keeps in mind that *Liebe* in German is the name for love.

With the ambiguous term *libido*, Freud included *jouissance* (naturalized, quantified metaphorically) in a theoretical trajectory compatible with his writings and clinical practice. This trajectory included clinical histories, the conception of the "choice of neurosis," genetic postulates regarding the displacement of libido across different parts of the body, ending with the primacy of the genital zones that, for Freud, was the phallus; there is only one genital, which is masculine and only one libido, linked to the male organ in the boy as well as in the girl. The psychoanalytic clinic thus proves to be the history of the wanderings of *jouissance*: its "fixations," "regressions," transformation into symptoms, "introversion" toward the phantasm, that imaginary formation that replaces action on the outside and is a "natural reserve" of *jouissance*. In the phantasm, *jouissance* is nonsubjective; it manifests itself in symptoms, hysterical repressions, obsessive reactive formations, distancing and phobic precautions, as well as unstoppable invasions that determine the psychotic break with an exterior reality and coagulations in staged scenes. The theory of the cure is permeated with this wandering of libido on exterior objects; that is how the figure of the analyst is conferred a select privilege. The theory of *jouissance* is thus the unacknowledged foundation of the transference, which is at the same time resistance and motor of the treatment, a magnet that attracts libido and an unfathomable abyss from which it will have to become unstuck for the end of analysis to be possible. In synthesis, the theory of libido is the theory of *jouissance*. All of the above is very succinctly developed but "refer to [Freud] and you will see," (AE) as Lacan said on another occasion and to which we will return.

The subject is born because she or he is exiled from the Thing, the non-symbolized *jouissance*, and is oriented toward the "primacy of the genital zones," which is the primacy of the signifier, taking this signifier as a foundation for the phallus, the support of all the processes of signification. So much so that to say "The Signification of the Phallus" is redundant because, as Lacan said ironically of one of his *écrits*, there is no other. From the Thing to the phallus—that is, to castration—this is the sense of the path Freud laid out in his psychopathology, giving a central place to the castration complex and its vicissitudes. The complex reorganizes, by retroaction, all that comes before phallic primacy. The process of subjectivation can be understood as a succession of migrations, exiles and emptying out of *jouissance*. Sexuality thus passes through "phases" that signal the journey from a previous real, outside symbolization (the Thing of the beginnings) to an ultimate real that is an unavoidable remainder left from symbolization, barely apprehended by words that scurry off. It is produced as an effect of discourse by the word, the object @, the elusive surplus *jouissance* (*plus de jouir*).

With its multifaceted manifestations, human sexuality is more a sublimation in itself than what is sublimated. To sublimate is to sexualize and not, as a hasty interpretation would have it, to desexualize. Sexuality is a symbolization of *jouissance* that is thus de-naturalized, humanized, spoken for in the relation between a woman and a man with their bodies and the body of the Other. It is at this point that Freud is confronted with the arduous question of the heterogeneity of *jouissance*. It is an enigma that leads to a succession of texts in which Freud attempts to account for the asymmetry of masculine and feminine *jouissance* through the asymmetry the castration complex (traversed by both) determines regarding the phallus. The question regarding the heterogeneity of *jouissance* occupies Lacan in his effort to respond to the Freudian question: what does a woman want?

I have already mentioned that the most tenuous observation on love, the basic things heard in an analysis, serves to show that human beings, speaking beings (*parlêtres*), are not governed by the pleasure principle. Freud noted it constantly. If love cannot be understood without taking into account the terrible fate of having to inscribe itself as *jouissance*, even less can the pleasure principle explain the other activity that appears as its opposite: war (CF, 28–40). His remarks on war and death during World War I converge with the observations on love. The article dedicated to the taboo of virginity (1919) concludes that the different *jouissance*(s) do not come together but rather compete with each other (SE XI). A year earlier, Freud had observed and established that feminine desire was not oriented toward the man but toward the penis and that the organ could be symbolically substituted for the child (SE XVII). The man was, for her, a necessary appendix, but ultimately expendable. For his part, a man dissatisfied rather than satisfied his sexual aspirations with a woman who was merely the replacement (*Ersatz*) for the prohibited mother.

Beyond Pleasure

One must keep all this background in mind to comprehend Freud's work at the beginning of 1919, a time in which one could say he does not work on two tables but on three, leading to a conceptual reformulation and a new beginning for psychoanalysis. In fact, although *Beyond the Pleasure Principle* is published in 1920, it was drafted from March to May of 1919, the month that the second and final version of "The Uncanny" (*Das Unheimlich*) was completed. Additionally, Freud finished "A Child Is Being Beaten" in March of 1919. The diaphanous unity between these three texts has never been sufficiently stressed, not even by Freud himself, nor has the light they all shed and receive from the concept of *jouissance*.

Beginning with the uncanny: why does cultural production adhere to these uncanny creations, and why do these horrific representations have the importance they do if man's imaginary is governed by the pleasure principle? Why would the subject repeat nightmares that show him harassed, with no recourse, the object of cruelty and abuse? Why cling to the advance of death and holocaust, to premonitions of failure or fantasies of shame, to the havoc and unraveling of guilt, demonic possessions, the presence of an unthinkable and inexpressible horror? Why the need or desire to create hydras and dragons, incubi and succubi, hells and miseries?

A first response would be the conscience that "declares us guilty." The payment due for the pleasure experienced or fantasized and which Freud revealed during those years to be the superego.[7] It is not mere coincidence. The first response that occurs to us springs back as a question: why is there a superego in an organism supposedly governed by the pleasure principle? Clearly, the superego does not conform to the search for the least tension, but rather deploys an efficient machine for not dozing off in the arms of pleasure and demands retaliation for any crime committed, if only in thought more than in action. Such is the case that the psychoanalyst Edmund Bergler once suggested that the superego is governed by the "torture principle."[8]

The superego controls and punishes all transgressions, the legal and penal code, the legal and police force that organizes the torment inside oneself. In Freud's graphic image (to which we cannot assign an ontological status), it commands restlessness, requires satisfactions that are not those of needs or demands, and deems desire to be dangerous and unfulfillable. Wielding the threat of castration in men and the loss of love in women, it perpetuates its imperative for sacrifice, unpayable debts, and subjugating possession by the Other. Its incessant exhortation can only be expressed with the imperative: *Jouis!*

Thanks to the superego, eroticism is stained with a now eroticized guilt; love is linked to transgression; pleasure enters the register of debt; sin becomes *jouissance*; consciousness gets acquainted with the oral *jouissance* of remorse (*remords*); the flames of hell cast their shadow on our flammable flesh, us beings deprived of the sexual relation. The superego switches pleasure for *jouissance* and sustains *jouissance* so that it not be extinguished by the effusions of an accomplished satisfaction. For this reason, Freud emphasizes that the superego's characteristics are all the more compelling the more sacrifices it receives, which Lacan's seminar on ethics puts in perspective.

The fascinating endorsement given to the uncanny by the constant vigilance of the superego is proof of a primordial masochism that overpowers the pleasure principle. The proof Freud provides in the 1920s is well known. The compulsion to repeat, discovered years earlier in analytic transference, shows us *parlêtres* as beings devoid of intelligence (the intelligence that governs the animal kingdom); it makes us trip on the same stone twice only to look for it a third time and ask why we stumbled on it on the two previous occasions, not satisfied until we bend over backward to remove it from the path . . . only to be able to stumble on the next one. Let Sisyphus say it and Prometheus recount it, let the Danaids explain it, as well as the martyrs and truth-loving scientists.

Similarly, there is the constant impossibility of distancing oneself from the traumatic memory: the accident, the humiliation, the painful recollection that attacks us from inside. Or the child's play that summons the phantasm of being abandoned (*fort-da*), devoured, poisoned, seduced, beaten, watched, persecuted, harassed, tortured, maligned, or punished (FL, 151–172). Or the experience confirmed again and again in analysis of a negative therapeutic reaction, in which the subject is not worthy of alleviating his suffering and insists on sustaining it to the point of abandoning the analysis rather that allow a cure. They love their delirium, their symptoms more than themselves and give testimony to the fateful imperative of *jouissance* on their flesh. The defense is a defense of suffering, and psychoanalytic technique is misguided if it does not take *jouissance*, rather than pleasure, as the point of departure in the approach to each case.

The superego marks the subject with the command of *jouissance*, but that directive is also a calling: "You are not at your own service, but of something beyond you that is your cause, your Cause. Your existence is borrowed and you must account for it even if it was not wanted, you must offer the pound of flesh to an implacable God." What links subjects (*re-ligare*, religion) is "the guilt of existence" that can only be subdued by adoration and gratitude toward He who made us debtors and is our creditor. The principle of sacrifice is the basis and not the effect of religion; *jouissance* is inherent in sacrifice. The subject sacrifices himself in the tribute he offers: subjects himself to a yoke that inscribes him in the community, includes him within a social link and makes him a participant of the clan (*socius*).

It is well known that for Lacan, contrary to Freud, castration is not a threat, but rather a saving grace. The real, terrifying threat is that castration be lacking. The clinic shows again and again that lack (*faute*) in the function of the father (to inscribe the subject in the symbolic order): the cause of the desperate, pathetic call for a castrating intervention to separate the child from the *jouissance* and desire of the Mother. When that lack is lacking, the symptom is its substitute. Such is the case in Lacan's (not Freud's) illuminating reading of Little Hans. The child had nothing to fear from a domesticated father that too easily yielded his place in bed next to Hans's mother. The horse in this case is not the symbol or equivalent of the real father but rather the figure of an Ideal Father called on to amend the paternal lack.

Similarly, the phantasm in "A Child Is Being Beaten" is centered on its second phase, which is the repressed formula "my father beats me." There, the whip does not nullify the subject, but rather invokes his ex-sistence, signals him as debtor and dislodges him from the mother's mortiferous *jouissance*. It is an instrument that functions as a signifier (S_1) whose result is a subject ($) that will have to account for his acts by means of the word in the world of language. If the whip causes pain, it is because the Other demands that pain as a pledge of reparation and redemption; the Other demands the tremor of bruised flesh, the cry and promise of submission. It is the proof of "someone cares about you." If the birth of the brother (the one who is flogged in the first phase of the phantasm and was the *colactaneum*—the one nourished at the same breast—of the venomous gaze observed by St. Augustine) threatened the subject with extinction, or disappearance from the field of the Other, the whipping in the second phase of the phantasm not only punishes the sadistic thoughts expressed in the first phase, but also makes existence possible and is paid on account of life's debt (FL).

I've already mentioned the seminar on March 5, 1958, in which Lacan detailed the relation and opposition between desire and *jouissance* as fundamental for understanding what occurs in the psychoanalytic experience. That day he wrote the protocol for the birth of the innovative concept of *jouissance*. In the preceding class on February 12, 1958, Lacan noted that the whipping expelled the subject from a place of omnipotence and sent him toward existence. The child being beaten is not all or nothing. The lashings are *given*; they imply the gift of a signifier that return the subject to an alienated ex-sistance: not in the One but in the Other. To be beaten is a way of ratifying the desire of the Other put in doubt by the appearance of a rival. This is frequently ascertained in children that have been repeatedly traumatized and must overcome the mortiferous hostility of their mothers, or in abuse victims and in the accidents and manifestations of an inflexible and atrocious destiny. The whip eliminates the subject but also constitutes it in its very division; his wounds function as a call to life. The phantasm of being beaten is beyond the pleasure principle. Yes, it is *jouissance*, certainly, but also the principle of certainty, being an object that counts in the Other's desire. "It's because I love you that I make your life so miserable" is the latent signification in Job's phantasm: it secures a place for the subject in the discourse of the master, calling for resignation or rebellion. This is also the case in Christic *jouissance* where the debt is inverted in the form of an invocation: "My God, my God, why have you forsaken me?" To exist is to exist for the Law and be subject to it. Human beings thus pass under the rod and receive their being, as well as the mark of the Other's desire. Historically, the discourse of the master presents and justifies itself in this way.

For these reasons Freud posited the existence of a fundamental death drive, the life drives being deviations, ramifications that pass through the narcissistic image of the ego. Succinctly, the death drive is *the* drive. Psychoanalysis recommences in the 1920s when naturalist explications are questioned. Freud's own push to preserve them under the guise of a "mythobiology" are clumsy and emphasize, by contrast, what is at stake. This occurs at the same time Freud is forced to abandon his project for a metapsychology based on the pleasure principle. The interruption of a series of articles on metapsychology, after the first five, is due to the fact that its real continuation lies in *Beyond the Pleasure Principle*. Anticipating later chapters in our study, we can say that human existence does not tend toward pleasure but rather to a historical inscription of subjective suffering. The clinic repeatedly shows the efforts made by a speech that wishes to be recognized as a sign or writing of life's afflictions; a demand for the Other to recognize the subject's signifying existence; the Other's tolerance always being put to the test, a maximum forcing and stretching of the libidinal lamella.

Not all Lacanians will agree with this, but in the above a particular characteristic of *jouissance* can be observed. *Jouissance* is *dialectic*, although different from the dialectic of desire. First, we must understand that the reference to the dialectic in Lacan is not Hegelian because in Lacan there is no final moment of synthesis due to the "cunning of reason." In fact, one cannot sustain that the dimension of desire is dialectical while *jouissance* is not. That is the position sustained by J-A. Miller in his unpublished seminar *L'exitimité* of May 2, 1984: "The very concept of *jouissance* is fundamentally a nondialectical concept in relation to desire." In this class, Lacan's legal heir incisively explored how Lacan's teaching had adopted a contrary position to that of the dialectic, specifically in his 1960 text "Subversion of the Subject and Dialectic of Desire in the Freudian Unconscious." Miller's position here is consistent with his conference "Theory of *Jouissance*," where he claims that one can straightforwardly say that desire is the desire of the Other, but not that *jouissance* is the *jouissance* of the Other.[9] In this we agree. One's *jouissance* is not to be confused with the "*jouissance* of the Other." However, although we do not wish to incur such confusion, *jouissance* is linked to the dimension of the Other and the dialectic of the subject. We also cannot agree with Miller when, in that same 1984 conference, he states that from 1960 to 1964 (from "Subversion of the Subject . . ." to "The Position of the Unconscious") Lacan phases out any reference to the dialectic.

What is problematic about Miller's assertion can be ascertained by following the thread of Lacan's seminars, particularly the May 31, 1967 class in "Logic of the Phantasm" (S XIV). On that day Lacan recalled that Hegel introduced the notion of *jouissance* given the contradiction between the *jouissance* of the Master and the *jouissance* of the slave, between the leisure of the one and the *jouissance* of the thing in the other: "Not only in so far as he provides that thing to the master, but has to transform it in order to render it acceptable" (S XIV). Lacan included the following wonderful reference in order to comprehend the dialectic of *jouissance*:

> Oedipus did not know the object of his *jouissance*. I posed the question of whether Jocasta knew it and even, why not, if Jocasta *jouissait* letting Oedipus remain in ignorance . . . what part of Jocasta's *jouissance* corresponds to the fact that she left Oedipus in ignorance? It is at this level that, thanks to Freud, serious questions are henceforth posed regarding truth . . . What Hegel surmised was that at the origin the position of the master is a renunciation of *jouissance*, the possibility of forcing everything on the disposition or not of the body. And *not only his own, but also the body of the other*. And the Other, from the moment the social struggle introduces the fact that the relations between bodies are dominated by what is called the law; *the Other is the set of bodies* (S XIV, original emphasis).

In sum, these references to Lacan's 1967 seminar confirm that *jouissance* is considered dialectically, although the dialectic is Lacanian and not Hegelian; it does not lead to any synthesis. For Lacan it is a question of the particular, but of a particular that appears as such only inasmuch as it departs from the universal. *Jouissance* is of the One, but that One cannot be known outside of its relation to the Other and the Other's division between desire and *jouissance*. Also, there is a *jouissance* that depends on the ignorance of the Other, which is extracted, just as in Jocasta's case, from knowing that the Other does not know. That is the dialectic of *jouissance*: oppositional, dissenting. The different forms of *jouissance* are not defined in themselves, only diacritically, in their difference with respect to what is not *jouissance*. The opposition of *jouissance*(s) between the master and the slave, between masculine and feminine *jouissance*, between the one who deprives and the one who is deprived, between the one who knows and the one who knows not, between one race and another. Why not propose, much like we have learned regarding the signifier, that the value of *jouissance* has no other substance than a difference in relation to what a certain actual *jouissance is not*.

There is more to be said regarding the binary opposition Lacan poses between *jouissance* and desire. The desire for recognition (of desire), a key notion in the first Lacan, implies the dialectical struggle with the desire of the Other and, therefore, the *jouissance* of the battle, the war to make one's own desire when faced with the desire–nondesire of the Other (desire–nondesire inasmuch as the desire of the Other is a desire to be recognized and not to recognize someone else). This is key in the Freudian texts on masochism, beginning with "A Child Is Being Beaten." It is also central in the clinic of life and history. The struggle to the death between master and slave (in all its versions) has its foundation in the concept of *jouissance* (as opposed to desire).

"If they punish me it is because my desire exists; it has not banished in the desire of the Other. In the punishment I regain my *jouissance* at the price of alienating it in a relation of opposition to the Other." *Jouissance* becomes possible at the same time as it is subdued by this intervention of the Other, accepted as a salvation with respect to the Other *jouissance*, a nondialectical, unbridled, and terrifying *jouissance* of the One without the differentiating intervention of the Other. The whip, the object, is a signifier that functions as a call to existence, to circulate in a relation that is dialectical and contraposed to the different *jouissance*(s): articulated to the dialectical relation of desire, but not confused with it, with its "agreements" and symbolic pacts. Hegel's words, quoted at the beginning of this chapter, remind us that the juridical notion of *jouissance*, which is particular, differs from that of desire, which is universal. Also, in Lacan's short article dedicated to Freud's *Trieb*, desire comes from the Other, while *jouissance* is on the side of the Thing, the One (E, 722–725). This does not exclude *jouissance* from the plane of the dialectic, given that *jouissance* of the One can be reached only if torn away from the *jouissance* of the Other, safeguarding it from its attacks. The *jouissance* obtained by the beatings that come from the Other, from destiny or God, is a mark that signals the desire–nondesire of the Other: a way to force it in order to recognize one exists.

Jouir implies the usufruct of something. To "use and enjoy the property of another" implies someone's dispossession, one who does not dispose of the same right to usufruct. The first property is the body and, at the same time, the battlefield between the *jouissance* of the One and the *jouissance* of the Other. To whom does the body belong? Is the slave mine to dispose of as I please or, on the contrary, am I the slave of the Other, who can dispose of me and that body that I, phantasmatically, in my position as "figurehead," think I "have"? What happens with the Other, what hole do I dig in him if I condemn this body to death (the suicide of separation) or I mortify it with drugs that anesthetize and prevent it from responding to its demands?

Jouissance is on the side of the Thing, as Lacan noted with rigor, but the Thing can only be reached by turning away from the signifying chain and therefore recognizing a certain relation to it. No one illustrates this more than the suicidal person, but it is also seen in addicts, psychotics, and writers, for whom the pen presents a way of escaping from the links established by discourse. These forms of addiction will be discussed in chapter 7.

Pleasure is on the side of reflex action. It's what makes a frog's leg contract when an electric current makes contact with it. This type of reaction does not produce something new. Speaking beings (*parlêtres*) inscribe their works and discourse in time. They live to die, leaving testimony of their suffering, seeming, to-be(ing). The true substance of the death drive is on the side of *jouissance*, suffering, exploit, the act.

In psychoanalytic terms, death is not the intended inertia of an inanimate nature, but a register that inscribes the impossible passions of subjectivity in its tribulations, errancy, and anti-economic struggles, and that go against the pleasure principle. Lacan's sarcasm toward Freud is justified, then, especially when the latter speaks of the unifying virtues of Eros and when he sustains that human life is oriented toward the creation of vast and ever superior entities. It is not necessary to mention nuclear fission to understand that on that point Freud is not even coherent with himself and that his reflection on human history in *Civilization and its Discontents* manifests the omnipresent death drive as the final substratum of all individual and collective human action.

The goal of the drive is not appeasement or satisfaction (*Befriedigung*: *Fried* [peace]), but rather the lack (*faute*) that tirelessly re-launches forward the movement of the drive. Our history, each of ours, is the history of the many ways of missing the mark of the impossible object, the result of the nonexistence of the sexual relation. This is also true for the history of culture, the organization of the modes of confronting that inexistence.

The subject has a sub-stance that is "*jouissological.*" The first Freudian theory of the psyche proposed a subject governed by the pleasure principle, for whom sexuality was an impurity and tension produced by the seduction of an Other, the perverse adult. The second theory shows the increase in excitations as something that begins in an interior (the very idea of the death drive) that adheres to fantasies and requires an Other for it to be dialectically integrated in the manner specified in the script of the phantasm, the apparatus of *jouissance.*

A reflection and rewriting of Freud's complete works in light of the concept of *jouissance* is possible and even necessary, since it allows for a renewal of Freud's words. We are now in a position to recreate the history of psychoanalysis in view of the shifts it has suffered and pinpoint four or five essential points. The first is the discovery of the unconscious and its processes in relation to the pleasure principle (1895–1915). The second is the moment Freud transcends naturalism and proposes the scandalous theory of the death drive (1920–1930) that, as is well known, was not accepted by the official psychoanalytic movement, which preferred to accept psychoanalytic thinking and actions more in line with homeostatic objectives. Against this inclination, Lacan's "return to Freud" (1953–1958) centered on what was evident but yet unknown, even by Freud: "the unconscious is structured like a language." This third crucial moment in the history of psychoanalysis made possible the fourth turn (as of 1958), the one in which we include analysts after Lacan. The central thesis is that the unconscious is structured like a language, yes, but depends as such on *jouissance. Jouissance* is "processed" by the *langagière* apparatus that transforms *jouissance* into discourse.

It is evident that each of these four moments (or five if we include the period between the second and third [1938–1953]) corresponds to different modalities of conceiving psychoanalysis: its practice, the position of the analyst, and the process of his formation. In sum, the ontological concept and the ontic existence of *jouissance* allows and demands the rewriting and remaking of psychoanalysis.

Chapter 2

Jouissology

Logic of *Jouissance*

Between *Jouissance* and Language

Every subject is called to being, but it is not a summons from "inside," an interior force arising from within or a biological need that promotes its development. The injunction makes a subject, it subjectifies. A demand is made for the subject to speak, assuming the name the Other gave him. He must speak, say who he is, identify himself. The Other requires his speech: if language kills the thing by replacing or making it absent, speech must necessarily represent and order the recognition of that Other of language, which confers life by marking a distance or mortifying it. The subject comes into being, attains ek-sistence, but incurs a debt. In many ways, the Other indicates that the life a subject receives is not free; it requires payment.

How can the *infans*, the subject before the function of speech, pay the price of existence? To pay means to accept the debt: the payment is the receipt. All payments made, whatever they may be, are a renunciation of *jouissance* and cannot be used again once handed over. The purchase of every new object or service mandates another payment; the loss is irremissible. To live, one has to pay, part with *jouissance*, reluctantly. In fact, the clinic shows the devastating effects on those for whom existence is free, the ones who do not stumble with a demanding Other in a system of mutual equivalency, who receive before asking, outside a system of exchange, when the anticipated satisfaction of the demand crushes the very possibility of desire.

The tit for tat of milk and shit (*El toma y daca de leche y caca*), which I mentioned on another occasion, makes it so that life develops in a marketplace of *jouissance*, where nothing is obtained without payment (LI, 172). The transaction is never acceptable or willingly accepted. One does not know if the price paid corresponds to the value of what has been received in return and must resign oneself to the loss implied in surrendering something real for symbolic compensation, a quantum of *jouissance* in exchange for the inconsistent glow of images, precarious certainties attached to words of love or misleading signs that come from the Other, an Other that also asks himself why he should renounce *jouissance*. The Other, with a capital O (*A*, *Autre* in French), is represented for the subject by someone in the imaginary, an other with a small o (*a*), which allows us to begin to sketch the function as well as the impasses of love.

The conflict between the subject and the Other would be fatal if no symbolic instance existed to regulate these exchanges. It is the Law that, although blind, is never neutral, given that it is the Law of the Other (culture), inherent in language and manifested for each *parlêtre* (the speaking subject of the unconscious) as the obligation to make a supposedly maternal language one's own. The Law is nothing if not the imposition of these limitations and losses of *jouissance*. To be a good, prudent, well-educated child; in other words, following the etymology, well led from the outside, able to accept that the mother belongs to the Other. The mother as such exists because the Other (Law of the prohibition of incest) bars her with an interdiction: the breast is an impossible object that exists in the reign of hallucinations, excrement can be surrendered to the Other as educator, one's own production cannot be one's own *jouissance*. One can, at most, speculate with that good, delay its surrender or release it when least expected, but the Other's reason (*logos*) will eventually impose itself on the *jouissance* of accumulation and tension. At the limit of that natural barrier, which is the law of pleasure, the Law of the Other imposes itself, proclaiming its impossible crossing. The *jouissance* of seeing, being seen, beating, spitting, biting, vomiting, being beaten, speaking, hearing and being heard, screaming and being screamed at, all are subject to education, repression of the drive representatives, the discursive suppression of inconvenient words, turning round the subject's own self, the reversal into its opposite, the sublimatory displacement of drive objects and goals to un-knowledge: the conversion of *jouissance* into shame, disgust, pain, and morsels of remorse.

The preceding paragraphs can be summarized in this way: the incompatibility between *jouissance* and the Law—the Law of language, the Law of the Father (according to Lacan's first seminars) that orders to desire and renounce *jouissance*. It compels us to live, transforming the aims of *jouissance* in terms of articulated discourse, allowing and enforcing entry in the social link. Demand is conditioned by what can be demanded. Nothing remains from an original *jouissance* but the nostalgia that creates and mythologizes it retroactively, beginning with the fact that it has been lost, is irrecoverable in its "original" form, and must be veered through other means, per-verted. The body, an unlimited reservoir of *jouissance* in principle, is progressively emptied of that substance (mythical libidinal fluid) that moved through its pores, flooded its recesses, and settled in the borders of its orifices. Now it can be reached, yes, but only through the detour of narcissism, the field of images and words, as a *langagière jouissance*, outside the body (*hors corps*), subject to the imperatives and aspirations of the ideal ego that commands them with the false promise of its recovery in the ego ideal [I(A)].

From *jouissance* of being to phallic *jouissance*: from the absolute Thing of the beginning (absolute because it knows nothing of limits or renunciations), only the phantasmatic objects that cause desire remain. These veer toward other things (the things of the Other), the only ones that can be inscribed once they are reached, due to the disappointing difference with what is sought: the (lost) Thing. The object @, as surplus *jouissance*, is the measure of the missing *jouissance* and, for that reason, being the manifestation of a lack in being, cause of desire. Because the subject must pact with the Other, which gives only by taking away, *jouissance* of @ is residual, compensatory, an indicator of the missing *jouissance*. Just like surplus value is the surplus of value that the worker produces, but is snatched away by the Other in the very act of production (as stipulated by the work contract), leaving him with a remainder of pleasure in the form of a salary that re-launches the process and makes him return the next day, so is surplus *jouissance* the *jouissance* that is the very reason of the movement of the drive and, simultaneously, what the subject loses, his minus, the pound of flesh or the usurped value given over once and again to the insatiable greed of the Other (Shylock).

However, no one resigns himself willingly to the demand for surrender. The rejected *jouissance* returns to claim its privileges; it insists and is thus the foundation of the compulsion to repeat. What is lost is not forgotten; it becomes the basis for even more memory, an unconscious memory beyond its erasure—an infinite longing for recovery that manifests itself in another discourse, the unconscious: the chain of enunciations that runs underneath, that feeds and disturbs the chain of the statement. In order to have and conserve life, one has to accept losing one's money: the thief is never forgiven.

Jouissance Is (Not) the Satisfaction of a Drive

There are perils to disseminating, commenting on, and attempting to broaden Lacan's teaching. Drawing new conclusions that go beyond the letter of his texts is not without danger. Many times, a reader quotes a phrase, an aphorism that is easy to memorize, and is seduced by the simplicity of the expression. But a quote is essentially an interpretation (the analyst knows this well when he repeats an analysand's expression assuming the quotation marks are understood): a selection that retains its meaning only in the specific context in which the text has value. The problem is more pronounced when, as frequently occurs, the commentator knows and skillfully handles the quoted text, directing it to a public that in turn becomes its second-hand commentator, thus establishing a common *doxa* that undermines the teaching without literally altering it.

This preamble is necessary as an introduction to the sad destiny of one of Lacan's sayings, precisely due to its exegetes. I am referring to the oft-quoted expression, "*Jouissance* is the satisfaction of a drive," which appears as a subordinate clause in a sentence in the seminar on ethics (SVII, 209). Jacques-Alain Miller quotes it in his 1984 seminar, and Diana Rabinovich takes it up in an absolute sense: "*Jouissance*, always defined by Lacan as *jouissance* of the body, receives its clearest definition in the *Ethics* [*of Psychoanalysis*]: *jouissance* is the satisfaction of a drive."[1] It is appealing to have such a concise definition, apparently irrefutable and endorsed by the words of the Master. But nothing is more dangerous. The misunderstanding is exacerbated by the way in which Miller, as editor, titles Lacan's seminars. It is well known that Lacan never titled his classes but only each seminar as a whole, and even this was not always definitive, as Seminars III, VIII, and XI prove. These were later edited with titles that differ from the ones they had when they were just courses. The misunderstandings are less possible to avoid when the seminars are broken up into fragments that also receive unwanted titles.

Lacan's class of May 4, 1960, has the acceptable title of "Death Drive." What is problematic is that the second part of the same text has the subtitle: "*Jouissance*, satisfaction of a drive." It is therefore necessary for us to return to Lacan's precise words to avoid the false idea that the drive is compatible with the notion of satisfaction, a profoundly anti-Freudian notion. For Freud, it is necessity that can be satisfied, while the drive is a mythical being: indeterminate, a constant force, an incessant exigency imposed on the psyche due to its link to the body—spurring onward ("*ungebändigt immer vorwärts dringt*" [Mephistopheles in Goethe's *Faust*, Part I, scene 4]), beyond any possible domestication. The drive is not satisfied: it insists, repeats, and always misses the mark, "though with no prospect of bringing the process to a conclusion or of being able to reach the goal" (SE XVIII, 42). Its objective cannot be reached with the satiety or peace (*Friede*) of appeasement (*Befriedigung*), but with a new shot of the arrow, always taut, tense: the bow of aspiration. Freud said, "The aim [*Ziel*] of an instinct [drive] is in every instance satisfaction, which can only be obtained by removing the state of stimulation at the source of the instinct [drive]" (SE XIV, 122). He then immediately refers to the drives that are inhibited in their aim and that are "also" associated with a partial satisfaction. It is different to have an aim than to reach it. The aim [*Ziel*] is aspired to.

It is neither futile nor the task of scholars to dissolve the ambiguity. On the contrary, if *jouissance* is *not* the satisfaction of a drive, we can learn from the discussion what it *really is* or, better yet, in what particular and restricted sense, as Lacan actually said, we can speak of *jouissance* being the satisfaction of a drive, quite specifically the death drive, which is not what one thinks of when speaking of drives, much less the *jouissance* of satisfaction of all or a particular drive, a more-or-less indefinite *Trieb* in the set of drives.

In order to clarify these points, we must turn to Lacan's seminar on ethics and contextualize the quote:

> It is a curious and even paradoxical fact—but analytical experience can be registered in no other way—that reason, discourse, signifying articulation as such, is there from the beginning, *ab ovo*; it is there in an unconscious form before the birth of anything as far as human experience is concerned. It is there buried, unknown, un-mastered, unavailable to him who is its support. And it is relative to a situation structured in this way that man at a subsequent moment has to situate his needs. Man's captivity in the field of the unconscious is primordial, fundamental in character. Now, because this field is

organized logically from the beginning, it embodies a *Spaltung*, which persists in the whole subsequent development; and it is in relation to this *Spaltung* that the functioning of desire as such is to be articulated. This desire reveals certain ridges, a certain sticking point, and it is for this reason that Freudian experience has found that man's route to the integration of self is a complicated one.

The problem involved is that of *jouissance*, because *jouissance* presents itself as buried at the center of a field and has the characteristics of inaccessibility, obscurity, and opacity; moreover, the field is surrounded by a barrier which makes access to it difficult for the subject to the point of inaccessibility, *because jouissance appears not purely and simply as the satisfaction of a need but as the satisfaction of a drive—that term to be understood in the context of the complex theory I have developed on this subject in this seminar.*

As you were told last time, the drive as such is something extremely complex for anyone who considers it conscientiously and tries to understand Freud's articulation of it. It isn't to be reduced to the complexity of the instinct as understood in the broadest sense, in the sense that relates it to energy. It embodies a historical dimension whose true significance needs to be appreciated by us.

This dimension is to be noted in the insistence that characterizes its appearances; it refers back to something memorable because it was remembered. Remembering, historicizing, is coextensive with the functioning of the drive in what we call the human psyche. It is there, too, that destruction is registered, that it enters the register of experience. (SVII, 49, my emphasis)

Having said this, Lacan goes on to illustrate the concept with the system of Pope Pius VI, a fable by the Marquis de Sade that proposes it is through crime that man participates in the new creations of nature. Lacan reads to his audience what is perhaps the longest quote in his twenty-eight years of teaching to show that the death drive is split between what results from energetics or the Nirvana principle (leading to zero, the inanimate, or annihilation) and, *on the other hand* (my emphasis), the death drive. He then adds:

The death drive is to be situated in the historical domain; it is articulated at a level that can only be defined as a function of the signifying chain, that is to say, insofar as a reference point, that is a reference point of order, can be situated relative to the functioning of nature. It requires something from beyond whence it may itself be grasped in a fundamental act of memorization, as a result of which everything may be recaptured, not simply in the movement of the metamorphoses but from an initial intention. (SVII, 211)

Lacan follows Bernfeld here ("one of the most orthodox Freudians") in distinguishing between the movement of energetics toward zero and what we analysts call the drive, something that is beyond the tendency to return to an inanimate state. Along with the drive, we find in our experience something else that comes close to a will to destruction: "Will for an Other-thing, given that everything can be challenged from the perspective of the function of the signifier" (SVII, 212). This will to destruction is, following Sade, a will to create from zero, to begin again. This destructive and creative force is linked to history insofar as it is memorable and memorized, registered in the signifying chain. The death drive for Lacan is therefore "creationist sublimation."

We have to review Lacan's position in this class in order to articulate the triple sense of the drive. The energetics level, outside the register of psychoanalytic experience, is Freud's "meta-biological" speculation. This is the level of the *drive* described in "Instincts and their Vicissitudes [Drives and their Vicissitudes]" (1915), which always hinges on the partial sexual drive. Lacan says of the latter that it borders the object @ toward which it tends and fails, in contraposition to the death drive, memorized, historicizing, comparable to the will to destruction, leading to the inscription of the subject in the signifying chain. These two, the partial and death drives, are the pertinent ones for our field and can ultimately be joined together given that the end of every drive is the inscription of life in the symbolic: through inanimate writing, not through obedience or the transgression of the pleasure principle.

As I stated in an earlier commentary:

In *Civilization and its Discontents*, Freud posits that history is the result of the eternal struggle between the death drive and the life drives. History, says Heidegger in his *Introduction to Metaphysics*, is the result of the eternal struggle between *diké* and *tekhné*, between the instituted norm that brings together ever more complex units and *tekhné*, the dissolving activity of man that challenges the established orders to destroy the existent and create new forms of existence. In an earlier work we claimed that both conceptualizations overlap and converge, but that Heidegger's is more exact because it avoids the biologizing ambiguities linked to the concepts of life and death. (LI, 64)

If the drive is part of the demand that provokes the fading of the subject ($\lozenge$D), the drive stumbles with its impossible realization. Lack is structural: it is inscribed in the Other to whom the demand is directed—S($\cancel{A}$). In other words, if we consider the drive in relation to the field of language and not a debatable biological or hedonistic transcription, we cannot accept the phrase "the satisfaction of a drive." This phrase is neither Lacanian nor Freudian because it confuses drive with necessity and the difference between these two registers has always been clear in our experience. If *jouissance* has to do with the drive it is insofar as the drive leaves a remainder of dissatisfaction that spurs repetition and, for that reason, the drive both historicizes and dissatisfies. We can also affirm that *jouissance* is the remainder of the drive's movement around the object because what is contoured is the void in the Thing, stumbling with the real, impossible to avoid.

The other consideration that allows us to understand the drive essentially as death drive is Freud's indication regarding the drive's fundamentally conservative nature, which tends toward reestablishing a previous state. What is the previous state to which the *parlêtre* could refer? There is no need to imagine a previous mineral stage in life or metabolic exchanges, borrowed from dubious biological discourses, to answer what we can elucidate with psychoanalytic terms. Death is what curtails all possible *jouissance* in the *parlêtre*, because there is *jouissance* only of the living body. Such is the consubstantiality of the death drive and the symbolic order already established, beginning with Lacan's second seminar dedicated to the ego (S II). If life is defined beginning with an inscription in the structures of subjectivity, which are transactions with the Other, that is, starting from the flesh becoming body due to the interference of the signifier in the vital processes, the movement of the drives can be seen as the force that propels the recovery of a state before the word, or the recovery of the Thing as the absolute object of desire: a *jouissance* of being, from which the subject comes to ek-sist.

Once again we posit the opposition between the first *jouissance*, the *jouissance* of being and the word that comes from the Other and gives the Other prominence, compelling a renunciation of *jouissance* in exchange for pleasure and blocking the *jouissance* of being, thus requiring that the latter be directed and misdirected through thought. It is accessible to the subject, but as another *jouissance*, a second-order *jouissance*, semiotic, *langagière*, talkative, outside the body, which theory considers and designates with the doubtful, ambiguous, and nevertheless necessary name of *phallic jouissance*. We have to see why, since it is not evident and leads to discussions and misunderstandings.

There is an unfathomable and unavoidable point of departure: cases where the function of speech do not exist or have been annulled and the living being, even within the field of language, is not included in discursive exchanges. As an example or paradigm, think about autism or catatonia. Or, to begin at the absolute beginning, in the newborn's condition in relation to the Other: being an object at his disposal, discretion, or arbitrariness. It is the state of indistinctness between ego and world, "the world" being essentially the mother's body. In his 1915 text, Freud calls this original and mythical Thing, prior to any differentiation, the real-ego: it is first, a being in the real, prior to any recognition by the Other or the establishment of the pleasure principle that will construct a pleasure-ego, the definitive ego, the one that accepts in greater or lesser measure the pressures of reality that modifies and gives continuation to the pleasure principle. We will return to this discussion later in the chapter. It is in relation to this initial real-ego that the invoking call of the Other has impact since it is a subjectifying call. The intervention of the Other is antithetical to *jouissance*: it displaces the subject from this absolute real, expels him from Paradise, and constitutes *jouissance* as such, insofar as it has been lost.

Speech is always the word of the Law prohibiting *jouissance*. Paradise exists from the beginning with the two trees whose fruit must not be eaten. After the expulsion, the return to the Thing (real-ego) is obstructed and only exile and a resigned living in language remains. An angel that brandishes a flamboyant sword ensures the observance of the Law. As Lacan notes in Seminar VII:

> We have presently reached that barrier beyond which the ana-
> lytical Thing is to be found, the place where brakes are applied,
> where the inaccessibility of the object as object of *jouissance* is
> organized. It is in brief the place where the battlefield of our
> experience is situated. The crucial point is at the same time
> the new element psychoanalysis brings, however inaccessible
> it may be in the field of ethics.
>
> In order to compensate for that inaccessibility, all indi-
> vidual sublimation is projected beyond that barrier, along with
> the sublimations of the systems of knowledge, including—why
> not?—that of analytical knowledge itself. (SVII, 203)

Either the inaccessible Thing or the Other. The Other is the object of a
primitive hate that justifies absolute negativity as the original vocation of
being. For this reason, every drive is at bottom a death drive, an attack on
the alienating imperative of making *jouissance* pass through the chain of
discourse. Freud says nothing else: "Hate, as a relation to objects, is older
than love. It derives from the narcissistic ego's primordial repudiation of
the external world with its outpouring of stimuli" (SE XIV, 139).

If Eros tends toward connection, the constitution of links, it is a
question of links between signifiers, the vector that goes from one signifier (S_1) to another signifier (S_2). Lacan is ironic, with reason, regarding
Freud's delirious statement when he claims that the links between cells
that constitute multicellular organisms or complex societies could be
proof of the work of Eros. It is true that the drives are mythical beings,
but we only know of them because of our *langagière* practice. Since it is
not a concern in their field, biologists can say nothing about our Eros
and Thanatos, as they emerge in psychoanalytic practice. The death drive's
actions fall on the interval of the chain and tend to dissolve the relation
that is discourse. It thus negates the Other and expresses the irredeemable
longing of a return to the *jouissance* of being. It is an iconoclastic activity
that always seeks to begin again. The destructive negativity that takes hold
of desire, emphasized by Freud, Lacan, and Hyppolite in their discussions
of *Die Verneinung*, can be understood by considering how the *jouissance*
of being is included in the theory.[2]

The drive is not something that is satisfied and gives access to *jouissance*, but essentially an aspiration to *jouissance* that fails for having to
recognize the Other and pay the charge of his lodging with *jouissance*.
The drive is fundamentally destructive and cannot be pacified. One

must again turn to Freud for his surprising expression and clarification regarding *jouissance*. Regarding the death drive, he writes in *Civilization and its Discontents*:

> But even where it emerges without any sexual purpose, in the blindest fury of destructiveness, we cannot fail to recognize that the satisfaction of the instinct is accompanied by an extraordinarily high degree of narcissistic enjoyment, owing to its presenting the ego with a fulfillment of the latter's old wishes for omnipotence. The instinct of destruction, moderated and tamed and, as it were, inhibited in its aim, must, when it is directed toward objects, provide the ego with the satisfaction of its vital needs and with control over nature. (SE XXI, 121)

In the previous paragraph we noted a phrase that is not Freudian; there is satisfaction, but not of the drive because Freud speaks of the *satisfaction of the ego*. We can now better define the purpose of our claim by analyzing Lacan's aphorism, from which this section of chapter 2 takes its title. The purpose is to avoid the continued repetition of a facile and decontextualized formula that makes us lose sight of the sense of the relation between drive and *jouissance* in Freud and Lacan. Concretely, I have tried to emphasize the originality of the Freudian concept of the drive once transformed, in its roots, by the introduction of the revulsive death drive. Specifically, once that concept has been divorced from the idea of pacification or satisfaction and referred to *jouissance* as "beyond the pleasure principle." Lacan's commentators know this well, but the doxa they create contradicts Lacan's teaching in fundamental points.

The drive does not satisfy or satiate. The drive historicizes, makes what is memorable transgressive; it borders on failure by tending toward the real as impossible, and that is how it reaches its aim. It is now time to continue to another point in order to avoid more ambiguity, the Manichean and hasty conception of the Other as "evil," which distances the subject from that supreme "Good" (the Thing).[3]

Speech, Diaphragm of *Jouissance*

Due to the intervention of the Other and his Law that demand *jouissance* be handed over in the exchange market, what remains of the *jouissance* of being is lack in being (*manque à être*): desire. Something is lost of bodily *jouissance* because of the Other. It is the basis of the well-known aspiration of Freudian *Wunsch*: the recovery, either through a short-circuiting hallucination or the long road of the transformations of reality, the identity of "perception": something that resembles the forever lost *jouissance* of the Thing. What is inscribed of *jouissance*: the Freudian *Id*, *Ça*, the drive that has been renounced, all this is chaotic and disarticulated. They are *impressions*, signs that cannot be subjectified and presupposed as being someone's. The "thing-representations" (*Sachvorstellungen*, not *Dingvorstellungen* because there is no representation of the Thing) must access the preconscious system by linking up with "word-representations" (*Wortvorstellungen*), although this process is not simple. Word-representations, the signifiers in language, do not only overinvest or provide an extra charge of "energy" to the signifiers of desire aspiring to recover *jouissance*. The signifier substitutes the thing-representations and imposes other laws that are not those of *jouissance* (*qui n'a jamais connu de loi*) but of discourse and language. Only metaphors and metonyms remain of *jouissance*; they come from the symbolic to take charge and "denaturalize" the anterior real that is now inaccessible and irrecoverable, symbolizing the lost, renounced *jouissance* handed over to the demand of the Other. For Freud, its proper name is *Triebverzicht*, drive renunciation.

Articulated language, speech, is a road that leads astray. In order to travel, one must follow where it leads: exile, reality, the things of the world that are other names for the original loss. Articulated in "thing-representations" (according to Freudian terminology), unconscious desire is inarticulable, having to accept the laws of the signifying chain: to translate *jouissance* in few words and through circumlocutions that necessarily distorts it. It must be articulated as a demand, recognize and accept the Other as a condition of satisfaction. The central idea I wish to emphasize here is that the signifying chain does not have a common measure and no possibility of signifying the *jouissance* to which it aspires; the signifier is incommensurable with *jouissance*, and the lack of such a common measure is what defines *jouissance* as a type of substance that "runs underneath," is constantly produced and at the same time escapes, because discourse brands it as impossible, unsayable. What name other than "libido" would correspond to this fabulous and slippery substance, this *hommelette*?

To repeat some basic elements of the Lacanian concept of discourse: the subject is the effect of the signifying chain, in place of a signified of one signifier (S_1) that represents it before another signifier (S_2), a chain is made between them. The product of this articulation between the two signifiers is an irreducible remainder, a real that is an in-significant remainder, the unreachable object cause of desire that represents the lost *jouissance* as plus (or minus) *jouissance*. Between the subject and the object @ produced as the remainder that falls out from the encounter of the two signifiers, there is a disjunction, an essential failed encounter. One must now write the relation between the two effects of the function of the word (the subject as signified and the object as the lost *jouissance*) with the double bar of disjunction or with the *losange* ($\lozenge$) of the formula for the phantasm ($\$\lozenge a$). The encounter between the two is, with the exception of psychosis, impossible.

$$\frac{S_1}{\$} \quad \xrightarrow{} \quad \underset{\text{//}}{} \quad \frac{S_2}{@}$$

$$(\$ \lozenge @)$$

In this formula one notes the radical heterogeneity between the signifiers and the subject, which is the effect of signification, on the one hand and, on the other, *jouissance*, indicated by object @. Let us recall that "everything is structure but not everything is signifier"; object @ is what is unrepresentable in the structure: not a signifier (E, 253).

With Freud, since Freud, we know that this displacement, which is also an emptying out of *jouissance* in the signifying articulation (in discourse), is also a scansion, a dividing up of moments, dramatic points as cuts or interruptions that Freudian theory has defined as phases or states of psychosexual evolution. Everyone remembers the chronological outline that places certain age groups in the abscissas and the evolutionary phases in the ordinates, making it appear as if psychoanalysis were just one more chronology of development. With Freud, since Freud, we know that all those phases, characterized by a renunciation of *jouissance* (first oral, then anal, with no well-established interpolations regarding urethral, muscular, visual *jouissance*, etc.), are preparations for a final renunciation that retroactively re-signifies them as well as their corresponding phantasms. After the pre-genital prelude follows the Oedipal passage of castration; all the bodily renunciations of *jouissance* are produced and only the pure disposition of the subject to assimilate her- or himself to the "formative" (alienating) word of the Other remains. Not by a casual coincidence does that period of latency coincide with so-called "school age." What is not dissolved by castration returns from the repressed in the form of symptoms, monuments that commemorate the abandoned *jouissance*, although transposed into *langagière* terms. The symptoms are translatable, interpretable, effects of a "conversion" of *jouissance* (to which they will always refer): forms of phallic *jouissance*. Everything functions thus until the impact of puberty reactivates the demands of sexuality; these have to be channeled through the dictates of the primacy of genitality—that is, of the male genital, leaving the young girl divided between a *jouissance* that is phallic (the clitoris, the same or comparable to that of men) and another *jouissance*, vaginal, which is complementary to phallic *jouissance* and therefore included within its orbit, under its aegis and supremacy (a thesis that Lacan later corrects and resignifies). With Freud and since Freud, we know about the process of renunciation of the most archaic object of desire, whose dynamic is played out on the stage of the Oedipal Complex and culminates, on the masculine side, in identification with the rival father and, on the feminine side, in a demand made to the father. After accepting the disillusionment of an irremissible maternal castration, there is a remainder of penis envy and a desire to recover it in the form of its symbolic equivalent: a child.[4]

After this process, sexuality, with its polymorphous arrangements, "perverse" sexual components, initial multiplicity of zones and objects, is balanced out. Where *jouissance* spilled out anarchically in the green paradise of infantile love, there is now a law, the effect of castration and the prohibition of incest, which determines the objects and the modes of accessible satisfaction to the one who speaks.

Freud thoroughly analyzed this process in many texts and forms, but perhaps most clearly in "Formulations on the Two Principles of Mental Functioning" (1911), where he describes the replacement of the pleasure principle by its modified substitute, the reality principle (SE XII). In this article, the term *Lust* in *Lustprinzip* should not be understood as "pleasure," the limit and barrier to *jouissance*, but rather as *jouissance* itself, while "reality," master of convenience and regulator of ideals, is that obscure reason of the Other that superimposes and displaces the *jouissance* of the body; the subject is thus divided between two Others difficult to reconcile. These are the body as Other, alien to him inasmuch as it sustains aspirations to *jouissance* that are prohibited (*jouissance* of the Other) and the Other of language, demanding renunciations of *jouissance*, accepted without enthusiasm and the basis for symptoms and the psychopathology of everyday life. This process of "dis-*jouissance*" (to use a necessary neologism) justifies that we read the article on the two principles transgressively. In this text, *Lustprinzip* corresponds to the initial *jouissance* that Freud called real-ego in 1915 (SE XIV). The reality principle is the proper name for the principle of pleasure-unpleasure. The two principles, pleasure and reality (linked), accordingly act as barriers interposed on the road to *jouissance*.

The *jouissance*(s) succumb to castration and transform themselves for having to be signified, making their way through the funnel of speech, having to accept its Law (culture), always evoking the renunciation of the drive that deviates (perverts) it through a narrow pass. For this reason Freud proposed the "partial drives" as precursors of castration since it is only with the latter that they reach definite signification, which includes the imaginary function as $-\varphi$. With symbolic castration, the objects of desire must carry the weight of their own impossibility. As far as Φ, the Phallus as signifier of the *jouissance* prohibited to those who speak, whatever *jouissance* is accessible is also barred and displaced along the signifying chain, outside the body (*hors-corps*). For this reason, with the object @ of the phantasm, one must also infer the function of castration; although not written, for the sake of brevity it should be object @/-φ.

The flesh is incorporated in language and made into a body. The aspirations of the drive require the Other to whom demands are made. For this reason, Lacan writes the drive as $\$\lozenge D$. The subject constitutes itself based on the ways in which the Other signifies and responds to the demand, imposing its conditions, what it will or will not do. The subject exists as the effect of the action of the Other of language on the flesh made body insofar as it accepts the cuts that language makes on the vital flow. The body becomes a map, a parchment where the letter is written with blood (*la letra con sangre entra*).[5] A body is human if it partakes of this system of transactions that exchanges *jouissance* for words. The division of the subject (\$) alludes, among other things, to this process of alienation that constitutes the pole of the drive as Id, *Ça*, and leaves the ego in charge of relations with the Other, as well as to organize defenses against the excesses of *jouissance*. Emerging from the repressed, the drive proceeds as the exigency of work, a tension imposed on the psyche because of its relation to the corporeal, a transgression of the pleasure principle, an aspiration to *jouissance* that does not have sympathy for the orders and restrictions imposed by the Other (S XI). The "dynamic" of Freud's metapsychology is the conflict between transgressive *jouissance* and homeostatic pleasure, between an infantile sexual desire that is never enough and the wish to continue sleeping.

Jouissance can be declined (in the grammatical sense of declension and the subjective form of "to decline"). There is now a clinic of *jouissance*: ways of conjugating, evoking and missing its mark, refusing and recovering it without wanting to know much about it. It reappears after *langagière* metamorphoses in the formations of the unconscious, the unconscious that works with raw material (*jouissance*) and transforms it into a product (discourse), its condition being an instrument structured like it ("language is the condition of the unconscious," Lacan said): the battery of signifiers that serve the ends of *jouissance* (AE, 393–403). It is not a question of language but of *lalangue*, the Lacanian *linguistérie* (even *linguystérie*, *linguysterics*) that is the flesh of the phantasm (L, 213). The unconscious is able to smuggle *jouissance* by contraband, but in order to say no to the Law one must accept being its subject, as well as recognizing its constraints. The transgressive night-time dream, as well as the joke, do not abolish but confirm its rule. Repression recognizes it with extreme pain in the symptom; what is incommensurable in *jouissance* is condemned to vegetate in those falsely natural reserves: the well-delimited spaces of the phantasm. *Jouissance* takes refuge in the unconscious fantasy, whose archives and protocols Melanie Klein explored: a crazy fantasy, irreducible to reason, cut to pieces, corrosive, wild, asocial. The "gutsy genius" (*tripière de genie*, as Lacan called her) evokes a suffocating and devouring *jouissance* of the Other linked to the mythical body of the Mother as representative of the Thing.[6] The repressions and renunciations of the divided subject, the good neurotic child, are based on these horrific imaginary formations of *jouissance*.

These formations belong to the world of communication, meaning and the reciprocal specular satisfaction of egos. The subject cannot recognize himself when placed under the emblems of an in-itself, a *self* that sticks to the pieces of *jouissance* in a unified and totalizing image of itself and the other, the "object," as it is called by the proponents of the "theory of object relations." The latter aspires to be a "new paradigm" for psychoanalysis and has rapidly conquered the will of large numbers in the world association of psychoanalysis, avidly seeking any novelty allowing it to recede to theoretical pre-Freudian times. This is not the appropriate text to review and critique this psychology of the total person that flourishes in our times, waving the flag of a concealed "return to . . . Adler." Not for being embarrassing is it less flagrant, a "scientific regression," as it is called by one of the supporters of an earlier regression to ego psychology, criticized by Lacan (F, 133–150).

We are now at a time in which the proponents of a model that reigned during the 1950s and '60s turn out to be too Freudian, conservative (two words that are synonymous for the "innovators"), traditionalist. The *self* and the total object (the other person) are the tools that make it possible to reject the unconscious and the always partial objects of an "antiquated" Freudian theory of the drives. I cannot emphasize enough that at the center of this theoretical project is the emptying out of *jouissance* from psychoanalytic theory, so as to convert it into a conception of interpersonal relations controlled by the ideals of harmony and completion. We can imagine how lovely psychoanalysis is when we manage to remove the drives, castration and Oedipus, *jouissance* and unconscious desire. Freed from such weight, it wishes to show that the cure can be reduced to a detailed narrative of the interactions between a friendly therapist and a patient that learns to integrate a previously dissociated self due to the defects of a not-good-enough mother.[7]

So it goes, from one digression to another, toward our already proposed understanding of a *langagière jouissance* we would know nothing about were it not for discourse. The latter imposes its legality and divides *jouissance* into a *prior jouissance*, the retroactive mythical effect of the word and a *subsequent jouissance*, produced as it escapes traversing the minefield of language. We would know nothing of *jouissance* were it not for the effect of the word. Lacan speculated about a *jouissance* of the tree and the oyster. It is not a question of following him there; *jouissance* is not a vital function, but appears because speech and the Law mortify life. It is question of *parlêtres* (speaking beings, subjects of the unconscious). Speech extracts *jouissance* from the body and gives a body to *jouissance*, another body (of discourse). This process is never complete or peaceful; the formations of the unconscious are memorials to the impossible translation of the emergence of a *jouissance* that should not be. Discourse is, rhetoric aside, the bearer and product of the *jouissance* that passes through language, managed by a strict economy of *jouissance*.

Articulated speech lets it pass, controls and regulates its voltage. The signifier does not exist in the heaven of Platonic ideas. Its place is difficult to pinpoint. Lacan states that Descartes's substance (*cogitans* and *extensa*) is not enough to localize it because "the signifier is situated at the level of a *jouissante* substance (*substance jouissante*)"—that is, at the level of the body that is felt, irreducible to physics or logic. Or rather, the support of a different logic from that of the logicians. If the signifier is there and *jouisssance* exists only because of its mediation, it is because "the signifier is the cause of *jouissance*;" by imposing limits, the signifier also gives *jouissance* its reason for being: "the signifier is what brings *jouissance* to a halt" (S XX, 24).

What about this "*jouissante* substance"? The best illustration I can offer is the oft-repeated analogy that compares the *parlêtre* to a computer. What is in it? A body, the effect of a signifying creation: a product of technology that is its physical materiality (hardware), totally stupid in itself, even when it is the support of the activities of the machine. It is a crude body that has no use until it is programmed by a structured organization of signifiers, codified information without a body (software). With the "I am" of the hard and the "I think" of the soft, we have Descartes's two substances in view. The machine can function to perfection, faster and more efficiently than the dumb machines of us *parlêtres*. For the former, what is of no use, errs, or is ambiguous, is material to be discarded, to be Descartes. If it is sufficiently advanced, it learns from its mistakes and corrects them; it is neither complacent nor rigid. Its hardware is indifferent to the composition and operations of its software. The one does not affect the other, if technically compatible. There is no phantasm, imaginary, neurosis, nor compulsion to repeat. That is the difference between the machine and the *parlêtre*; the latter is the seat (not the subject) of a *jouissance* that passes through him, felt in the confluence of the body and language that does not recognize a principle of efficiency and is the source of complacency in error and erring. What would be the purpose of a *jouissante* machine if a computer technician were to invent it? In the computer, thinking (not *savoir* as Lacan notes in his seminar of March 20, 1973) proliferates in an absolute desert of *jouissance*, in the coupling of the hardware and software (S XX). In a man and a woman, made from a *jouissante* substance not even dreamt by Descartes, the signifier allows for copulation, not happiness.

It is in this sense that I propose speech is the filter or, appealing to a photographic analogy and without ignoring its other connotations, the diaphragm of *jouissance*. That is, in relation to the "*jouissante* substance," the Freudian libidinal fluid or the mythical, elastic Lacanian *lamella*, speech has the function to intercept and protect against undesirable (or too desirable) excesses. *Diaphrasein* in Greek is to separate, intercept, erect a barrier.

Speech is the medicine offered by the Other, the drug introduced in the *parlêtre* at birth, now considered a regulating thermostat, the diaphragm that regulates the passage of light, the pupil that dilates in the darkness and contracts with the luminous rays. We know that too much light drowns out the photographic plate, exposing the image, and that the lack of light does not allow the plate to impress a definition on the image. We also know that the diaphragm needs to be sensitive, like the pupil, and regulated to accommodate different conditions and hours of the day, much like the sphincterian diameter.

Such is the function of speech. In the psychotic it does not function, exist, or its apparatus is destroyed. In that case, *jouissance* inundates the speaker and sweeps subjectivity away: the barriers that limit the penetration of the Other's words break; the body is exposed to uncontrollable metamorphoses that the subject witnesses in amazement. In neurosis, on the contrary, we see the spasm or contraction of this diaphragm that loses flexibility and shows us the entire phenomenology of the classical mechanisms of the ego's defenses: *langagière* methods to reign in a *jouissance* experienced as dangerous or intolerable. We find special situations not reducible to the simple opposition of the open or closed diaphragm in perversions, drug addictions, and psychosomatic illnesses. We will discuss these in the chapters dedicated to the clinic, but it is important to emphasize how the opposition and articulation between *jouissance* and discourse is useful in the clinic; it is central in the experience of analysis insofar as the latter works on the diaphragm of *jouissance*.

The conditions for a cure are not only *not* the same, but must be radically different for cases in which the diaphragm does not exist (psychosis) or is occluded (neurosis). The Freudian framework emerges from the experience of neurosis and consists in creating the conditions of possibility allowing the passage from *jouissance* to speech. This also gives us another point of entry to what is at stake in the transference, which is transference of *savoir* certainly and even of a subject supposed to know, but only to the extent that this supposition is a *savoirjouir* that opens the way to both the perverse and analytic act and where only the desire of the analyst determines the difference.

The Thing and Object @

Jouissance exists because of the signifier, if the signifier does not detain and subject it to a norm, which is phallic. Language is what functions as a barrier to a *jouissance* that would not exist otherwise. However, we have referred to a *jouissance* that inundates being and is only devastated by the demand to organize it in words. There is no mystery nor contradiction in saying that language produces a *jouissance* that existed before the former's intervention. It is a function of language to kill the thing by giving it a new existence, a displaced life. It was the issue I posed in the first chapter: what came first, *jouissance* or speech? It is the classic problem of the chicken and the egg—that is, of structures that do not recognize before or after, although the question regarding their genesis always returns. If *jouissance* is a retroactive effect of the speech that limits it, we must explore its origin and point of departure. Or, if the universe is expanding, then we must ask at what moment it was concentrated at one point; Italo Calvino wrote about this in his memorable story "The Cosmicomics." The question regarding an origin necessarily leads to an answer that is in the realm of myth. We psychoanalysts do not reject myth. The drives are mythical beings and great in their indetermination, said Freud; Oedipus is a complex because it is mythical; the fundamental phantasm was first developed by Lacan as the "individual myth of the neurotic;" the Lacanian libido is a mythical fluid; and so on (N 405–425). For Lacan, the original myth of *jouissance* and its subsequent loss articulates a Freudian term with a long philosophical tradition: the Thing; Kant with Freud. In a brief definition, quoted previously regarding the relation between the Thing and speech, Lacan states: "The Thing is that which in the real, the primordial real, I will say, suffers from the signifier . . ." (S VII, 118).

The Thing, a pure real, prior to all symbolization, exterior to any attempt to apprehend it, and wiped away by speech. An enclosed impossible nucleus that is at once intimate and inaccessible to the subject. Lacan referred to it with a neologism in Seminar VII, *The Ethics of Psychoanalysis*: extimate (*extimité*). Any representation distorts it. Anyone can imagine the breast, the mother's body, intrauterine life, the womb and what resembles it, knowing that these images are not the Thing; they emerge due to the existence of a world produced and structured by the symbolic that allows for such imaginary productions, those representations revolving around a real impossible to recover. The phantasms, including those of the Thing, are the effects the real suffers due to the action of the signifier. Symbolization, the intrusion of language on flesh, imposes a lack in being that characterizes the subject and launches him on the paths to desire.

Nietzsche anticipated this idea in 1873, in a brief, essential essay published posthumously: we know nothing of the real if not through fictitious constructions enabled by language.[8] We live in a world of lies, fictions. Lacan states that all discourse is *semblant* and its function is to represent and mask the truth from which it derives. For this reason, knowledge is impossible and what remains is *savoir*, a phantasm.

How is one to return, if not on the basis of a peculiar (*spécial*) discourse, to a prediscursive reality? That is the dream: the dream behind every conception (*idée*) of knowledge. But it is also what must be considered mythical. There is no such thing as a prediscursive reality. Every reality is founded and defined by a discourse (S XX, 32).

As the place of *jouissance* without limits and the myth of the lack of lack, the Thing appears as the absolute end of desire, the place or state that can do away with the lack in being, to reach the state of Nirvana, the suppression of all differential tension with the world, between being and nonbeing, death. The inclination toward the Thing is the death drive as the final destination of all vital human pursuits. This myth of full satisfaction makes one consider the logic of the myth: the point of origin and place that is on this side of desire, as well as the point of destination, the state of absolute inertia reached as ultimate quietude once the fire of life is consumed. To live, for the being that speaks, is to choose the roads to death, wander on misdirected paths, and look toward an errant *jouissance* in view of its recovery.

The Thing, as absolute object of desire, opens thinking to an uncanny and abysmal dimension of the *jouissance* of being, prior to ek-sistence: a retroactive effect of language that, by being placed beyond the thing itself (what the linguists call the referent), creates the intuition of an "on this side of." This supposition cannot be eliminated, says Lacan: "Language, in its meaning effect, is never but beside the referent. Isn't it thus true that language imposes being upon us and obliges us, as such, to admit that we never have anything by way of being (*de l'être*)?" (S XX, 44). What propels us not to seem (*paraître*) but rather to-be (*par-être*), to exist sideways, in the field of the *semblant*, given the "insufficiency" of language?

I have emphasized the point enough. The Thing is an effect of language that introduces a lack allowing for separation. The Law of language, of human societies whose final effect and foundation is the law of the prohibition of incest (reintegration with the mother), creates the Thing and defines it as lost. When the first access to the symbolic is produced, a first intrusion of the symbol in life, the Thing is obliterated. *Jouissance* is thus marked by a *minus*, and the human being is called to being in an obligation to say itself, to articulate signifiers that express the only fundamental content: the lack in *jouissance*, the only referent, "the only avowed ontic" for us psychoanalysts ("*Avec cette référence à la jouissance s'ouvre l'ontique seule avouable pour nous*" [AE, 327]). It is because of the gap produced in beings for having to say themselves that being is—the being of all those *parlêtres* exiled from the Thing.

In the previous section we addressed the question of discourse and noted that the articulation of signifiers supposes an anterior real, an "on this side of" the Thing, which produces an un-comparable and incommensurable remainder: a lost *jouissance*, cause of desire that is the object @, an ulterior real. This is how the thread of desire moves; through the demands repeated to the Other from whom the subject receives signs, manifestations, and attributes that, because they have to be put into words, cannot fill the open void of *jouissance*. It is not because the Other is malevolent; it is simply that the Other cannot respond to what is demanded, and "limps" (*ça cloche*) due to the lack of a signifier, which is barred (*barré*).

Given that the Thing is unrepresentable—an empty scene, a space beyond the impassable surface of the mirror—a virtual space emerges that is nothing more than an illusion; the objects that wished to substitute, populate, and furnish that space can achieve only an imaginary, spectral status (*mirages*). They are the objects of the phantasm before which the subject fades ($\lozenge$@). The essential dissension between the Thing and objects (*das Ding, die Sache, die Objekte, die Gegenstände*) is thus introduced. It is here that we can consider the object @ that causes desire and moves the drive. Inasmuch as the Thing is missing, the objects of the world appear and multiply. The *parlêtres*, through language, make a world for themselves and enter the market of *jouissance* with the Other. Due to this original displacement, subjects are constituted in their division, which is now a division between the Thing and objects (following Freud, this includes the ego, considered a particular object on which a particular case of narcissistic investment falls). All objects are derived from what was lost, its substitutes and phantasmatic representatives: from *Jouissance*, the initial and mythical Great *Jouissance*, to *jouissance*, the small @ of the objects that cause desire and vectorize it.

Early on Lacan proposed explaining this difference topologically. This is why in 1960, the same year he introduced the Thing, he conceived an apologue, a simple topology that convincingly illustrated the difference between the Thing and the object. I am referring to his famous mustard pot. God knows why it had to be a pot of mustard. What is important is that in this industrial product we can recognize three elements: (1) the pot, its surfaces: a human invention, a manifestation of the creative power of language; a signifier that produces (2) something that intuitively would have been first, the void, wrapped by the sides of the pot which would not be so were it not for the action of the signifier which (3) invites and allows it to be filled with something definite, mustard, that without the pot and the void would not have any other end than to spill and be lost irremissibly. This apologue shows the signifier's *ex nihilo* creative function, which produces the void as that Thing that would have been there before (which is false) and proposes the object as able to (deceptively) occupy that void. Two years later, in his seminar on identification, Lacan shows the existence of a topological figure that more rigorously demonstrates the structural missed encounter between the objects of the drive (variable, able to be substituted, as Freud noted) and the Thing as the absolute object around which all the movements of the drive circulate.

What I propose is to illustrate the distance between the Thing and object @ topologically with the torus, knowing full well that it is not in relation to their difference that Lacan developed this figure in 1962. For those who may not know what I am referring to, it is best to think of the image of a ring intuitively, or the inner tube of a wheel.[9] In the tube of the torus are two voids that, much like the void of the mustard pot, are created by the walls in the surface of the torus. A peripheral void, closed, covered by the gum of the inner tube, called the "soul" of the torus, and the other which is the central hole, "the hole through which air flows," as Lacan once explained, and is not covered. It is clear that there is no communication between the two voids and that they belong to different dimensions.

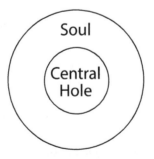

What does this toric structure show us? The activity of the signifier, the articulated demand that repeats and insists, functions like something that walks on the internal surface, spinning constantly around the closed void, which is the soul of the torus. The interior space generated is the space of desire, the activity of the drive that borders the object @ permanently, misses, and launches itself again untiringly in its pursuit. The return errs at the point of arrival as well as the point of departure and is comparable to the bow Lacan describes in Seminar XI (S XI, 178). The repetition of demands that leave an unpaid remainder of desire tighten the bow from which the arrows discharge, only to return like boomerangs to the point of departure. It is worth noting that this repetition is not the intentional act of a psychological subject; the subject is the effect of the successive discharges of the arrow. The drive is acephalous. Every subject's history is the result of the modes of missed encounters with *jouissance* and the incessant re-launchings in its pursuit.

For this reason, it was necessary to clarify that *jouissance* is *not* the satisfaction of a drive. The torus does not exist since forever or from the start; it is the effect of the eternal return of the drive from which the other empty space is configured: central and open, the space of the Thing, totally indifferent to the circular returns of demand. The incommensurable distance between desire and *jouissance*, between objects and the Thing, between allowed *jouissance* (wordy, unsatisfactory) and prohibited *jouissance* (empty, central) is clearly manifested in this topological figure.

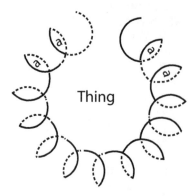

The drives circulate around the soul of the torus; they are aspirations to *jouissance* submitted to the Other's demands, $D; Freud called them erotic or life drives. In their orbit, the drives create a central space, the insurmountable hole that is an unapproachable beyond. The topological representation also allows us to apprehend the difference between the realm of the pleasure principle, with its inevitable lack figured by the soul of the torus (a peripheral void), and its beyond, the area of the Thing, unnamable *jouissance* where the silence of the drives reign. It is irrational, inasmuch as there is nothing there, thus confirming that *jouissance* is a surplus value introduced into life. Those empty spaces are, as in the mustard pot, sites of enigmatic attraction. The void asks to be filled and the subject, inspired by a passion that is *horror vacui*, sets itself the task, only to fade in the *jouissance*-filled pursuit of doing so. It is the activity of the drive displaced from any natural end or satisfaction of needs, a work of sublimation that is, according to the definition Lacan gives in 1960, the elevation of an object to the dignity of the Thing (S VII). This is not the site of distinguished artists or exceptional beings, but rather the home of all speaking beings (*parlêtres*) as such. It is Winnicott's transitional space, the area of *jouissance* where the child plays, the phantasm proliferates, or the *jouissance* of the One and the *jouissance* of the Other are confronted: an impossible space located in the confluence between the imaginary and the real, without symbolic mediation—where the subject precipitates itself and dissolves.

Thanatos's empire is surrounded by a space of signifying creation that surrounds without ever penetrating it; it is where the eagles do not dare fly, or a still living Antigone descends to find her sepulture, fascinating and dangerous, the seat of a lethal *jouissance* the word discerns and sustains at a respectable distance. By way of illustration, consider the final lines of F. Scott Fitzgerald's *The Great Gatsby*:

> Gatsby believed in the green light, the orgiastic future that year by year recedes before us. It eluded us then, but that's no matter—tomorrow we will run faster, stretch out our arms farther. . . . And one fine morning—
> So we beat on, boats against the current, borne back ceaselessly into the past.[10]

This image of life bordering, avoiding, and postponing the final and definitive encounter necessarily leads to considering the barriers to *jouissance*, developed later in this chapter. First we must review the Phallus as concept.

Castration and the Name-of-the-Father

I realize that topology is not popular, but the simplest and most exact way of approaching the central topic of a chapter that distinguishes the forms of *jouissance* is through the strange and disturbing figure of the torus, with its creation of new dimensions and incommunicable spaces. One can spend an entire life travelling on the inside surface of the inner tube of an automobile tire without having the least intuition or representation of the central hole, the pivot around which one has circulated. In comparison with what it would be like to discover that we live in a toric space, the celebrated Copernican Revolution seems to be a modification of small importance regarding the conception of the world in which we carry on our lives.

I will get right to the point with a dogmatic affirmation that may appear hurried, but I will attempt to develop it in due time: the surface of the inner tube that separates the two voids in an irreversible manner and places them in heterogeneous dimensions is the function of language, separator of the Thing, effect of the law of culture—language that establishes the cut of symbolic castration, revolving around the signifier of the Phallus (Φ). The symbolic Phallus, which is impossible to make negative, represents unreachable *jouissance* for those who speak, given that with a penis or without, this organ cannot *be* it, even if it represents *jouissance* in the imaginary. Every relation with *jouissance* passes through this prohibition; it is the reason why the objects @ to which the subject may accede always entail the dimension of castration: the name of @ / ($-\varphi$) we mentioned in a previous section.

This is a complex and much-debated point regarding Lacan's teaching and his reading of Freud. Much has been written regarding the theory's "phallogocentrism," the proximity between the function of language and the phallic function (CF, 112–120). Derrida's and Irigaray's objections do not fail to recognize the evident, massive fact of the phallic prerogative.[11] For Derrida, "Phallogocentrism is neither an accident nor a speculative error that can be imputed to any given theoretician. It is an old and enormous root that must also be accounted for" (PC, 481, note 60). This is the argument Derrida recognizes as valid, although he is not in agreement regarding its use, because what passes as a description of a fact ("an old and enormous root") in fact induces "a practice, an ethics, and an institution, and a politics that insure the truth of the tradition" (PC, 481). The complaint is a valid warning regarding the danger of passing from phallocratism in the theory to oppressive phallocratism in concrete life. Charybdis and Scylla are now the renunciation to thinking what actually occurs and has been occurring (phallocratism) and, on the other hand, accepting in a conformist way that a structural reason imposes passivity regarding the modes of rectifying the injustices of phallocratism. The question is: how can the excesses of domination be confronted if the fundamental principles of its power are ignored?

The solidarity between signifier and phallus can be questioned only if we accept that the human order, the Law, has been phallocratic. Of course this does not justify the prevalent androcentricity throughout history. Psychoanalysis does not take sides; it explains the need for this articulation and recognizes that the mere knowledge of a need can open the way to a possible liberation of what previously appeared fatal. This is precisely the key to the Lacanian position concerning feminine *jouisssance*, which we will study in the following chapter. It is at the center of what is at stake theoretically, clinically, and even politically regarding how to distinguish the differences in *jouissance*, which must be considered in their specificity.

The Law has an effect that does not frighten or cause anguish: castration. Symbolic, for sure, what other type could it be? The separation between desire and *jouissance* is possible due to castration. What is prohibited becomes the basis of desire, and the latter must be put into words. As we have already seen, in Freud and since Freud, all renunciation to *jouissance*, all payments made on the Other's account—that is, the emptying out of *jouissance* and the education of the drives—ends in the castration complex that resignifies all the previous losses in relation to the phallus, the universal signifier of lack for *parlêtres*. It also divides the field of sexuation in two noncomplementary halves, which are the One and the Other, man and woman. Sexuality and the differences between the sexes thus becomes a question of logic that signifies and resignifies the anatomical difference. Between man and woman lies a signifier that divides them according to the particular way in which they position themselves; there is a wall erected with bricks of language that separates them.

The signified of the Phallus (signifier) is the impossibility of the *jouissance* of the Thing or the *jouissance* of being. Castration does not mean anything but this: all human beings who speak are subject to the Law of the prohibition of incest and have to renounce the Mother, the first and absolute object of desire. Having the phallus or not, no one, not the child, not the Mother, nor the Father can *be* it. The Phallus is the signifier of that absolute prohibition; that is how language substitutes the point zero of language that is the Thing. Its value is identical to the name-of-the-Father that in its metaphoric function substitutes the signifier of the Desire of the Mother. Attention. I am here proposing an equation:

Phallus = name-of-the-Father. Following Lacan, this is essentially correct, but later will have to be corrected in order to explain, in relation to the clinic, why psychoanalytic theory needs two different terms and the reasons for their duality.[12]

The Phallus (Φ) is the plug, the core of the signifier; it signals the place as well as the impossibility of the Thing. It has a central place in the torus, the hole through which "air flows," as the finger through the ring. It thus has the function of being the support of the Law and designating the lack in the Other, the castration of the Mother (her incompleteness), which makes her a desiring subject not to be completed in relation to her child. That is, S($\cancel{A}$), a matheme that expresses *jouissance* as impossible to subjectivize and makes it necessary to move through the roads of desire and exchange. In other words, one desires in function of castration and the objects of desire carry a mark: (-φ). The twists and turns of desire, what remains unsatisfied in the drive, occur around the soul of the torus (the peripheral void that has the form of a ring), delimiting the central void plugged up by the signifier of the Phallus, the signifier of the desire of the Mother, continued and displaced by the name-of-the Father.

Having completed this part of the chapter, we can now propose a double equivalency and proportion, which is not to be taken in a mathematical sense, but rather as a topological relation between irreducible and incommensurate places. In the central hole of the torus we find the Thing as a real with its signifier in the symbolic Phallus (Φ), while in the soul of the torus we have an incessant going around @, real and lost retroactively in its turns. The signifier that polarizes that search is the phallus as the part lacking from the image desired (φ), a semblance, an imaginary signifier that can be made present only with the sign of negation; castration thus makes the subject a desiring subject and @, the cause of desire. We thus propose the following elastic, topological relation, with no presumption of calculating accuracy:

$$\varphi : \Phi :: @ : \text{Thing}$$

The road to *jouissance* is blocked, and one must take the detour of speech, leave the *jouissance* of the body and enter through the sliding signifier, from one to the other, looking for the elusive *point of capiton* (quilting point). The *jouissance* of castration is phallic *jouissance* (*jouissance* of the signifier, semiotic *jouissance*), a *jouissance hors-corps* (outside the body). Phallic *jouissance* must be distinguished from the others, which are *jouissance* of being and *jouissance* of the Other (these are *jouissance* of the body and therefore *hors-langage*, outside the word, ineffable).

To differentiate and separate *jouissance* of being and *jouissance* of the Other is a theoretical risk I take, knowing full well these are synonymous in Lacan's teaching, established by his disciples and commentators.[13] With the help of the topology of the Mobius strip, in the following chapter I explain the need to differentiate them and show the clinical difference between the *jouissance* of being, linked to the Thing, and the Other *jouissance* (*jouissance* of the Other), which is also of the Other (feminine) sex. Feminine *jouissance* may be crazy and enigmatic, but that does not mean women are crazy and need injections of the unconscious, as was once suggested.

The Phallus, the signifier to which all the others refer, the organizing function (in the logical-mathematical sense) of the avatars of the *parlêtre*, is absent from the chain, unpronounceable, a circle that is traced with a −1 in relation to what can be said (E, 697). It is not a signifier, an organ (the penis) or its image, but what prompts that all images appear marked by lack, incompleteness. If it is −1 it is because it designates the lack of a signifier in the Other. A signifier of the lack of a signifier, then, a pure positivity barred with negativity, condemning all that is articulable to being nothing more than *semblant*. The Phallus bars it with negativity and makes it *paraître*, *par-être*, being aside, in the sense that everything affirmed, whether attribute or existence, involves a shadow: every signifier is such because it is not the Phallus. By recognizing the Phallus in this central yet eccentric place one can explain that there is no basis for phallocratism and, yes, the theory is phallocratic. Castration is central to the advent of the subject and therefore not exclusive to either of the sexes or a reason for pride or shame.

The signification of the phallus as −1 is not zero; it is not an absence, but rather an affirmation that the battery of signifiers, the system of the Other, is inconsistent. It entails an absence that makes it a closed set since, without such an absence, it would not have limits and exist as a set. That is why the Phallus S($\cancel{A}$) and the prohibition of *jouissance* (of the Thing) as absolute are equivalent. Phallus is the name of the signifier that deviates the intangible Thing toward the objects of desire.

The subject of demand, the effect of the repetition of the turns round the soul of the torus to the drives' inexhaustible demand for satisfaction (a satisfaction that does not exist but is still demanded), is the subject that fades, to be replaced by what it demands of the Other ($\$\lozenge D$). This subject necessarily trips due the lack of the signifier in the barred Other, a desiring Other whose desire is an enigma ("What does the Other want from me"?, *Che vuoi?*). The signification of that lack, S(A̸), is prohibited *jouissance*: "It can only be said [dite] between the lines by whoever is the subject of the Law, since the Law is founded on that very prohibition" (E, 696).

These differences can be discerned intuitively in the upper part of the graph of desire in "The Subversion of the Subject and the Dialectic of Desire." The horizontal vector that goes from *jouissance* to castration intersects the retroactive vector that runs from right to left and leads from the drive to the signifier of the lack in the Other.

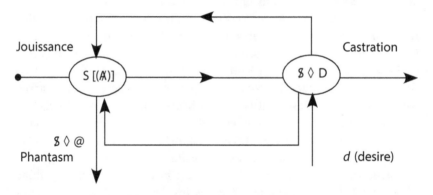

One can see the topological difference between the *drive, desire* (*d*) (which is the rest produced by the dissatisfaction of the demand), the *phantasm* ($0@) (the imaginary response to desire on the one hand and the lack of *jouissance* on the other), *jouissance* (what must be abandoned in the enunciation given that *jouissance* is its cause and *raison d'être*), and, last, castration (the result of the always unsatisfied passage through the drive and the lack of the signifier in the Other, which could allow a "happy" alienation and complete both the battery [of signifiers] and be a support of *jouissance*). The capital letters below, which correspond to the drive and to the prohibition of *jouissance* or the Law, indicate they are symbolic terms, while the small letters and italics (the *d* of desire and @ of the object of the phantasm) graphically show their imaginary dimension.

The condition of enunciation is that lack not be lacking: that symbolic castration be complete, the cut making the subject a subject to the Law. In more Freudian and less Lacanian terms, this means that the Oedipus complex must fulfill its mission.[14] The Thing is prohibited and the Phallus, the unpronounceable signifier, S(A̸), takes its place and establishes the irremissible lack in the subject. It is to this lack (the effect of the Phallus that puts the Thing at an insurmountable distance) that another signifier responds, constituting itself as the articulating pivot of the spoken word—a signifier that structurally makes castration possible: the name-of-the-Father as separation from the desire of the Mother. This articulable signifier functions as one (S_1), an unavoidable place for the link with a second signifier (S_2), which is an economic way of writing the set of signifiers that only reach signification inasmuch as they are articulated with the primordial S_1, the name-of-the-Father. The unconscious as *savoir* (unknown knowledge) is the S_2 with S_1, the name-of-the Father, as support. The latter is an articulated word that comes to the place of lack deployed by the Phallus as -1 in the battery of signifiers (the Other), signifying the Law that decrees the exclusion of the Thing as an impossible Real.

As an effect of the articulation of the signifying chain $S_1 \longrightarrow S_2$, there is a rest that is object @, a real bordered by the drive and outside the symbolic, which the subject experiences as an affect, the effect of its fall. It appears thus from the beginning of Lacan's reading of Freud: "In this text by Freud [*Die Verneinung*], the affective is conceived of as what preserves its effects right down to the discursive structuration on the basis of a primordial symbolization" (E, 320). In his Seminar *L'extimité*, J-A. Miller made an illuminating commentary on Lacan's text. He noted that "primordial symbolization" is made from an anterior real (the Thing, we could say) while the later "effects" (of that real) that subsist in the discursive structuration, representing what is otherwise un-articulable in discourse ("affect" for Freud), is a real that discourse engenders, but is not discourse; it is the object @ which falls away from it. It is worthwhile to maintain the distinction between the anterior real and the real subsequent to discourse that remits to a logical and not a chronological time and shows the function of the cut in speech between the Thing (anterior) and the object @ (ulterior), between *jouissance* of being and another *jouissance*, the effect of castration (Law of language), a phallic *jouissance* chasing after object @, cause of desire. It is not difficult to discern in this early formulation of Lacan's the formula for the discourse of the master, consubstantial with the discourse of the unconscious, where S_1 (in this case the name-of-the-Father) occupies the place of the agent or *semblant*.

$$\frac{S_1}{\$} \quad \rightarrow \quad \frac{S_2}{@}$$

Earlier I wrote an equation that the name-of-the-Father and the Phallus were the same, without considering a difference that now must be clarified because "the privilege of the phallus is that it can be called, frantically; it will not say a word" (S XVIII, 172). It cannot be articulated: in order to speak, it is necessary to link one signifier to another signifier, given that a signifier cannot signify itself. For this reason, the Phallus is a silent signifier without equal. While the name-of-the Father is "the phallus, for sure, it is also the name-of-the-Father . . . if this name is effective, it is precisely because someone stands up to respond" (S XVIII, 172). Therefore, being the Phallus, it also fulfills a function the Phallus cannot fulfill: being the core and point of reference that makes discursive articulation possible. We can consider the Phallus as the signifier at point zero and the name-of-the-Father as its metaphor, the master signifier that comes to its place.

Before going any further, it is necessary to develop this point, since it has caused confusion in the theory of *jouissance*. I will quote from an unequivocal affirmation made by Lacan in 1971, where he maintains the identity between the name-of-the-Father and the Phallus. Lacan knows he is modifying an essential point from an earlier version of this formulation; concretely, the common understanding of the paternal metaphor in his essay on psychosis. That is why he laughs at his follower's consternation ("God knows the shock of horror this caused in some pious souls" (S XVIII, 172) and explains that when he proposed the paternal metaphor in 1957 he could not articulate it any better. In the earlier formula we find the reason why Colette Soler, an astute reader of Lacan, says that the name-of-the-Father achieves "the production of the Phallic signifier" and that the Phallus is secondary to the metaphor: "The name-of-the-Father produces another signifier without equal, the Phallus. It produces it . . . as signification. This can also be seen in the writing of the metaphor: the phallus is below the bar, in the place of the signified. Therefore, the production of the phallus as signification, but also the production of signification as phallic."[15] In the same conference, Soler offers a solution to reconcile the contradiction, which is essential for our discussion. It entails distinguishing between the Phallus (Φ) that "cannot be negativized" (E, 697) and the phallus ($-\varphi$), signifier of desire, subsequent to the intervention of the name-of-the-Father. It presents itself to the subject as the "image of the penis—. . . negativized where it is situated in the specular image. That is what predestines the phallus to give body to *jouissance* in the dialectic of desire" (E, 696). Experiencing its lack, it allows the subject to invest the object by giving it a value lacking in him, thus emerging as a desiring being: "it is . . . the assumption [*assomption*] of castration that creates the lack on the basis of which desire is instituted" (E, 723). The lack imposed by castration and accepted by the subject as such in the imaginary is indicated algebraically as ($-\varphi$), minus phi.

We have to accept the idea of the Phallus as split inasmuch as it is a signifier, the result of the metaphoric intervention of the name-of-the-Father. On the one hand, as D. Nasio noted in a 1982 conference, in the formula of the paternal metaphor "the Name-of-the-Father is the signifier that substitutes and condenses the phallus as the signifier of the desire of the Mother" (R, 295). In this sense it is a signifier of prohibited *jouissance*: a signifier without equal, consubstantial to the Law of the prohibition of incest, marking the objects of desire as its representatives in the imaginary and granting them phallic signification. Thus the formula for the paternal metaphor:

$$\text{Name-of-the-Father} \left[\frac{A}{\text{Phallus}} \right] \qquad \text{(E, 465)}$$

This formula can be understood in the following way: the name-of-the-Father, an articulable signifier that calls for a response, substitutes the Phallus as desire of the Mother (developed in the first part of Lacan's essay on psychosis, E, 445). It emerges as one signifier (S_1) taking the place of the Thing, that element of the Real that suffers because of the Phallus, an un-articulable signifier that situates itself at the limit of the battery of signifiers, outside A/Phallus, not between brackets (as shown in the above formula). Its effect is that, at the level of the signified, below the bar, all that is signifiable is invested with the phallic function. In light of our discussion, the word "phallus" should be written in small letters, as a signifier of desire (φ) that is represented for the subject in the form of castration ($-\varphi$): "What analytic experience attests to is that castration is what regulates desire, both in the normal and the abnormal" (E, 700).[16] In other words, the name-of-the-Father does not "produce" the phallic signifier, as C. Soler claims, but rather phallic signification, which does not produce the quilting point (*point de capiton*) or allow apprehension, but always appears as minus ($-\varphi$) in relation to the real and launches the contingencies of desire. To sum up, in the Lacanian formula of the paternal metaphor, a "spelling error" occurs in writing the word "phallus" with a capital letter. What the name-of-the-Father "produces" is phallic signification, which is an articulable, sayable substitute for the Phallus, signifier of *jouissance* and unspeakable source of speech.

For this reason, the function of the name-of-the-Father is pacifying for the subject (Lacan plays with "pacifying" and its homonym *pas si fiant*, not to be fully trusted). By introducing symbolic castration, it puts limits to a *jouissance* without limits that is "the worst." In the clinic, the latter manifests itself as a psychotic invasion of signifiers without an anchoring point, the foreclosed signifier of the name-of-the-Father. It is the chaos of the S_2 due to the lack of an S_1 that can only be resolved and stabilized when delirium occupies the space of the missing name-of-the-Father (S_1). The metaphor of delirium seeks to patch up the missing signifier.

In reviewing our trajectory thus far we find the following: (1) The Thing, real and mythical; the retroactive effect of primordial symbolization; an always already lost absolute object of desire. (2) The Phallus, signifier without equal, zero degree, indicating the radical impossibility of accessing the Thing: a symbol that inscribes the division of the sexes and *jouissance*(s); it executes the cut of symbolic castration that places being (of *jouissance*) and thinking (of speech) at different levels. By establishing the lack in the *parlêtre*, castration at the imaginary level, and what is missing in the image desired, the Phallus induces phallic signification and leads to desire. (3) The name-of-the-Father, signifier one (S_1), articulable, diacritical (characterized by its difference with the rest of the signifiers), instigator, producer, and also representative of the subject ($) before the set of signifiers, the Other of language. (4) The unconscious *savoir* (S_2), speech that expresses the impossible integration of the subject in the real—the necessary exile that leads him to inhabit the Other of language after having refused (by way of the Phallus) the *jouissance* of being in order to reach an Other *jouissance*: *paraître* through the *semblant*. (5) @ as effect of the real produced by discourse, brought about by castration, an inevitably lost object, which is also surplus *jouissance* dependent on the social link established between $, the subject, and Ⱥ, the Other, castrated and desiring.

The Thing, like the past, is irretrievable; the object, in its condition as real, like the future, is impossible. The subject is also divided between a past *jouissance* and a future *jouissance*, and is excluded from both. The name of this exclusion that imposes a lack in being (*manque a être*) is desire. The Thing and the object escape the reach of symbolization. Speech, always in the present, cuts time; maker of the future, it is the scissor that divides the *jouissance* of being (of the Thing) and the Other (feminine) *jouissance*, a *jouissance* of the Other that we will discuss in the next chapter. There is also a common *jouissance* that is essentially different from the two already mentioned. Being marked by castration, it is phallic *jouissance*, outside the body: an evocation in language of the possible and absent *jouissance*, past and future. This *jouissance* in speech is a translation that denaturalizes (as if anything related to *jouissance* can be said to be "natural") and at the same time makes possible the part of *jouissance* accessible to the *parlêtre*, the speaking subject of the unconscious.

This *langagière jouissance* requires the consent of the Other, which the subject knows without wanting to know: an unknown *jouissance* on which the unconscious depends, because it is structured like a language and charged with the function of deciphering *jouissance*. There is *jouissance* for the subject who speaks, but the subject struggles against this *jouissance*, limits and restrains it, because it is asocial and maledictory. Speech (*parole*), common discourse, opposes the seriousness of language and consensual reason to the unreason of *lalangue*, poetry, jokes and the emergence of truth in discourse. Again, speech is the diaphragm of *jouissance*.

Lacan's words should be understood in the context of this definition of castration: "Castration means that jouissance has to be refused in order to be attained on the inverse scale of the Law of desire" (E, 700). In Lacan's concise synthesis we learn that it is not a question of one *jouissance* but of two, the one rejected and the one to be reached; these two are separated by the emergence of a third that divides them, a scissor or scythe that imposes the requirement of traversing the funnel of castration. It subjects the organ that represents the phallus, the bit of flesh that can be present or missing, protrude or remain half-hidden in the mucous membranes, to forever remain below the function assigned for providing *jouissance*. A cut is traced around it, producing a division of the sexes that cannot be closed (mythologized by Platonic androgyny and the destiny of an eternal search for the lost, cut half). It produces *angst* in the male neurotic that wishes to ignore that the feared castration has already been practiced from the beginning; with his desire he has little to lose and everything to gain. The female neurotic, thinking she is outside phallic *jouissance*, envies it, thus closing herself off to another *jouissance* that requires the phallus, without being limited to it, as we will see in the following chapter on *jouissance* and sexuality. We find a discussion of the different species of *jouissance* essential for a new approach to the psychoanalytic clinic, given that the misnamed clinical structures (neurosis, psychosis, and perversion) are better understood as subjective positions regarding *jouissance*.

Briefly, as a preview of what we will develop in greater detail in the following chapters, we must speak of a *jouissance* produced by the non-inscription (foreclusion) of the name-of-the-Father, a *jouissance* not regulated by the signifier and castration, outside language (as subjection to the laws of exchange and reciprocal regulations) and outside the Law of desire. This *jouissance* does not await or receive a response from the Other to his lack in being: a psychotic *jouissance*, on this side of the word, overwhelming, invasive, unlimited. We know of this much-discussed *jouissance* of being because of the need to conceptualize it. But also because it appears clinically in those subjects whose bodies are the scene where the Other's limitless word spills out in waves, vibrations and rays supposing unusual transformations; where the word functions as a hallucinatory real and language can, through delirium, put a precarious curb on *jouissance*.

There is also *jouissance* due to castration, phallic *jouissance*, which cannot be symbolized through speech and exchange, where castration is not the road to saying well (*bien dire*) but rather a threat that blocks the insistence of desire; phallic *jouissance* is therefore sequestered, repressed, and manifests itself in symptoms that affect the body (in hysteria) and thought (in obsessional-compulsive neurosis).

Another example is the voluntary exit from the system of exchange through drugs, which can transform itself into an addiction (a-diction, @-diction). Here *jouissance* of being is reached by way of a shortcut that leaves the body at the mercy of the Other and his desire. There is also the attempt to control the levers of *jouissance* with know-how at the disposition of a subject who, through techniques of the body, is able to liberate himself from an intolerable castration. How? By displacing it onto a degraded object dominated by perverse practices. All this without realizing that the phantasm of knowing the ways of *jouissance* is in turn a defense against the threatening *jouissance* of the Other.

Finally, after the inscription of the name-of-the-Father, there is *jouissance* that is a di-version from the original *jouissance*: a regulation of *jouissance* by symbolic castration, displacement, change of register, translation to another code, denaturalization, irreversible metamorphosis that leads to its transaction in the marketplace that discusses and decides the *quantum* of *jouissance* reached on the road to desire. Nosological traditions force us to say that this *jouissance* is "normal," which implies that the others are "abnormal." However, it is well known that psychoanalysts do not speak in these terms, although we can refer to Lacan's play on words, never as clear as in this context: it is a question of the *norme mâle*, the male norm.[17] A clinic of *jouissance*, then, one that ethically regulates the analytic act and can distinguish the psychotic, perverse, addict's and neurotic's significations or articulations of *jouissance* in each changing subjective position: a clinic that is the reason for these chapters, a long road in the twists and turns of *jouissance*.

The Barriers to *Jouissance*

Jouissance is prohibited, but not because of a badly organized society, as some foolish people think. It is not that the Other does not allow *jouissance*, but rather that *jouissance* is also lacking in the Other; plenitude is a neurotic's phantasm in these frightfully tormented times of idyllic exigencies. The essential point, also found in Freud, is that the sexual relation does not exist; love is not the recommended road to alleviate the discontent in culture; desire, beleaguered by a malignant god, errs in its misadventures through the deserts of *jouissance*. As Lacan notes: "This drama is not as accidental as it is believed to be. It is essential: for desire comes from the Other, and *jouissance* is located on the side of the Thing" (E, 724).

This is where we started our journey: by distinguishing *jouissance* from what may seem similar, but is actually its opposite—first from pleasure, then from desire. We now find these again as barriers to *jouissance*. Pleasure, a vital link, soother of discomfort, destroyer of differences, is an almost natural barrier for the barred S: $. In the paradigmatic experience of copulation, the orgasm with its subsequent detumescence limits *jouissance*. Pleasure is therefore the antidote to *jouissance*.

Erected on the basis of this homeostatic law, the Law of language also imposes a renunciation of *jouissance*. Language empties the body of *jouissance* and signifies itself around the Phallus, along with its correlate, castration; it makes the subject appear as lacking and institutes desire, the constant turns around the interior surface of the torus and its hidden obscure object @. *Langagière*, worded desire, is a transaction and defense that keeps *jouissance* in its horizon of impossibility; desire has to yield to the Law due to the paternal function. That desire is the desire of the Other means it is subjected and has to accept the Law. It tries to do what it can in its exile from the Thing, displacing itself toward the objects that are its cause, but also deceive it. The initial structural dispossession must be accepted in order to reach some relation with those objects in the economy of gains and losses. In Seminar X, *Anxiety*, Lacan stated: "desire and the law . . . are one and the same barrier to bar our access to the Thing" (S X, 81).

Desire traces the roads to the drive, which are roads of dissatisfaction: "This occurs because the drive divides the subject and desire, the latter sustaining itself only by the relation it misrecognizes between this division and an object that causes it. Such is the structure of the phantasm": ($◊a$) (E, 724, translation modified). Desire does not know itself in the imaginary formation of the phantasm that stages the aspirations to *jouissance* and, consequently, is another barrier to *jouissance*. Not only if the subject imagines it neurotically without imposing it on reality (introversion of libido, as a Jungian Freud used to say), but also if he acts it out in a perverse manner.[18] In both cases he realizes that it's not *it*: the object is lost not only in the masturbatory phantasm, but also in the perverse intent to demonstrate that *jouissance* can be achieved through a bodily know-how, his own and that of his *partenaire*. The phantasm proposes different kinds of object @s as conditions or instruments of *jouissance*. As we've seen, these objects are effects of the Phallus and castration that give them a negative phallic value. These objects, as Freud indicated in 1917 in his well-known work on the transmutation of the drives (closely resembling the function and concept of the object @ in Lacan), are subject to symbolic substitutions and displacements in a system of equivalencies that exist between the penis, the child-*Lumpf*, shit, the gift, money and, for the woman, the male child as the extension of the wished-for phallus and her children as narcissistic (phallic) extensions of herself.

Objects, the things of this world, are nothing more than screens offered to the phantasm as the promise of imaginary gratification. This is how commodities are priced by advertisers to then increase their value and be recommended to consumers, without realizing that this process operates based on Lacan's object @. Reality and the multiplicity of objects are also defenses against *jouissance*. Lacan's discourse here comes close to Marx and Marx's to Freud. Surplus value and surplus *jouissance*, merchandise and fetish, money and phallus, gold and shit, exploitation and gains or losses, salary and plunder, *jouissance* of the One and *jouissance* of the Other, contract and theft and property as theft, exchange value and use value (of *jouissance?*) are all references that bring together political economy and another libidinal economy that is its foundation, the economy of *jouissance*. In the words of the economist Karl Polanyi:

> For it is on this one negative point that modern ethnographers agree: the absence of the motive of gain; the absence of the principle of laboring for remuneration; the absence of the principle of least effort; and, especially, the absence of any separate and distinct institution based on economic motives.[19]

For Norman O. Brown, who also refers to Polanyi, "The ultimate category of economics is power, but power is not an economic category . . . power is in essence a psychological category."[20] To sum up, we will refer to an unexpected guest, Aldous Huxley, from *Point Counter Point* (1928):

> The instinct of acquisitiveness has more perverts, I believe, than the instinct of sex. At any rate, people seem to me odder about money than about even their amours. Such amazing meannesses as one's always coming across, particularly among the rich! Such fantastic extravagances too. Both qualities, often, in the same person. And then the hoarders, the grubbers, the people who are entirely and almost unceasingly preoccupied with money. Nobody's unceasingly preoccupied with sex in the same way—I suppose because there's a physiological satisfaction possible in sexual matters, while there's none where money's concerned. When the body is satiated, the mind stops thinking about food or women. But the hunger for money and possessions is an almost purely mental thing. There's no physical satisfaction possible. That would account for the excesses and perversities of acquisitiveness. Our bodies almost compel the sexual instinct to behave in a normal fashion . . . But where acquisitiveness is concerned there's no regulating body, no lump of all too solid flesh to be pushed out of the grooves of physiological habit. The slightest tendency to perversion is at once made manifest. But perhaps the word "perversion" is meaningless in this context. For perversion implies the existence of a norm from which it departs. What is the norm of acquisitiveness?[21]

The economy, production and consumption, find its reason beyond the pleasure principle. Psychoanalysis questions both classical political economy and its Marxist version. The number, accounting, and accumulation recognize their foundation in castration and in the investiture of money as $@/ -\varphi$.[22]

A particular case that would have given Huxley room for reflection is Don Juan, who classifies women geographically (per country) and counts them: as a seducer he is more concerned with the catalogue of conquests that his servant keeps at hand than with the object itself. In Don Juan's case it is a question of going beyond the limit that the relation with a body imposes on sexuality. In the catalogue, in the collection of photographs of "his" women that a neurotic carries, thinking he has possessed them, making sex accountable, one finds a particular way of making pleasure a barrier to *jouissance* and sustaining the turgid image of the phallus beyond its declining destiny. Needless to say, it is castration anxiety that Don Juan, a singular collector, sustains and wishes to disavow.

The objects, fetishes, commodities, all constitute reality, which has the same substance as the phantasm. Like the phantasm, they veil the real, much like screens imposed by the Law that place the Thing at a distance. The Law does not prohibit but rather imposes desire (to desire in vain): to struggle and strive after the object that is nothing more than deception, appearance, slippery *semblant*.

Faced with this impossibility and disappointment, a particular type of phantasm is constructed as a way to register, in the imaginary, a *jouissance* the subject can access, possess, and dominate: the phantasm of reaching *jouissance* through knowledge, the articulation of signifiers allowing the appropriation of a real and a *diction* able to confirm the possession of truth. The phantasm of a *savoirjouir* links the discourses of the master, science, and perversion. This knowledge wishes to close the unfillable hole that makes the sexual relation impossible, because the Phallus is a signifier without equal that organizes asymmetrical positions and nonreconcilable *jouissance* between a man and a woman. Precisely because there is no Other signifier that is proper to her, She does not exist.

In sum, there are defenses around *jouissance*. The Thing is surrounded by barbed wire, circles of fire like the ones that protect Brunhilde, electrified fences—Berlin or Mexican walls that make it an object of desire precisely because of the halo of impossibility that surrounds it. The Law and the symbolic order on the one hand; on the other, the phantasmatic set of imaginary presentations, knowledge and reality included and, finally, desire itself. All these constitute the set of defenses that *jouissance* finds beyond the first, almost natural defense: pleasure. In this context, sexuality, a function linked to desire and pleasure, regulated by the Law, is a lure offered and a barrier to *jouissance* as well.

With so many obstacles, having to go through so many layers of the onion in order to reach the nucleus of *jouissance*, the central vacuole of the Thing, it is easy to think it is unreachable. Given that the Phallus is the signifier of impossible *jouissance*, the barrier erected on the road to *jouissance* is castration. It appears thus in the upper horizontal vector in the graph of desire we discussed earlier. From *jouissance* to castration and, having undergone castration, on to desire, aspiring to recover the rejected *jouissance* by way of the deceiving road of the *semblant*. The *semblant* of discursive articulation invents a world that is rhetorical: a deceitful play of metaphors and metonyms, primary and secondary processes. *Jouissance* is of the body (the Other), but it is not reachable if not through language (again the Other) . . . that transforms them in an irreversible way and makes them unrecognizable.

> The Thing is that which in the real, the primordial real, I will say, suffers from the signifier—and you should understand that it is a real that we do not yet have to limit, the real in its totality, both the real of the subject and the real he has to deal with as exterior to him. (S VII, 118)

It is clear that the difference between exterior and interior is not pertinent because that difference is, precisely, an effect of that signifier the Thing suffers from and bars; it subtracts being from the central hole of the torus and propels the *parlêtre*'s drives to circle around the torus' soul. The Thing does not know about inside and outside; the subject is outside and exiled in relation to the origin, outside the *jouissance* of being. Yet, as already noted, something of the Thing, the primordial real, conserves its effects even in the four different discursive structures Lacan points out ("Radiophonie," AE). The passage from the Thing to discourse is neither easy nor direct. Between *jouissance* and desire there is *angst*, which will be discussed at the end of this chapter.

The hinge that articulates *jouissance* of being and phallic *jouissance* is the unconscious. It has a double function: to allow for *jouissance* and, by imposing the Law, to deem it impossible. It orders the conversion from the real to the symbolic and induces imaginary effects, and it must be spoken and live as *semblant*, on the borders of the real. Neither a panegyric nor denigration of the unconscious is appropriate. Depending on the point of view, it can be one or the other. It's best to say it *happens*. It is not some*thing*, but rather an event, with the difficult task of articulating it the Other, which is the body submitted to symbolic castration, within which active pockets remain that resist normalization; it faces the Other of language, who "teaches" reality through its ally: the ego. Thus, the unconscious is neither the Id of the demands of the drives nor the Ego of defense mechanisms. We will discuss these topics in more detail in chapter 4.

Together with these considerations regarding the barriers to *jouissance*, we must add what is *not* a barrier to *jouissance*: the name-of-the Father, although it could be thought otherwise. That signifier makes *jouissance* possible through translation, the position of the signifier phallus as a hinge that allows for the subjectivation of *jouissance*. We must distinguish between the real father and his function from the signifier that represents him in the subject, the name-of-the-Father or, as we saw earlier, as representative-of-the-Phallus (with no name). The function of name-of-the-Father is to conjugate the Law (an obstacle) with desire. This nonpatriarchal consideration of the Father, thanks to whose name neither a man nor a woman remain attached to the mother's sexual demands, allows us to understand the Oedipus and castration complexes, leaving aside the imaginary. Castration loses its threatening and ominous aspect and becomes its opposite: a function that allows for *jouissance*, the condition for a relative and precarious immunity against the malicious *jouissance* of the Other that leaves the subject outside the symbolic. The function of the name-of-the-Father is made possible by the unconscious, charged with transporting *jouissance* from the body to speech. It is no secret that it is structured like a language.[23] Language is not a barrier to *jouissance*. On the contrary, it is a device (*appareil*) for *jouissance*; it presents and represents this *jouissance* whose absence would render the universe vain.[24] What lies beyond the pleasure principle is supported by language. If something in language is a barrier to *jouissance* it is that speaking produces effects of signification and comprehension, a welding of the symbolic and the imaginary, reciprocal narcissistic confirmations between interlocutors that are clearly obstacles to *jouissance* produced by blah, blah, blah (S XX, 55). Here the different functions of Freud's psychic apparatus can be traced: the diverse topics of the metabolic machine of *jouissance* he invented.

Phallic *jouissance* is inscribed in the articulation of the real (what remains of the Thing once displaced toward desire) and the symbolic (what can be constructed by disguising *jouissance* in speech, ordered by the signifier), between an Other and an other where the subject must inscribe itself. *Jouissance* of being has an*other* type of inscription: ineffable, outside the symbolic, an imaginary quality we invent as if it were the *jouissance* of the Other; a devastating Other that, due to the absent inscription of the name-of-the-Father (foreclusion), reappears in the real. It should be understood that it is not the Other that *jouit*. There is only *jouissance* for the subject who *jouit*, attributing *jouissance* to an Other that could supposedly take him as object.[25]

In this two-by-two grouping of registers proposed by Lacan, a third space of superposition remains: the imaginary entangled with the symbolic (without reaching the real), which is the realm of meaning, *jouis-sens*, jouissance of meaning. Thanks to meaning, the objects of reality (not "the real") are constituted, consensus is reached, and agreement guaranteed by speech (ideology). Bodily *jouissance* is excluded here, and all the instances described earlier are its defenses. Meaning functions as a tool to recognize the world. In our times its architect is the communicator, the big Other of the mass media that brings together representations from behind the liquid screens, globalizing how *jouissance* should be kept at bay. It also configures the egos that reciprocally recognize themselves in a common ideal, undergoing a mass de-*jouissance*, according to a Freudian formula of 1921 (SE XVIII, 110).

Lacan inscribed these relations in the Borromean knot during his third Rome conference, each ring being the representation of one of the registers. A triple superposition of the real, the imaginary and the symbolic remains where the object @ is placed, thus conserving a triple status and belonging. In the knot one can see three areas of double superposition that exclude one of the registers: *Jouissance* of the Other (without the symbolic), phallic *jouissance* (without the imaginary), and field of sense (*jouis-sens* without the real).

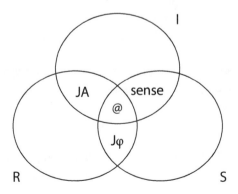

It is worthwhile noting that in this version of the knot, Lacan writes phallic *jouissance* with the initials Jφ: he uses the small *phi* that refers to the imaginary signifier, the phallus as *semblant*, not the Phallus, signifier of *jouissance* that allows the name-of-the-Father to function, barring entrance to a *jouissance* of being. It is important to make this distinction.

Even if going beyond what he explicitly states in that conference, I do not think I force Lacan's conception by proposing the following: (1) science, the activity that proposes appropriating the real through the symbolic, is homologous to phallic *jouissance* inasmuch as it repudiates the imaginary and also wishes to know nothing of the *jouissance* of the Other, the Other sex (in this it approaches perversion, as we will see later); (2) ideology, an agreement regarding reality, occupies the place of sense that fears the real; and (3) religion, devoted to the *jouissance* of the big Other, ineffable and mystical, is at the intersection between the real and the imaginary. Psychoanalysis, a Borromean *savoir* based on this structure, finds its place around the object @, a fugitive even from knowledge (an object for which no science could exist), located over the three registers, marking the necessary incompleteness that affects all attempts at full speech and the master's dream of an Absolute Knowledge.

The "Causation of the Subject" or Beyond *Angst*

As this chapter comes to a close, it takes on a cyclical (Franckian) structure by returning to the beginning: "The subject is and is called to being." In other words, the subject does not grow in a flower pot or as a natural product, but is rather "a response of the real."[26] For the subject to exist, it is necessary that someone call him or her (in the double sense of to call and to name). Because of the Other's invocation, the signifier enters the real and, as a response, produces the subject, an effect of signification. This is how Lacan understands the process throughout his teaching.[27] The flesh becomes body, someone's body: "sexuated," subject to the Law, exiled from *jouissance*, wordy, *langagière*.

"In the beginning was *jouissance*," but *jouissance* was not, because it can only be recognized after its loss and subsequent translation into speech. *Lost in translation*. The Thing is the real, but only inasmuch as it is mortified by language. For an early Freud, there was the erroneously called "(original) reality-ego" because the correct translation of *Real-Ich* should be "real ego," while "reality" should be, depending on the different cases and moments of Freud's writings, *Realität* or *Wirklichkeit* (SE XIV, 136).

I placed "original" in parentheses above because the term is an adjective that characterizes the "real ego" (to point out that the "real ego" is there from the beginning) and does not form part of the noun inasmuch as it is not contrary to a second supposed "definitive reality-ego," this being a formula that appears in a supplemental note in the *Standard Edition*, which belongs to James Strachey and not to Freud.

Freud never opposed two different forms of the "reality-ego." It is true that he spoke about it in two different ways and at separate times and this has caused confusion among his commentators. In fact, he defines a *Real-Ich* for the first time in his 1911 article "Formulations on the Two Principles of Mental Functioning," in which "real ego" has the sense of an ego that recognizes the reality principle as its guide (SE XII). It is therefore a "reality-ego." What Freud proposes in 1915 is a complete inversion; it is not a question of the addition of another initial "real ego," different from the "definitive" one (as in the 1911 article) that would allow the passage from the "original moment" to the "definitive moment" and give way to an intermediary, the *Lust-Ich*, "the pleasure-ego" (SE XIV, 136).[28] The expression "definitive reality-ego" comes later; it does not appear in the article on the drives and their vicissitudes. It appears only one time in Freud's works, in a 1925 article on negation, and there it is clearly opposed to the "original pleasure-ego" (SE XIX, 255–256).

To summarize, it is important to note that in Freud there are three oppositions of two terms, but never the ordered or successive relation of the three: (1) in the 1911 article on the two principles it is a question of the two working modes of the ego (*Lust-Ich* and *Real-Ich*), in function of the pleasure and reality principles, the former having chronological precedence. This is clear if we translate *Lust* as *jouissance* instead of pleasure, following the Lacanian differentiation between them. Derived from the Freudian development of the dualism of the drive in the 1920s, we give primacy to the ego of *jouissance* over the "reality-ego." In this first Freudian differentiation there is a "pleasure-ego" (*jouissance* of being) and a "reality-ego" ("connected with verbal residues," SE XII, 21). (2) In his "Papers on Metapsychology" of 1915, in the article dedicated to the drives, the opposition is the same, but the relation is exactly reversed because what is original is the "real ego," and the "pleasure-ego" develops because of the former; secondarily, an ego regulated by the pleasure principle develops (SE XIV, 136). (3) Finally, in his short essay on negation of 1925, the first terms of the opposition (of 1911) are again taken up between an original "pleasure-ego" and a definitive "reality-ego." Only Strachey's footnote to this last essay considers a third moment in Freud's reflections.

Laplanche and Pontalis's *The Language of Psychoanalysis* contributes to the confusion. After acknowledging that in the 1925 text Freud does not use the expression "original reality-ego" that he employed in 1915, they establish that "the expression 'definitive reality-ego' is here used to refer to a *third* phase."[29] This confusion wreaked havoc, even in the most authorized reader Freud could have imagined, Lacan, who in his Seminar *Encore* reproaches Freud for positing that *Lust-Ich* precedes *Real-Ich*. Lacan skips over point 2 (above), the formulation of 1915, which coincides completely with his own ideas (S XX, 55).

I think we must follow the 1915 text: in the beginning was the "real ego," a being there (*dasein*), thrown (*geworfen*) into a state of helplessness. Later it is possible to theorize the "pleasure-ego" and the "reality-ego," integrated to reality and the conventional world of sense, at the intersection of the imaginary and the symbolic, the result of the paternal metaphor. The ego integrated to reality, what Freud called secondary narcissism, is the continuation and modification of the *Lust-Ich*, the "pleasure-ego" that learned by experience that it is "convenient" and "adaptive" to accept what exists even though it may be unpleasant or contrary to the pleasure principle. The ego of reality, the one from 1911 that returns in 1925 with the added adjective "definitive," is not "beyond the pleasure principle." Its principle is not *jouissance* as the "real ego" of the 1915 text, which hates the Other even before reality imposes the benefits of loving him. We can thus conserve the three Freudian articulations: the one from 1915, on the one hand, and the two from 1911 and 1924 on the other, distinguishing the "real ego" from the ego of reality—that is, from the phantasm, because reality (*Wirklichkeit*) is nothing other than a phantasm that puts *jouissance* at a distance and offers protection from it. There are very few times that Lacan spoke of the "subject of *jouissance*."[30] We can only do so in relation to the "real ego," before the symbolic and submerged in the world of the Other: a subject buried in the "*jouissance* of being."

For Lacan, the "subject of *jouissance*" only exists as a necessary myth because ["it can in no way be isolated as a subject"] (S X, 173). The notion of a subject of *jouissance* before the intervention of the signifier, a pure real, is correlative to the other mythical being that Lacan rescues from Freud's writings, the Thing. If the subject emerges from the call of the Other, what is there *before* so that a subjective invocation may resound? What is the real that responds? On the one side is the Other's invocative desire, on the other, *jouissance* of being. On the one side appealing speech, on the other, a sheer cry. The subject of the signifier emerges from their intersection: a subject of desire. Lacan writes the subject of *jouissance* even though he does not name it; it is the S without the bar that appears in the L schema, defined in the *Écrits* as a subject in "his ineffable and stupid existence" (E, 459).

The sheer cry resounds in the Other and calls for a response. The cry becomes a signifier for the subject and shows the way: the *jouissance* machine can now only provide for his needs within the dimension of speech. *Jouissance* leads to ek-sistence. The "pre-subject" S of *jouissance* is confronted with an omnipotent, absolute, unbarred Other, which presents itself and later represents itself as Mother. In this schema we find the figuration of primary *jouissance*: being or the Thing. We can represent it as two separate circles.

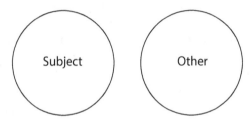

The mythical unbarred subject must inscribe *jouissance* by making itself heard by the Other, transforming itself into what it delivers, a cry of helplessness. Thus, it appears in the field of the Other as @, an object that evades the function of the signifier: a body offered to the gaze, a crying voice to be heard, a mouth that calls for the breast. At this point the subject finds that the Other is not omnipotent, but equally subject to castration. That is, the Other is not complete, but desiring, and its desire appears as an enigma for the subject, without any possible response. In this second moment we find the subject entering the field of the Other, making itself into an object that fills the lack in that Other. It is the moment of alienation or *angst*, a total dispossession at the service of an Other, voracious and insatiable. Here *jouissance* is horrific and found in fragmented and uncanny fantasies: the confrontation with a lack in the Other filled by the child as object.

Escaping from the *jouissance* of being leads to *angst*, which antic-ipates and is the correlate of alienation. The subject would just as well find satisfaction in satisfying the Other; this is the basis of the neurotic position of the child, propelling the *infans* to subject himself to the alien-ating demand of the Other and thus to be free of life's burdens. However, alienation consists in this not coming to fruition:

Alienation has a manifest aspect; it is not that we are the Other, or that the "others," as they say, by overtaking us, disfigure or deform us. The fact of alienation is not that we are taken up, remade, represented in the Other; on the contrary, it is essentially founded on the rejection of the Other, in so far as this Other—which I indicate with the capital O [*Autre*]—is what has come to the place of this question of Being . . . Would to heaven then that alienation entailed finding ourselves comfortably in the place of the Other! (SXIV, 1/11/67)

But heaven would rather not have it this way, and so we must "sweat blood," push along and go after what may compensate for the division of the subject, produced as the effect of being rejected from the place of the Other: the imposition of a separation in relation to that Other whose essence is lack. The subject must go through *angst* and alienation to emerge as desire, accept an unavoidable castration, and recognize himself as a subject divided by the signifier and, for this reason, separated from the object of the phantasm. To separate from the Other without renouncing him, but leaving something in its wake, object @, saving one's life at the cost of losing one's money in response to the imperious warning: "your money or your life!" Money (*jouissance*) is left in his hands and, although essentially curtailed, something of life can be saved. From then on, the relation to *jouissance* does not begin with S, but rather with $ through @. From now on life is lived in the phantasm.

At this point the operation can be represented with classic Eulerian circles.

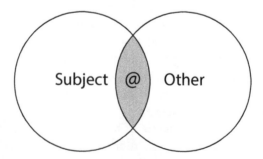

The subject's being must pass through the network of signifiers, the Other. Alienation stumbles with desire and the rejection by the Other. That Other is barred by a lack S(A̶) that is not filled by the subject who offers himself to the task. The question regarding the Other's desire remains open; it is an enigma as well as the key to existence. The subject does not find that his own sense is filled absolutely in the Other and thus separates from him. He withdraws from the intimation of the Other's incompleteness and asks what the Other would lack should the subject not recognize the Other as Other; this is how the subject recovers being. The relation between the subject and the Other can neither be one of inclusion or exclusion, as it was at the beginning, when the two circles were separated. There is an intersecting space where the lack in the One is superimposed on the lack in the Other. It is the area corresponding to the object @, the effect of the bar on both the subject and the Other.

What part of Lacan's teaching have we just reproduced? The opposition and path from *jouissance* to desire. Between 1963 and 1964, Lacan dedicated Seminar X, *Anxiety*, and Seminar XI, *The Four Fundamental Concepts of Psychoanalysis*, as well as his essay "Position of the Unconscious" in *Écrits* to this question. He did so in two successive and different ways that, much like the Eulerian circles, lead to a choice supposing loss. Chronologically first, the seminar on *angst* revolves around a schema regarding subjective division. In the table represented in the seminar, the word division alludes to the barring of the subject, but essentially concerns the adoption of a mathematical model of division: how many times can S be divided by A? It is the first moment of *jouissance*. The table shows that the subject can be in A only in order to inscribe his *jouissance* as @ but, as a result of this operation, a quotient is produced that is the barred Other (Ⱥ); this is the second moment of *angst*, which gives way to the third moment of division: @ divided by S, the subject. After going through the position of object @ for the Other, the subject becomes a barred subject, a subject of unconscious desire. Between the Subject and the Other, "the unconscious is, between the two of them, their cut in action" (E, 712). The remainder from this operation is $.

A	S	jouissance
@	A	angst
$		desire

This arithmetical model of division did not seem to satisfy Lacan, although he never explained why this formulation does not reappear in his teaching, neither in the *Écrits* or any other subsequent seminar. It was substituted the following year by a reference to the logic of disjunction, the two forms, *vel* and *aut*, with the conjunction "or," and by the topological reference to the Eulerian circles: from "subjective division" to "causation of the subject" through a double process of inclusion-exclusion, conjunction-intersection, or alienation-separation.[31] At this time Lacan is interested in the notion of cause: the object @ as the material cause that operates in psychoanalysis because of the meddling of the signifier. For this reason he introduced the neologism (or barbarism) "causation" of the subject when he could just as well have said "production of the subject."[32]

It is not an archeological interest but a clinical one that makes me recall this brief moment in Lacan's teaching. Seminar X is dedicated to *angst*, the only affect that does not deceive. As nightmares show, it appears with the approach of *jouissance*. If dreams are oriented by the fulfillment of desire, and slumber offers protection by a series of distractions (why not translate the *Entstellung* of the primary processes this way as well?), *angst* is that point of subjective dissolution (aphanisis) in which the subject disappears before the inscrutable lack in the Other (castration here understood as castration of the Other, the Mother):

> Let us recall that Freud unties the knot in his discussion of the lack of the mother's penis, where the nature of the phallus is revealed. He tells us that the subject divides here regarding reality, seeing an abyss opening up here against which he protects himself with a phobia, and which he at the same time covers over with a surface upon which he erects a fetish—that is, the existence of the penis as maintained albeit displaced. (E, 745)

The subject fades before the *jouissance* of the Other that appears in multiple ways: as the open jaws of the voracious monster in the nightmare; a devastating or inscrutable destiny; the uncanny noise of a scream that envelops us (the scream of nature that resounds in Munch's painting, the scream not heard by the characters who turn their backs to the mouth uttering the cry and go on their way); the *semblant* of *jouissance* that in the imaginary the neurotic attributes to the black widow and the praying mantis, that ineffable feminine *jouissance* that is "beyond the phallus" and beyond meaning. The unforgettable *jouissance* of the Other condemns the sexual relation to nonexistence. For this reason we are always summoned to treat the ambiguous relation between *jouissance* and sexuality.

Angst has an intermediary function between *jouissance* and desire, between S and $, between the unborn, abolished subject, of the former and the divided subject of the latter. There is a point of passage from *jouissance* to desire that is clinically considered *angst* in neurosis and perversion: between the lack of lack, in psychotic *jouissance* (the top part in the table of subjective division) and the *langagière* lack that defines the desiring subject, the final objective of analytic treatment. *Angst* does not depend on lack; on the contrary, *angst* emerges when the object of desire makes itself present. Against that *angst*, the subject resorts to the strongholds of phobia or the fetish.

In both neurosis and perversion, the subject identifies with what he is for the Other: he becomes an object to satisfy his demand in neurosis or the instrument destined to preserve the Other's *jouissance* in perversion. Freud's position was that both stumble with the intolerable lack that compels them to retreat in relation to desire. Lacan on this point differs from the founder of psychoanalysis; castration is not a gloomy phantasm (in neurosis), or unacceptable (in perversion). Neither is it a point of restraint or the bedrock on which analysis stumbles, but rather a point of departure. Precisely because it is an object of lack "what you've got to teach the neurotic to give is this thing he doesn't imagine, it's nothing— it's precisely his anxiety," instead of offering himself as object to satisfy what the Other demands, supposing in that way he will be able to pay the Other off (S X, 52).

The subject is mistaken in supposing that the Other wants his castration, or that the subject's castration is lacking in the Other. He does not realize that symbolic castration imposes itself as soon as he enters the *langagière* universe. Instead of standing before the Other as a desiring subject, the subject offers himself up and figures in his phantasm as a pervert offering his little "things" in order for the Other to *jouit*, to be happy and love him: that is, to have a stable place in the Other. He gives up on desire, and thus protects himself from its dangers. He specializes in affirming his ego, covering up the lack he inhabits; it is a strong ego, concealer of castration. Drawing on this paradigmatic position in neurosis, in his seminar on *angst* Lacan left us with memorable aphorisms on love: love is giving what one does not have, and love is the only thing that can make *jouissance* acquiesce to desire.

Lacan's position here differs from Freud's. The father does not prohibit; neither is he terrifying, or a rival or *jouissant*. The father is the name-of-the-Father, pure signifier of the Phallus, which distances the subject from the Desire-of-the-Mother and, through castration (-φ), marks the objects of desire. These become signifiers of lack and are therefore invested with phallic value. Lack is not to be feared; on the contrary, to accept one's own image as lacking allows the body of the Other to transform itself into object cause of desire. It is the element that prohibits and bars, with guilt (autoeroticism) that is not psychological but structural. Finally, lack is what channels "the transfusion of the body's libido toward the object" (E, 696).

The choice for the subject is clear: between *jouissance* and desire. It is one or the other; *angst* because of the lack of lack ("Don't you know that it's not longing for the maternal breast that provokes anxiety, but its immanence? What provokes anxiety is everything that announces to us, that lets us glimpse, that we're going to be taken back onto the lap" (S X, 53) or love, which is to bear the lack, castration (-φ), allowing one to condescend to the other. The experience of psychoanalysis moves entirely through speech and the two bridges that go from *jouissance* to desire: *angst* and love. Traversing *angst*, beyond the phantasm, toward love . . . with its fatal destiny.

Chapter 3

Jouissance and Sexuality

Equivocations of Sexuality

Many possible points of departure are possible for this chapter, leaving me
to wonder how I should write on this topic, rich in misunderstandings.
One must choose, though I may err or even lose. I could begin by going
back to classical mythology, the chronology of Freud's developments,
the modifications made to what Freud said in Lacan's teaching or even
to some points developed in the preceding chapter. Or take up literary,
philosophical, political, or film references. One must wager and attempt
to link these possible beginnings. A brief quotation helps us delve into the
task at hand: "the fact that the genital act must find its place in desire's
unconscious articulation is the discovery of analysis" (E, 529), which can
be completed with the following:

> If the recognition of the subject's sexual position is not tied
> to the symbolic apparatus, then nothing remains for analysis,
> Freudianism, but to disappear—it means absolutely nothing.
> The subject finds his place in a preformed symbolic apparatus
> that institutes the law in sexuality. And this law no longer
> allows the subject to realize his sexuality except on the sym-
> bolic plane. This is what the Oedipus complex means, and if
> analysis didn't know this, it would have discovered absolutely
> nothing. (S III, 170)

When Freud approached this topic over a century ago (in 1905), he
needed to demonstrate, against popular opinion and the state of knowledge
at the time, that sexuality was present beyond the enclosed restricted field
of adult relations in sexual intercourse and reproduction. Today we find

101

ourselves taking the opposite direction: questioning and putting limits on an ideology that sees sexuality and its symbols everywhere. In our time, to affirm the sexual meaning of a subjective action is to state the obvious and surprises (or interests) no one. The paradoxical effect of psychoanalysis' success is that its theses have left a mark on modernity and provoked a new closure of the unconscious. The mysticism of repression has been substituted by a newer one of liberation and acting out, although it maintains the same repressions of older constraints. As the two quotes above show, it is not a question of mystifying a natural tendency for satisfaction now understood as *jouissance*, but of demonstrating the ways in which the "symbolic apparatus" organizes sexuality in men and women, *parlêtres* (subjects of the unconscious). That rich *langagière* device can also be employed to maintain sexuality under the domination of newly upholstered but obsolete ideologies.

Perhaps it is a question easier to understand than articulate in a comprehensible manner because two apparently contradictory theses must be maintained simultaneously. Freud himself was aware of the difficulties, as he notes in the final paragraph of the 1920 prologue to *Three Essays on the Theory of Sexuality* (SE VII, 133–134). There Freud sustains that the great source of resistance to psychoanalysis lies in "its insistence on the importance of sexuality in *all* human achievements," while also calling the claim of pan-sexualism attributed to psychoanalysis a "senseless charge" (SE VII, 134, my emphasis).

The two previous chapters mentioned the difficulties involved in maintaining the affirmation and negation simultaneously. It is not so much a question of the pan-sexualism of the theory, but the phallogocentrism of the psychoanalytic clinic: the field of language and therefore culture marked by the function of castration, a limit to *jouissance* accessible to *parlêtres*—the razor that cuts and separates the *jouissance* of being, the signifier and the Other, as well as the *jouissance* of men and women, straddling the razor's edge. Sexuality is not the cause or explanatory principle at play in analysis, but its effect—that is, the consequence of how speaking beings position themselves in relation to castration, which regulates all exchanges and is the condition of possibility for discourse as social link. The question remains whether psychoanalysis can be a way to think and go "beyond castration" in new and different historical circumstances, when traditional discourses have been overtaken by discursive formations that challenge universal solutions and propose, according to the spirit and letter of the Freudian discovery, the singular consideration of each case.

In other words, the object of psychoanalysis that is cause of desire and surplus *jouissance*, @, is certainly @-sexual, but not for that reason is it independent of the Law whose signifier is the Phallus, represented by the name-of-the-Father. A historical and theoretical phallocratism is the foundation of the patriarchal order. Is it a structural and universal necessity for all human societies or a way to rationalize domination? This is the topic of many passionate contemporary debates that question as well as vivify challenges to psychoanalytic discourse. What is the destiny of the work of love "in the age of its mechanical reproducibility"?

Theoretical pan-sexualism, then? Certainly not, although there is a phallic reference, given that the phallus is the basis of the symbolic order, "the signifier that is destined to designate meaning effects as a whole, insofar as the signifier conditions them by its presence as signifier" (E, 579). It is the hinge joining *logos* and desire and the decisive reason why the unconscious is structured like a language, according to Lacan's teachings before 1970. The accusation of psychoanalysis' pan-sexualism should not provoke an excessive defense leading to disregard the central role of the *Bedeutung* of this signification or reference, according to the preferred translation of Frege's concept.

The first problem that afflicts a thinker (psychoanalyst or not) who approaches the question of sexuality is how to distinguish between biology or nature (the organism) and psychoanalysis (the subject), separating the ideological representations that occupy the field for each. These representations are full of distortions, due to ignorance, repression, and hypocrisy, up to the exhibitionism of the supposed overcoming of prejudice. Ferenczi began his "theory of genitality" with a daring affirmation: "It was reserved for psychoanalysis to rescue the problems of sexuality from the poison cabinet of science in which they had been locked away for centuries" (TG, 5). In fact, very little had been locked away during those centuries. More than rescue, Freud's works called attention to what had long been ignored, distinguishing as a particular trait of his work "being deliberately independent of the findings of biology" (SE, VII, 131). If in 1905 he still insisted in the "fundamental nature . . . upon sexual chemistry" (SE VII, 216), by 1920 he silently removed the paragraph supporting this naturalist hypothesis.

The indistinctness between the biological and the psychoanalytic leads to the analogy between sexuality and the drives of nutrition, hunger, necessity, and satisfaction, which are always inadequate, or only serve to mark differences, given that sexuality is what appetite is not . . . unless it is sexualized, humanized, directed toward the breast before or instead of its milk. Freud was not always clear regarding this point. His first theory of the drives was based on the classic distinction between two major necessities, conservation (of the individual) and reproduction (of the species), expressed through the sexual drive with a specific energy: libido. Today he would have less opportunity for confusion; reproduction is not something needed by the species, but rather what threatens it (overpopulation, they say) and the reproductive function can be accomplished *in vitro* or other ways, without drives to spoil the outcome. Today, we witness promising and frightful progress in the application of genetic engineering; the frameworks that pretended to straitjacket sexuality as a source of pleasure have shattered, and when the question of its relation to *jouissance* resurfaces, it is to clear the way and act as a screen for concealment and defense, as we studied in the previous chapter. Today, psychoanalysis is challenged by advocates of new paths for sexuality, such as feminism and queer theory.

It is here fitting to denounce the obscurantism produced in wake of psychoanalysis' inroads, in spite of Freud or against Lacan. There is confusion between "sexual satisfaction," orgasm, the achievements of "mental health," a successful genitality, and related notions, such as happiness, maturity, completeness, and so on. This set of normative justifications and reupholstered ideals have as models the notion of satiated hunger, the reduction of tension, the discharge of excitation, and the emptying out of seminal fluid analogous to repletion. Intercourse and sexual copulation (preferably *hetero-*) was and often still is considered an ideal commensurate with the unitive aspirations of Eros; the road to happiness or social revolution (Reich); the possibility of fulfilling what is supposedly a universal dream, the return to an original unity, the womb:

> I had already reached the conclusion that the human being is dominated from the moment of birth onwards by a continuous regressive trend toward the reestablishment of the intrauterine situation, and holds fast to this unswervingly by, as it were, magical-hallucinatory means . . . in the sex act one succeeds in a real sense, even if only in a partial one, in returning to the maternal womb. (TG, 20)

There are also formulations of psychoanalytic theories centered on the paradigm of the male orgasm and supposedly physiological research that looks for and periodically affirms there is an "objective" (masculine) equivalent for the orgasm in women: ejaculations, pelvic contractions, climax scan, neural release of dopamine, and more.

The dissemination of a certain psychoanalytic knowledge elevated to the category of the gospel of *jouissance* also modifies subjective attitudes regarding intercourse. In Seminar XIII (April 27, 1966), Lacan noted that if in antiquity the poet was able to say "*animal post coitum triste est*," to which someone added "except the woman and the rooster," nowadays men no longer feel sad because they've had an orgasm in conformity with the psychoanalytic rule; while women, who were previously happy because only their *partenaires* were sad, now are sad themselves because they do not know if they have experienced *jouissance* the right way. Meanwhile the rooster continues to sing . . . and women wake up from the dreams of deep psychology.

It is true there is a relation between the orgasm (which can be obtained through intercourse, although not necessarily, as masturbation, erotic dreams, and seminal ejaculations in situations of *angst* attest) and *jouissance*. But that relation is not one of identity or completion, and neither is it the recovery of a mythical original unity. It does not in itself constitute a goal to propose to anyone and less from a Freudian perspective.

I propose the reader delve into the analytic indexes of Freud's *Standard Edition* and search for an article on "orgasm." He will be surprised to learn that the fingers in one hand are enough to count the references. The term appears only once in *Three Essays on the Theory of Sexuality* and then to note that the breast-feeder who nurses with delight achieves a muscular reaction "in the nature of an orgasm" (SE VII, 180). The founder of psychoanalysis never wrote anything able to support the current mythology of the beneficial function of an orgasm. The reader should review the other few references. Surprise may be mixed with laughter when in one Freud compares an orgasm with the anger of young girls after receiving an enema.

As far as his phenomenology, Freud compared the orgasm with the not-recommended model of an attack: epileptic or hysterical. He never spoke of "total genital satisfaction," and if he has something to say on this point, it is of a personal nature: "I know that even the supreme pleasure of sexual union is only an organ-pleasure attached to the activity of the genitals" (SE XVI, 323–324). We do not find many references to "sexual satisfaction" in Freud, but it is clear that for him it is not identical to an orgasm. He also states: "one of the forms in which love manifests itself— sexual love—has given us our most intense experience of an overwhelming sensation of pleasure and has thus furnished us with a pattern for our search for happiness" (SE XXI, 82). But in the following line he writes that this road is ill-advised for those who seek happiness, which is why "the wise men of every age have warned us most emphatically against this way of life" (SE XXI, 101).

Lacan is rigorously Freudian when he questions the religion of sexual *jouissance* of our now long "sexual revolution," as it is called with involuntary humor. In his most extreme formulation, he noted: "the great secret of psychoanalysis is that there is no sexual act" (S XIV). This explains one of the opening quotations in this chapter, where Lacan refers to the "genital act" as not having primacy; it must seek and find the ways of positioning itself in the *langagière* apparatus of "desire's unconscious articulation." It is desire that condemns the act to an essential dissatisfaction, consubstantial to the sexual drive itself, according to Freud. After much debate as to whether there is a sexual act or not, Lacan made a solemn pronouncement: yes, there is, but there is no sexual act that does not constitute a Freudian slip. This is because, between men and women, there is no sexual relation, sexual equivalency, sexual rapport, correspondence, or harmony that would predestine them to conjugate or unite under a common yoke (*conjugar/yugo*).

The sexual act constitutes a misunderstanding in relation to *jouissance* (one could even ask: who framed the sexual act?). An orgasm is not, in relation to *jouissance*, more than its end point, the abolishment of all demand in which desire is not fulfilled or satisfied, but rather misled by the bonus of maximum pleasure (fleeting and fugitive). This notion is denounced by the most lucid commentators of our time that speak of the "canonical novel of the orgasm,"[1] a neo-mythology whose principal effect is the pretense of assimilating feminine *jouissance* to a masculine model and to abolish the differences between the sexes by universalizing penile *jouissance* as the paradigm of a sexual satisfaction that does not exist. The disavowal of feminine *jouissance* as an Other *jouissance* is, according to our thesis in chapter 6, the essence of perversion: the belief that there is no other *jouissance* other than phallic *jouissance*.

As we know, *jouissance* is barred for both sexes because every subject is subject to the Law, its signifier, the Phallus destroyer of the Thing. And it is represented by the name-of-the-Father, which opens the way to the articulation of demands that separate the unsayable and unreachable object of desire. One approaches the sexual act as a subject of castration. The organ that represents the phallus in the imaginary, the penis or clitoris, is there as a signal of lack in relation to *jouissance*, promised as a supposed and unpredictable reproductive function which is a-subjective (for the woman there is no representation of fertilization; she can only know of this sometime later—as for the man, not even then). As beings of language we are subject to a limit in sexual *jouissance*, which is the end of an erection, detumescence; this is different for a man and for a woman. In the man, an orgasm represents the end point of all demand, while for women, the demand frequently continues: it is not exhausted in the other's ejaculation; something unresolved remains, motivating an *encore*, a longing for something more.

The climax of pleasure dissolves all relation with any object whatsoever. The organism's homeostatic function is a mechanism for halting *jouissance*. It is not the function of a subject but an instantaneous dissolution, the reduction to a piece of flaccid flesh remaining from the act. The end of intercourse leaves a remainder of castration. Intercourse is thus the privileged site for a couple's dissatisfaction. The end of an erection is experienced as loss, differently for the man who undergoes it than for the woman, who leaves this function in hands of her *partenaire*. In this sense, psychoanalysis positions itself against any mysticism regarding sexuality as a source of superior knowledge, transubstantiation, or a glimpse of ultra-terrestrial life. It is a question of the fading of a subject's being identified to its phallic appendage, the end of *jouissance*, and for this reason, a *petite mort*.

The remainder of the sexual act is separation, tearing away from the body of the other that one has embraced and now flees; from the child that could be engendered, from the organ of intercourse that separates the woman and man (due to detumescence), and from one's own satisfaction, which reveals itself in fading, the separation of the subject from itself. Far from recovering unity, the son does not reunite with the mother or the girl with the penis. *Jouissance* is revealed as utopic, subject to castration. For this reason Lacan uses the harshest words against those unitive conceptions he considered stupid and abject, branding Freud's idea regarding the tendency of cells and organisms to join together to constitute ever-more complex and expanding organizations, delusional.

However, because the sexual relation does not exist and conjunction is an illusion, sexuality exists in reality. It is precisely an effect of the fault and lack: human sexuality is "phaultic," turning round that fleeting third object in the sexual encounter, surplus *jouissance*.[2] In other words, in relation to the object constituted as lost. For example, when Freud imagines the theoretical child he created saying: "It's a pity I can't kiss myself," there is a cut in relation to his own self that leads him "at a later date [to seek] the corresponding part—the lips—of another person" (SE VII, 182).

The primordial division that launches sexuality in the psychoanalytic sense is a division of the subject in relation to *jouissance*, brought about by castration. The latter in turn leads to the detachment of the object @, the substitution for the missing *jouissance*. The object is eroticized insofar as it comes to the place of the missing part of the subject in the desired image (E, 696). Precisely because it can be separated, "that is what predestines the phallus to give body to *jouissance* in the dialectic of desire" (E, 696) and produces the transfusion of the body's libido toward the object, the "corresponding part" (in the body of the other) to which Freud referred.

The reduction of the sublime dignity that mysticism (old-fashioned and Eastern or modern and Western) attributes to the sexual act does not lead psychoanalysis down a regressive road advocating a return to autoeroticism and idiotic *jouissance*, always at the reach of the hand. Nor does it lead to the opposite, but reciprocal side of that regression—the exaltation of ascetic values and the renunciation of *jouissance* of the body—given that such *jouissance* would be limited by pleasure.

Psychoanalysis is something else. It is not a technique of the body, as Heidegger naïvely told Lacan (according to Lacan and what can be gleaned from interviews with the philosopher, who affirmed that the philosophical consequences of psychoanalysis were unsustainable because they made the essence of man biological), and neither is it a spiritualizing ideology that extols sublimation. Psychoanalysis is an ethics that manifests itself in a *langagière* technique centered on the articulation of unconscious desire. This defines the ways that one draws near or away from the genital act, affirming his or her difference and special characteristics, the manifestation of desire in the approach to *jouissance*.

In the clinic, one often observes the effects of guilt related to masturbation. Guilt does not depend on sanctions, external codes, or the ridiculous threat that "if you touch it, I'll cut it off." Rather, it implies accepting the organ's role in the function of exchange that, through the subjectivation of lack, gives *jouissance* its value. The value of *jouissance* corresponds to the organ; for a subject it becomes devalued as signification if it is a permanently available satisfaction that leaves no trace, removing the drive from its memorable and historicizing function linked to the proper name and the symbolic register. Marcuse's criticism regarding the "repressive de-sublimation" generously offered to the consumers of real and virtual sex is pertinent here.[3]

Lack, what Freud taught us to call castration, is the foundation of the sexual order. It is a lack in the image or, as Narcissus shows, the subject is separated from his image; there is a prohibition at play between the image and the subject. Narcissus can live happily if and only if he cannot find himself. The surface of the mirror registers the presence of the insurmountable Other that separates him from himself; it is one of the implicit meanings of the barred S ($), the matheme of the subject in Lacan. The vertical trait is made from a silvered crystal that introduces lack and registers the non-relation between oneself and oneself perceived as other. The prohibited object appears in the specular image: what you are in the gaze of the Other. It thus receives a "proper" name, the signifier whose signified is the lost *jouissance*. It is the first commandment to which the *parlêtre* is subjected: "You will not *jouirez* yourself; you owe yourself to yourself." The penalty is harsh and is called psychosis.

Symbolic castration allows passing from *jouissance* to desire and makes possible another *jouissance* minted by the Law of desire: a *jouissance* beyond lack in being. The lack, what one does not have, must be accepted in order to be able to offer what one does not have in love (relations), where *jouissance* is valued and becomes a value transferred to the body of the *partenaire*.

An opening regarding the nature and relation of *jouissance*(s) of the One and the Other is possible only if the illusion of a total *jouissance* able to fulfill a person in its encounter with another body is rejected. If we accept that an orgasm is "only an organ-pleasure attached to the activity of the genitals" (SE XVI, 323–324) or a deviation of those lips that cannot kiss themselves, a "masturbatory concession" (S XIV, 5/24/67), as Lacan said referring to intercourse, differentiating it from false notions regarding an "oceanic bath" or the recovery of primary narcissism, the comforting notion that in the sexual encounter something of the Other passes over to the One is dismissed.

Jouissance of Being, Phallic *Jouissance* and *Jouissance* of the Other

Following Lacan, in chapter 2 (section six), I placed the Other *Jouissance* at the intersection between the imaginary and the real, without symbolic mediation. It is best to recall it: "*Jouissance* of being . . . is ineffable, outside the symbolic, an imaginary quality we invent as if it were the *jouissance* of the Other; a devastating Other that, due to the absent inscription of the name-of-the-Father (forclusion), reappears in the real." Two paragraphs later I reproduced the schema of the Borromean knot from "The Third," where the space of what is called *jouissance* of the Other (*Jouissance de l'Autre*) can "be seen." But perhaps what escaped the eye of my reader is that I was using another expression, synonymous to *jouissance* of being, for what Lacan calls *jouissance* of the Other. Lacan does as well on occasion (in French, one phoneme distinguishes the expressions *jouissance de l'etre* from *jouissance de l'Autre*). In what is quoted above, I suggested it was a *jouissance* of being we attribute to the condition of being *jouissance* of the Other, even if it is not necessarily so. In the previous chapter we linked *jouissance* of being, comparable to the unthinkable *jouissance* of a tree or an oyster (*jouissance de l'huitre*), to the Thing. We also said that speech was the razor that separated another type of *jouissance* from the one filtered by castration—the Phallus being its foundation—which is called phallic *jouissance* (JΦ). Later in the previous chapter, I distanced myself from Lacan's teaching in order to account for the clinical necessity of distinguishing and even opposing *jouissance* of being and *jouissance* of the Other, understood as *jouissance* of the *Other* sex: the sex that is Other with respect to the Phallus, and therefore feminine. In *L'etourdit* Lacan states: "We call heterosexual, by definition, those who love women, whatever their own sex may be" (AE, 467).

As already noted, in what follows I distinguish the different *jouissance*(s) with the topology of the Mobius strip. A promise or threat, it is now time to fulfill it. First we must go through an invaluable and extensive detour in order to account for what the clinical experience of psychoanalysis and the analyst teach us. The detour will end with the second section of this chapter, in which the three types of *jouissance* are distinguished, and section three, where the causal role of castration is demonstrated. The topological discussion forms part of section four.

What I am attempting to demonstrate is that phallic *jouissance*, linked to speech, an effect of castration, expected and carried out by all *parlêtres*, a *langagière jouissance*, semiotic and outside the body, is the cut that separates and opposes two different bodily *jouissance*(s), outside language. On one side of the cut, *jouissance* of being, the *jouissance* lost due to castration, mythical and linked to the Thing, prior to phallic signification—noticeable in certain forms of psychosis. On the other side, *jouissance* of the Other, also bodily, not lost by castration, but emerging beyond it: the effect of the passage through language, but outside it, ineffable and inexplicable—feminine *jouissance*.

The frankly insufficient naturalist model must once again be criticized. That model relies on the cycles of necessity/satisfaction, hunger/satiety, erroneously analogous to the sexual activity of the male, but cannot adequately account for the females of the species, who are gripped by language constituted between both males and females. Freud began by extrapolating from this insufficient model. Going astray is unavoidable if one starts here in order to comprehend human sexuality: that is, from a biological or behaviorist basis and not the subordination of the genital function to the Law, the castration complex, as well the cut established between *jouissance* and desire.

With supposed simplicity, the hunger or instinct model functions only to obscure possible responses. The theoretical work of psychoanalysis, from its inception to the present, incisively takes distance from this only apparent "explication." Once the difference between sexuality and reproductive function was made evident and sexuality could not be understood according to the biological rationale of the pleasure principle, but rather on *jouissance*, another problem presented itself. How should *jouissance* be defined in masculine and feminine terms, as well as what in the *jouissance* of the other (lowercase) is subjectifiable for "each one" in the sexual (missed) encounter? This question refers to the heterogeneity of *jouissance*(s) and the difficulty, also recognized by Freud, of how to psychoanalytically define the differences between masculine and feminine. Freud resolved the issue in a way that was insufficient even for him. After affirming the masculine character of all libido, he proposed the opposition between activity and passivity in the framework of the drive. This thesis is both questionable and irritating.

This problem does not have a solution when knowledge confronts itself with *jouissance*, which in essence is irreducible to the word and often confused with what transpires in the body, of which nothing can be said. What can we know of *jouissance*, not only ours, but of the Other whose skin we cannot share? This is a problem that afflicts humanity from its beginnings: the division of the *jouissance* of manual labor for Adam and the pain of (obstetric) labor for Eve. Both are *jouissance* as effects of the Law, after the expulsion from the *jouissance* of a former Paradise that never was.

In the myth of Tiresias the seer, the question of *jouissance* and its differences is obvious. Tiresias, roaming through the hills, sees two serpents copulating and, according to two versions of the myth, either separated them or killed the female. The consequence was that (as punishment?)

Tiresias was transformed into a woman for seven years, at the end of which he again repeated the same viperish action and recovered his previous sex. Some time later, Jupiter and Hera were debating the *jouissance* of men and women in intercourse and decided that the best way to resolve the issue was to ask someone who had had both identities. Tiresias was called. Without wavering, he responded that if sexual pleasure could be divided into ten parts, nine would correspond to the woman and one to the man. Hera considered the secret of her sex betrayed and, thinking it should not be known, punished Tiresias with blindness. Not being able to absolve the sanction imposed by his wife, Jupiter compensated him with the qualities of a seer. That is how we find him in the Oedipus drama, as a blind seer. It is clear that Tiresias became wise only after having suffered the punishment and receiving the prize. If it had happened earlier, when he was called to give testimony, he would have known (now in the position of the analyst) that he should not have responded, but rather answered with a question. And, if he did respond, nothing sillier than to respond with quantities, as if the substance of the *jouissance*(s) of a man and a woman were the same and the question could be resolved in terms of proportion. Tiresias was the first victim of the horrors of quantification in relation to subjectivity.

What the kings of Olympus discussed involves the unthinkable and unrepresentable *jouissance* of the Other. *Jouissance* is such that each of the participants loses for not being that Other. *Jouissance*, of one and the other sex, functions in terms of loss. It is impossible, no matter how strong the embrace, to take control of the *jouissance* of the other in the subjective sense (I cannot live in the other's body, feel what he or she is feeling) as well as the objective (there is only *jouissance* in one's own body and then only partially, as *jouissance* of the organ, *Organlust*).

Jouissance is produced in the encounter of the erogenous zones and escapes from both members of the couple, given its very division. The *jouissance* of the Other belongs to the register of the phantasm but nonetheless has real effects on subjectivity. In many ways, most especially in dreams and symptoms, the psychoanalytic clinic has shown the sometimes inhibiting, anguishing, or stimulating effects, always enigmatic and mobilizing, of the unconscious *savoir* that results from the impossibility of appropriating the other's *jouissance*: *jouir* the body of the sexuated other (whether heterosexual or homosexual). Is it possible? Can one of the participants in copulation know what is happening to the other? Are the different *jouissance*(s) compatible or even comparable? Are they reciprocal convergent *jouissance*(s)? Lacan questioned these possibilities in considering the function of castration:

> The subject realizes he does not have the organ that I will call—since I have to choose a term—the unique, unary, unifying *jouissance*; what would make *jouissance* one in the conjunction of subjects of opposite sex [because] there is no possible subjective realization of the subject as element, as the sexuated *partenaire* of what he/she imagines as unification in the sexual act. (S XV, 1/11/68)

In psychoanalysis there is nothing comparable to *ying* and *yang*, the pleasant pair of little fish that together form a circle.

In the first chapter I proposed that *jouissance* is also a function included in the dialectic, but it was not a question of agreement between subjectivities, but a rivalry of *jouissance*(s) in which the lost *jouissance* is always at play; the incommensurability between the *jouissance* of one and the other, the lack of a common measure to assess what is the good (or evil) of each one. The dispute between Hera and Jupiter is the mythical formulation of that ancient discord between the sexes where Tiresias cannot be the arbiter, even less if he quantifies the sexual *rapport* that does not exist.

This is how the paradigm of penile *jouissance* has functioned traditionally, with its clear localization in the time of the orgasm and in the space of an erection-detumescence, giving a man the doubtful and much-debated privilege of a certain knowledge regarding genital satisfaction. It is well to recall that the fading of the subject's being in an orgasm corresponds to the loss of *jouissance* that escapes irretrievably in the semen. It is a short circuit; the fuses blow out, the light goes off. In the darkness that follows there is an attempt to localize, apprehend, and secure it. True knowledge is of an inevitable loss and remainder of discontent regarding the possibility of penile *jouissance* (phallic, inasmuch as the penis represents the phallus as signifier in the imaginary, due to the reality of its detumescence) able to ensure subjective satisfaction.

Localize it, but where? Geographically, as an exotic *jouissance* growing in *tristes tropiques*; ethnologically, as the patrimony of a fabulous tribe or race; historically, as the achievement of a previously wise, but extinguished, civilization? Or perhaps in religion as the extasis of saints incapable of transmitting sensation; or in mythology where Freud's construction of the primitive father of *jouissance* is its culmination and paradigm; in anatomy, where neurofibers and discharge patterns are examined; in politics and law, which pretend to administer, channel, and distribute a "legitimate" or contestatory sexuality; in chemistry, which promises to create an artificial paradise and sells substances that imitate sexual *jouissance*; or in cybernetics, which promises to abolish the biblical curse of work, relegating it to golems with no pretension of achieving *jouissance*, leaving it in hands of its inventors, without demand or envy. Or, finally, in psychoanalysis, where Freud brands *jouissance* unreachable due to the hard rock of castration, giving way to other quests that border on delirium (Reich and Ferenczi), until we reach Lacan's logical and topological articulation. The seed of our own discourse was planted in the space he marked out.

Localize it where? If the penis is an organ that cannot sustain its erection (an erection being the *jouissance* of the organ that fades with the orgasm) and if women show signs of another *jouissance* which is, in part, homologous to the male one (in the clitoris), but is not restricted to this *jouissance*, which may well be missing; if women can experience *jouissance*(s) that escape this and any other localization, there is the possibility that the *jouissance* the Phallus lacks may be a *jouissance* Other to the One. That is, Other to the phallic signifier that unifies the subject and recognizes him in the set of signifiers. The question of the *jouissance* of the Other, understood as the Other sex, that radical hetero-(*eteroz*) in relation to the Phallus, which is recognized and acknowledged, but which does not exhaust itself there—neither in itself nor in the universe of significations it imposes.

For these reasons feminine *jouissance* appears as *jouissance* of the Other. The attempt to control it in the field of knowledge has given place to the theories we summarized above and many others. If *jouissance* escapes knowledge (historically linked to power), knowledge engages in catching it precisely where its presumptions have slipped away, in Freud's "dark continent." At the end of his life, Freud concluded that he was not able to answer the question of what a woman *wants* and therefore what a woman *is*. Lacan added that psychoanalysis, the most radical mode for questioning *parlêtres* regarding their existence, when applied to women and even by women analysts, was not able to dispel the reigning perplexity regarding feminine *jouissance* by anything worthy of note. The enigma, apparently atemporal, has produced infinite responses by many an Oedipus and provoked the ruin of many sphinxes. We can describe these responses as neurotic or psychotic, but inasmuch as they are attempts to link *jouissance* and knowledge, they "open the door to all perverse acts," as Lacan used to say (S XIV, 6/7/67). When I discuss the topic of *jouissance* in perversion I will be able to further develop the relation between an impossible *savoir* regarding feminine *jouissance* and the perverse attempt to control what escapes this *savoir* by disavowing it (*Verleugnung*), reducing feminine *jouissance* to phallic *jouissance*, which is equivalent to considering women to be incomplete men. The question of feminine *jouissance* requires a new consideration of castration.

Neither men nor women are born as such, but come to be through an initial event, which is the attribution of a sex to a piece of flesh devoid of representations. The Other proffers a word at the moment of birth, "boy" or "girl," which functions as destiny, even beyond anatomy, given the case. The cut of castration is directed by speech, which sections ("sexions") bodies and sends them out to live in one of the two irreconcilable and noncomplementary homelands of the species. It is the real that mythologizes the Platonic androgen or the extraction of a rib (or from the tail, according to some Hebrew myths, in the language where the sound *tsela* has both the sense of "rib," as well as "misfortune, obstacle"): rib or tail belonging to Adam, an androgen before the divine surgery.[4]

The (*langagière*) cut in the assignation of a sex imposes otherness in each of the *parlêtres*. That is how speech becomes castration, separation, in essence.[5] Sexuality is established by discourse and the anatomical organs conform to it (or not). From and through discourse, the value of the organ is determined; with its presence or absence it "makes" the difference symbolized in the Other of language. As Freud noted, this difference, confirmed constantly in the clinic, is not important in itself (cases having to do with innervations, the bigger size of the penis in relation to the clitoris, premature sensations that can exist or not in a vaginal stasis or cultural determinations of phallic primacy) if not for the inevitable and late discovery that castration exists and operates in the mother, that primordial Other that must stop being phallic, for the boy and for the girl. This primordial Other also determines the possibility of normative identification of the boy with his father, who has it (the organ) and, on the feminine side, a demand directed to the one who has it so he may give it, displacing the Other of the demand of love from the mother to the father (*père-version*) and setting up a symbolic equivalence between the phallus and the child (*das Kleine*).

It is due to lack that the subject, man or woman, is forced to give up autoeroticism and renounce masturbatory *jouissance* with guilt not dependent on cultural codes. That guilt is inherent in the will to disavow castration, to function as a detour, a shortcut of self-sufficiency interposed on the road to *jouissance*. Sexual difference implies castration for both sexes. (Almost) no one has both. *Jouissance* is not able to materialize itself in only one, on one's own body; it pushes the aims of that body by filtering them through the field of the Other, the Other sex. It also constitutes the Phallus as a signifier of lack, what is looked for outside because it is not in place in one's own image. In this way the phallus is constituted as the third, between a man and a woman, looked for in the Other and always lacking. The missed encounter is fatal, structural, alien to his and her (best) wishes. What is absent is the cause of desire, which is the desire of the Other.

The lovers in the sexual act embrace and circle the lack at the center, an interior excluded from each one and desired in the Other. Freud was wrong when he wrote: "The sexual instinct [drive] is now subordinated to the reproductive function; it becomes, so to speak, altruistic" (SE VII, 207). The later introduction of narcissism corrects this idea that could well be the basis for the phantasm of oblativity and mutual offerings in obedience to the higher ends of the species. At play in the sexual act (which is always a *faux pas*) is the relation between a man and a woman with *jouissance* because the representation of the phallus rests on the Other of the embrace—that Other that later slips away in separation, when only the organ of copulation remains, now reduced to a remainder: lost for the woman, resistant to *jouissance* for the man, separated from both.

The Other is the phallus (lowercase) as regards the *jouissance* value the subject cannot satisfy by himself (-φ). For this reason the Other bears the message of the castration of the One ("When you see me you will see that something is missing in you"). Precisely because the phallus cannot be counted on, one enters into the sexual act. We can thus understand Lacan's adage that love consists in giving what one does not have: to give the Other one's castration. Whence Lacan's two propositions, only contradictory in appearance, noted in Seminar XIV (5/31/67): (1) the sexual act does not exist as far as the possibility of integration, restitution or contribution of what was lost in the "sexion" that constitutes man and woman as castrated, and (2) there is only the sexual act to allow the articulation by which a subject searches for the missing *jouissance* in the body of the Other: that is, the answer to his dissatisfaction. Whoever participates in the sexual act, whatever his or his *partenaire*'s sex, does so from a subjective position of enunciation: it is a declaration of sex. Unconscious, of course.

There is no complementarity between the sexes, but it is necessary there be two so that each one may define himself for not being the Other in a system of signifying opposition. Difference is irreducible. What they delineate between them is what they lack, the phallus as the third in the relation, whose representation relies on an organ marked by the castration complex and whose only role is the introduction of exchange, thus becoming the real *partenaire* of the sexual act: an act verified in the intersection of two lacks in which each of the participants is (-φ) for the Other.

There is no symmetry here. True, it is not possible to define the psychoanalytical status of "masculine" and "feminine," but the conditions of castration for each differs in the sense that for intercourse to occur (if one wishes to participate), an erection of the male member, on the man's side, is necessary and, on the woman's . . . the erection of the male member. On the man's side, desire is required, on the woman's side, consent. The possibility of rape, in principle only possible for phallophores, is the forcing of this consent.

The asymmetry of the respective sites of desire may explain the reason that for Freud the only relatively acceptable translation of masculine and feminine in the unconscious are activity and passivity. Of course this has nothing to do with the sperm's penetration in the ovule; this "interpretation" would be laughable. In relation to the sexual act, the man directs himself toward the woman, posing his desire as a demand for satisfaction, making it an object in the phantasm, attributing it a phallic value, an object of his eventual *jouissance*. Lacan states:

> one is not what one has and insofar as the man has the phallic organ, he is not it; this implies that, on the other side, one is what one does not have; that is, insofar as she does not have the phallus, she can take on its value. (S XIV, 4/19/67)

Not having it, she must be it, incarnate it: be clad in this value that can provoke the erection, since it is the condition for intercourse. Her desire cannot be manifested directly, but must be directed toward rousing the Other's desire. It is the feminine side of what we call the castration complex, which appears as the embodiment of the masquerade, the same function that confers a feminine aspect to any man that flaunts his male attributes.

The access to the genital act *appears* to be less charged with difficulties for women than for men, for the reasons discussed above. Once they have defined themselves (for themselves) as desiring beings, and not having the organ of connection, women have a smoother path; they can go toward the one who has it . . . and see how he manages. Frigidity therefore has neither the consequences nor transcendence that impotence has on the male side, where desire can acquire an inhibitory function, as the clinic shows. There is nothing to renounce and not much at risk, since castration is given from the start and not at the end, as for men. Freud posed this difference in similar terms, not in relation to every sexual act, but in relation to Oedipus, where transgression (incest between father and daughter) does not have, in general, the devastating clinical consequences of incest of a son with his mother. This "advantage" of the "beautiful-weak" sex is counterbalanced in Freudian discourse by the imposition of a double exigency: having to transplant the dominant and definitive erogenous zone from the clitoris to the vagina. On this point, no one agrees with Freud today.[6]

Intercourse requires the erection of the penis as a necessary condition for a man as well as for a woman, although it is not entirely sufficient (the desire of one and the consent of the other has to be added), setting aside other bodily variables as contingent. This banal observation, as well as the difference in positions established above, does not allow any privilege, advantage, or ease for any one of the *partenaires*, although in the imaginary one can find that either one, if neurotic, despises, is fearful or jealous (in her or his phantasm) of the position and *jouissance* of the other.

Actually, the condition for intercourse does not involve what one has, but what one no longer has due to sexual division. The phallus does not assure its owner anything other than being the missing part of his own ideal image—the cause of libidinal investiture in another body and the reason for refusing the *jouissance* of his own body: idiopathic, insignificant. The channel for the transfusion of libido to another body is produced in the case of homosexual or heterosexual object choice. What is decisive is not the organ involved, but the subjective position, the declaration of a sex. The phallus is the object of reciprocal dispossession that organizes the play of courtship and love; it is what women or other men look for in a man and (a perhaps scandalous theory) what men look for in women—or in other men—such as women look for it, not necessarily in a man, but in other women.

For Lacan, deception or the scam is constitutive of the sexual act. The man aspires to find a complement according to the biblical promise of "being of one flesh" and finds that there is indeed one flesh: his own. That is, in the end there is disillusionment regarding the scam of the false promise; searching for one flesh, he finds castration and the truth of the sexual act—*jouissance* is missing somewhere. We must also distinguish the disassociation between genital orgasm, which is the end point and limit of *jouissance* and intercourse that ends (or should) in an orgasm for the man *parlêtre* "encumbered by the phallus" (S XX, 76), but not for the woman *parlêtre*. It is clear that an orgasm does not require the conjunction of bodies and does not necessarily have to end in climax. This dissociation leads to the question regarding what represents sexual *jouissance* at the level of each subject. It is not a question of sexology but rather of erotology, "jouissology," even though the "object" *jouissance* is impossible to be apprehended as knowledge.[7] Certainly it is a question for psychoanalysis, a dimension open to the singular exploration of the roads open to *jouissance* for each of us, outside of any biological or cultural normativity.

The first use of the word erotology (*érotologie*) in French was in 1882. The *Dictionnaire Historique de la Langue Française* (Robert) provides the date and definition: "the study of physical love and erotic works." Freud never used the term, and Lacan used it on two occasions: in Seminar X (12/19/62), he noted that the practice of psychoanalysis, "deserves the name of erotology" (S X, 15). Nine years later, in Seminar XVIII (11/4/71), he affirmed "*jouissance* is of the order of an erotology." My friend J. Allouch takes up the term and insists on its consubstantiality with psychoanalysis, although in a later text he notes that the word is not very convenient ("it is a wager, crazy, no doubt, since no one ignores that the work of the little god Eros has neither rhyme nor reason").[8] The word "jouissology," linked to the Lacanian concept we are exploring, has the advantage of specificity, although we acknowledge there is no possible science of the slippery object @. In French we would have to coin the term *jouissologie*. What no one who has come this far can deny is that a definition of psychoanalysis cannot renounce the object of its practice and theory, *jouissance*, which is closer to Thanatos than to Eros. That is why we would gladly accept neologisms such as *erothanatism or erothanatology.*

Castration as Cause

Lacan tirelessly insisted on a point that today is frequently discussed (E, 575). The castration complex (an order of determination accessible to psychoanalysis and only to psychoanalysis inasmuch as it is a *langagière* practice) has the function of a "knot" in the production of men and women; the development of one and the other (in relation to the so-called libidinal states or phases); the determination of the clinical position of the subject (neurotic, perverse or psychotic, if we continue to speak with medical or psychiatric terminology); the possibilities and modalities for approaching the genital act and even the position vis-a-vis the child. Anatomy is not destiny but for the speech that signifies it. The function (of intercourse) does not make the organ; it is the organ (penis or not) that is appropriated by language. The symbolic order realizes an interesting function in relation to the organ, which is to transform it into a signifier of the loss of *jouissance* due to the intervention of the Law. In other words, the symbolic yields the castrating cut (S XIV, 4/27/66). The millenary practice of circumcision has no other meaning: the mark of the Other on the organ that represents the phallus.

Castration means that insofar as it is lost, *jouissance* must be signified, circumvented and evoked in the interweaving of signifying threads that outline where it is pooled: it contains, accumulates, and prevents its dispersion. Castration is a condenser of *jouissance*, making it subjectifiable. Subjective and at the same time strange, extimate, it vectorizes *jouissance*, channels, signals, and prohibits its ways. Because it is symbolic (not real) and asymmetric, as we've seen, it raises many questions regarding its effects on *jouissance*: the *jouissance* that is lacking, the possibility of recovering the loss; the *jouissance* of the Other, questions without end that multiply the responses in the uncertain world of knowledge, in the place of unarticulated truth. That is how they are transformed into statements: children's sexual theories, neurotics' family romances, sexological notions, sexual theories of adults, feminists, and analysts. Every one of these statements is ideologically charged and for this reason a debate that clarifies them is necessary.

The Phallus is primordially what makes the Thing suffer: the signifier inscribed in the real, the name of a lack in the Other, the barring of the desire of the Mother—what leads from the *jouissance* of the mother to the name-of-the-Father, making the Phallus a metaphor and thus sealing it off (in the sense of sealing a door or window). This point of impossibility and zero degree of the signifier introduces the S_1 that calls for another signifier and the rest of the chain (S_2), *savoir* in all its modalities. It is the indicator of lack (in *jouissance*); because it operates as signifier, the lack can be named. The Phallus indicates a place of absence to be colonized for what can be named, the *semblant* that comes to the place of truth and is the agent of all discourses. Because it is the localizer of lack (-φ), it organizes and commands desire and epitomizes the subject's response to lack in being. Thus, the objects that are cause of desire (@) reach phallic signification and are correlated to castration. The Phallus is the child's body, able to fill the lack in the mother, before it is barred by castration. What is lacking in the body is invested in the field of the Other. It must be looked for there.

As an organ, it allows for intercourse. It is crucial how having or not having it determines the subjective positions of the two in copulation[9]— and not only when they have the titles of "man" and "woman." Because its destiny is detumescence, the penis, a volatile and unstable organ that obstructs *jouissance*, also indicates the way. One of the essential meanings of the castration complex is the channeling that makes *jouissance* pass through the genitals in both *partenaires*. *Jouissance* is imaginarized by the flight of a bird that cannot sustain itself in the air and must separate from its part-en-air(e). As Freud noted, it is impossibility, not impotence, inherent to the sexual drive itself. As such, phallic *jouissance* is localized in the genitals (*Organlust*) and concentrated in the penis or clitoris. It is present in both sexes and there is no reason to suppose that it is different in one or the other, or greater on one side than the other, since there is no natural relation between *jouissance* and size or visibility. Any electrical technician knows that the valves are not superior to the transistors.

Perhaps Lacan exaggerated when in *The Logic of the Phantasm* he said:

An erection has nothing to do with desire, because desire can perfectly act, function, without being in any way accompanied by it. An erection is a phenomenon that must be localized on the road to *jouissance*. In itself an erection is *jouissance* and what is demanded, for the sexual act to take place, is that it not be detained: it is autoerotic *jouissance* . . . It is important to remember the operation essential to the sexual act in these terms; if it is in the register of *jouissance*, instead of desire, that we situate the operation of copulation, we are absolutely condemned to understand nothing at all of what we say about feminine desire, when we explain that it is, as in male desire, in a certain relation (*rélation*) of lack, a symbolized lack that is the phallic lack. (S XIV, 6/21/67)

The penile erection is directly discussed here, but does not mention that the clitoris is also an erectile organ whose erection is not a necessary or demanded condition for intercourse. The objections I make to Lacan's categorical affirmations above regards the supposed independence between erection and desire and the oft-repeated idea that an erection is a "test" of desire. Clearly, there are erections without desire and desire without erections, but intercourse is only possible if erection and desire converge. The function of an erection cannot be thought in isolation without taking into account its inevitable correlate, detumescence. The difference between both leaves a rest, a loss, which is the object @ as the intersection between *jouissance* lost and desire caused, reciprocally motivating one and the other in their repetition. There is no satisfaction here, only a reduction of tension due to organ pleasure.

We also have to doubt the following line regarding a supposed equivalence between masculine *jouissance* linked to an erection and feminine *jouissance* experienced as something women would call "*le coup de l'ascenseur*," which Lacan attributes to his experience as a man and not to psychoanalytic theory.[10] It is evident there are many differences between *partenaires* regarding *jouissance*. What cannot be said is that the differences are universal.

The relation to *savoir* and to *savoir* as a phantasm making prohibited *jouissance* possible is what is at stake here. The localization of male *jouissance* (and its interruption) is obvious and poses no doubt. Men are completely within phallic *jouissance*, without remainder in the *semblant* of *jouissance* that depends on an erection. But, what of the Other (sex)? This is Hera's and Jupiter's enigma and the sphinxes', as well as that of men and women, physiologists, neurotics, perverts, and psychoanalysts (male and female). The enigma perplexed Freud and finds a response in Lacan, a response of non-response, the affirmation of an unexplored *jouissance*: ineffable, in the body and beyond the language that outlines impossible *savoir* and sustains *jouissance*. It is linked to the impossibility of saying the whole truth that, as Nietzsche said, is woman.

The *jouissance* of women is partly phallic and partly enigmatic, linked to the unsayable, written with the matheme $S(\bar{A})$. For women, the *semblant* (a function of language, the imaginary effect of the signifier) and *jouissance* are dissociated. There is, yes, what is visible, sensible, sayable of *jouissance* . . . and there is more still (*encore*).

Does *jouissance* said to be experienced, but declared ineffable really exist? How can it be distinguished from a phantasm, a chimera, a dream sustained by a general and growing dissatisfaction with the doubtful promises of phallic *jouissance*?[11] Lacan himself gives feminine *jouissance* an uncertain status, that of belief:

> you are all going to be convinced that I believe in God. I believe in the jouissance of women insofar as it is extra (en plus), as long as you put a screen in front of this "extra": until I have been able to properly explain it. (S XX, 76–77)

As is well known, a belief is not certain, and whoever manifests it avoids committing themselves (like saying: "I think it's going to rain") or, at the other extreme, is a devouring certainty, something that may lead someone to die for their cause (e.g., "I believe in God," whose Lacanian equivalent is feminine *jouissance*).

In light of clinical experience, it seems certain there is a feminine *jouissance* that is beyond the phallus and the detumescence awaiting the organ that represents it: a *jouissance* in the body (*en corps*) that does not complement the masculine one, but rather presents itself as a *plus*, something more (*encore*), supplementary, and disrupts all attempts to restrict and localize it. The disavowal (*Verleugnung*) of this *jouissance* has motivated attempts to control it, from the most primitive forms (infundibulectomy) to the most scientific (modern sexology and massage therapy's search for encephalic centers or the vagina's G-spot). It is also present in the attempt to refer this mysterious *jouissance* to a supernatural contact of the soul with God, which makes ecstasy an orgasm. The ideology that proposes a mystical *jouissance* is the other side of the ideology of the sexologist. In Mexico: "same song, different tune" (*la misma gata, pero revolcada*).

Freud recognizes the split between a phallic *jouissance* (of the clitoris) and a different *jouissance*, a productive conception that suffered due to Freud's repeated intentions to localize it in the vagina. The unfortunate consequences of his affirmations are well known and can be seen in the tragic, paradigmatic, and extreme operations (three in all) to which the princess Marie Bonaparte subjected herself in order to make the clitoris reach the vagina; the most immediate effect was the dissatisfaction of many women with their *jouissance*. Possibly no other Freudian thesis has justifiably met with such heated and virulent opposition. Feminists sharpened their arrows against psychoanalysis and accused it in myriad ways of relegating and belittling feminine *jouissance* in function of the masculine model of erection-penetration-ejaculation, a model whose intent was to show, without success, to be the patrimony of both sexes.

The dissatisfaction with phallic *jouissance* promotes the search for other modes and modalities of *jouissance* based on the enigma of feminine *jouissance*. The task of defining and reaching *jouissance* through paraphilia and periphalia, for example, lengthening the duration of intercourse, asceticism, chemical displacements by means of substances able to provoke an erection, orgasms through stimulation of the central nervous system, aesthetic sublimation, or physical pain; all these capture the imagination and efforts of poets and scientists. But also of some psychoanalysts who think that fist-fucking, sado-masochistic practices, and multiple and anonymous sexual encounters can reveal new truths.

Beginning with what hysterics concealed and confirmed, psychoanalysis has made it its mission to respond to the question of *jouissance* differently from ortho-meta-para-phallic explications. What analysts proposed was disappointing, due to the common error of producing formulas that are supposedly universal. In 1960, a colloquium in Amsterdam brought together two works—one by Lacan, the other by Perrier and Granoff—that proposed something new based on analytic experience. It is the basis of the somewhat definitive development made by Lacan in Seminar XX (1972–1973).[12] In this seminar, the response to the age-old enigma takes the form of a logic that produces a series of formulas and formulations surrounded by an air of impudence.

The absence of a universal solution to the enigma of feminine *jouissance* led to the scandalous Lacanian proposition (but only in appearance because it is in fact an always recognized and banal truth) that Woman does not exist. This implies that women, one by one, must and can find their own response, not complementary or analogous to the masculine response, but rather independent and supplementary. And this is because, for Lacan, women are "not-all," they are "not-all" in phallic *jouissance*. With the phallus, "not-all" is said regarding *jouissance*. Men insist in speaking about Woman and finding a universal for the *jouissance* that women feel and men sense, a *jouissance* that because it escapes the network of knowledge is feared and even considered hostile.

The supplement of "extra-phallic" *jouissance* (*en corps, encore*) that could not be said, had to be written. To do so, Lacan laboriously worked on the formulas of sexuation, not of sexuality or sex (S XX, 78): the particular way each *parlêtre* positions itself before the phallic function, determined not by anatomy or culture, but by the avatars of the castration complex (determinant of unconscious *savoir*) and the desire that results from that complex (a means of subjectifying the lack in being).

I have decided not to include a reproduction of Lacan's formulas of sexuation that divide the part called man and the part called woman of speaking beings or to add yet another explanation to the ones that already exist. I refer the reader to Lacan's Seminar XX and its many enriching commentaries.[13] My reading marks a distance from explicit propositions that even coming from Lacan are confusing. Instead, I will approach and adopt suggestions from authors that treated the matter seriously in view of deriving a topological model.[14]

In a summary presented earlier in the chapter, we arrived at the point of separating *jouissance* of being and phallic *jouissance* and, following Lacan, placed them in different areas of the Borromean knot. In Lacan's teaching, the *jouissance* I call *jouissance* of being is also indistinctly called *jouissance* of the Other. What Other? It could be (1) the body as Other, a radical Other, outside language, the basis for a *jouissance* linked to the Thing, impossible to symbolize; (2) the Other, the great Other precisely as the Other of language, the Law and code (a code that could exist but doesn't), the Other where the message must signify, the Other indicated as A in the graph of desire; or (3) the Other that is the Other sex, and the Other sex is always feminine (*Eteroz*) because the sex that is One is always completely regulated by the signifier and the Law of the phallus.

The expression *jouissance* of the Other is unfortunate because given the polyvalence of the Lacanian Other and its matheme, the uppercase A, all *jouissance* is *jouissance* of the Other or Other *jouissance*: (1) the *jouissance* of the body outside language (that I call *jouissance* of being); (2) the *jouissance* that passes through a *langagière* articulation subjected to the Law and situated in culture (here called phallic *jouissance*, with Lacan); and (3) a third *jouissance*, supplementary and situated beyond castration and its symbol: a feminine *jouissance* for which I now propose reserving the name of *Jouissance* of the Other (sex). It is important to clarify that it is in the subjective sense—the Other sex as the one who *jouit*—not in the objective sense, because it is impossible *jouir* the Other as the object of *jouissance* of the One. We will return to this third *jouissance*, beyond the phallus, at the end of the chapter.

To say that the expression *jouissance* of the Other is unfortunate and then recognize its use in a restricted sense requires additional commentary. As we noted in the previous chapter, it is clear that "desire comes from the Other, and *jouissance* is located on the side of the Thing" (E,

724). In this sense, *jouissance* must always be considered as referring to the One, from which *parlêtres* are then displaced by the intervention of the invoking Other that splits subjectivity. *Jouissance* is what the Other lacks and at the same time what it prohibits in the One, as the mathemes of the barred Other and the barred subject show. In this way, and only this way, does *jouissance* present itself to the subject as being Other, the radical absence whose symbol is the uppercase Φ (Phallus), manifested in language as the name-of-the-Father.

For all these reasons, we propose the following synthesis:

1. *jouissance* of being (of the Thing, mythical)

2. phallic *jouissance* (of the signifier, *langagière*)

3. Other *jouissance*, not phallic, and *jouissance* of the Other (feminine, ineffable)

We agree with Lacan that *jouissance* of being (1) and *jouissance* of the Other (3) (JA, *jouissance de l'Autre*) are inscribed in the same region of the Borremean knot written on a plain surface: the region that intersects the real and the imaginary, without symbolic mediation—something bodily, outside the phallic function (of speech). As could not be otherwise, it is paradoxical that the *jouissance* called "of the Other" remains outside the symbolic, in the intersection of the Real and the Imaginary (see The Barriers to *Jouissance* in chapter 2).

The Three *Jouissance*(s) and the Mobius Strip

In articulating the three *jouissances*(s), it is important to remember that we are not operating in a speculative field but in constant reference to the clinic, which must be thought differently after incorporating the concept of *jouissance*. The list of three types of *jouissance* has something excessive or bizarre. It is much like the superposition of three heterogeneous substances: the three identifications defined by Freud in chapter 7 of *Mass Psychology* or the three masochisms in the article on the "economic problem," connecting things that do not seem able to be combined since they derive from different sets. It could not be otherwise, given *jouissance*'s relation to logic, from which it is excluded. Therefore, what is difficult to grasp with words in discourse is best to apprehend topologically.

One must begin with the clinic and extra-discursive *jouissance*(s) that do not pass through the focused diaphragm of speech, signal the dissolution of subjectivity, and are external to all life-relations. I am referring to bodies reduced to a corporeal existence of extreme alienation or intoxication, autism, *infans*-cy. This is one extreme. On the other, the ecstatic experiences of those who, having traversed all the barriers to *jouissance*, as well as its opposite, desire, find themselves in a direct, immediate relation to *jouissance*. Between these two poles are the "diaphragmed" *jouissance*(s), regulated by *langagière* sphincters, subjected to castration and its law, pursuing a phantasmatic object that inexorably escapes, like the tortoise for Achilles or woman for man. It is not wrong to say that this last (phallic) *jouissance* is "perverse" (thrown on its side, transferred, transversal, metaphoric) while the other two are mad.

We must take note of the two *jouissance*(s) that are outside language in order not to confuse them. They are not the same; one is the opposite of the other, or its inverse. Despite the classical psychiatric clinic that classifies it under psychosis, autism cannot be compared to paranoia. Between them, on this side of and beyond speech, is a field that insufficiently covers the real by means of language and gives us "reality," a certain substitute for *jouissance* that escapes us. It is the field Lacan called *semblant* and Nietzsche, more crudely, the lie. *Semblant* or lie (both tributaries of the phallus and *jouissance*) is discourse's condition of possibility because there is no discourse that is not *semblant*.

It is simple to show the relation between the three *jouissance*(s) topologically, on the surface of a sheet of paper. One traces three concentric circles that represent the existing relations between the three *jouissance*(s).

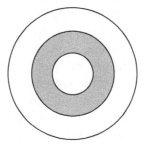

There is a central zone, the nucleus of being, the most intimate and inaccessible, an interior foreign land excluded from the Real and suffering the signifier: *jouissance* of being. The shaded middle area is speech that frames and defines the Thing, condemning it to silence and unexpected filtrations, the space of the signifier: phallic *jouissance*. There is also a zone of *jouissance* that is beyond, exterior, a *jouissance* that exceeds signification and the phallic function; it makes a woman "not-all" (*pas-toute*) and of which there are only traces (not knowledge) in the experience of mystics and paranoiacs. It goes beyond the organ (in the form of the phallus) that spoils everything: Other *jouissance* and *jouissance* of the Other (sex).

This exceedingly simple model does not show the continuity and opposition between the *jouissance*(s) of the body (the central and exterior circles) separated by speech, making *jouissance* pass through the funnel of the phallus. With the model of the concentric circles, separation is absolute, and between both *jouissance*(s) there is no opposition, but simply no contact. For this reason I propose another model and demonstration that Lacan himself used in a totally different context: the Mobius strip. It is important to recall what is essential about this topological figure. The reader interested in the technical details and Lacan's uses of this figure can refer to the already cited text by Granon-Lafont. I assume the topological properties of the strip are well known.

We are not confronted with the relation between three visible and clearly separated spaces, as in the three circles above. That is why we prefer the strip, the ribbon with a half twist. We know that the Mobius strip commonly used, the one we make by joining the top border of one of the ends with the bottom of the other, is a "false" Mobius strip because if with scissors we cut it in half or along it, what remains is simply a ribbon, a surface with two sides and two borders. We also know that the space opened by the cut cannot be cut simultaneously. That space, virtual and intangible, is the true Mobius strip. The intangible and incorporeal space of the cut is essential for our conception of the three *jouissance*(s) and the separation between them.

Jouissance of being and *jouissance* of the Other (sex), the two *jouissance*(s) outside speech, have the same false continuity that we noted in the false Mobius strip. There, the scissors, an object that indicates the function of castration and the incision of the phallic signifier (in more precise and less intuitive terms), produce the hole, the separation of a primordial *jouissance* that opens the gates to an accessible phallic *jouissance* for speaking subjects, made of *langagière* enchantments and deceptions. It is a *jouissance* without a body, outside the body, in language, that makes for division and conflict. The *jouissance* of the body is now divided in two, obverse and reverse, outside of language (figured as a cut in the Mobius strip) that separates it into a *jouissance* of being, before the cut, and a *jouissance* of the Other, its antithesis, antiphony, beyond: neither secondary nor conceivable without that cut.

I explained earlier why I reject conceiving the three *jouissance*(s) using the simple model of the three concentric circles. It lacks the heuristic richness of the Mobius strip and the opposition between the false and true strip. What I propose shows that castration is the cut that makes the substance of the two *jouissance*(s) of the body the same, although they are not the same; they are different, and it is not possible to pass from one to the other. There is a discontinuity between them that is essential. The body, with its surface is one, obverse and reverse. Language (the Phallus) is that virtual being that in itself produces the opposition and differentiation of the three *jouissance*(s), a subtle breath that marks the impossible reencounter with the lost *jouissance* of being and the possible, mutilated one possible through speech. The cut of castration is complete, total; on the side of the man, it leads him through a funnel made possible by the organ that represents it (it is not a question of anatomy, but a relation with an imaginary representation of the organ of lack in desire). The cut is incomplete in women, who do not stumble with the obstacle that in its corporeal image puts a barrier to *jouissance* as *semblant* of the phallus. In other words, it is a "not-all cut" which, once in effect, opens to a beyond and refers to the signifier missing in the battery of the Other of language: the enigma of femininity, an enigma from the point of view of the phallus, of course.

Due to the incommunicable heterogeneity of *jouissance*(s)—two of them are ineffable and refer to the lacking $S(\cancel{A})$—, the result is the necessary impossibility of the sexual relation in the real. If the Phallus were a signifier with an equal, if a signifier of ~~The~~ woman existed, the relation could be articulated and inscribed; that is, some type of complementarity would be possible. But because that signifier is lacking, an imbalance is established that configures and delineates *jouissance* linked to castration and the two *jouissance*(s): one nearer—*jouissance* of being—and the other farther—*jouissance* of the Other (sex)—from the cut. In summary, before speech there is *jouissance* of being and after, Other *jouissance* and *jouissance* of the Other (sex). Between the one and the other, semiotic *jouissance*, the one linked to the phallus and speech that separates the body.

Jean Allouch reconstructed the original text of a Lacanian reference in Lacan's Seminar XVII that speaks beautifully about the existence and differences of these three *jouissance*(s) (SM, 205):

> There is no more burning question than what, in discourse, refers to *jouissance* [*jouissance* of being], discourse is constantly touching on it, by virtue of the fact that this is where it orig-inates [phallic *jouissance*]. Discourse again disturbs it when it attempts to return to that origin. That is how it defies all appeasement [*jouissance* of the Other].[15]

It is crucial to point out the difference between the two *jouissance*(s) outside language and not assimilate them, even if doing so impinges on Lacan's text. If not read in this way, then Lacan's conception of feminin-ity would make women beings that can only ex-sist as *langagière*, linked to the order and Law of the phallus. The reproaches made by feminists would then be justifiable because, as women, they would not have any other recourse than the unthinkable space of the Thing, where silence is confused with screams, all significations disappear, and life gives way to death. Her *jouissance* would be phallic; if not, only the silence of the trees, the oyster, or the scream no one hears and says nothing would remain. In this latter conception, there would be nothing left for the feminine position but imposture or phallic masquerade on the one hand and, on the other, the passive acceptance of the place of @, an object for the phantasm of a subject's essentially perverse desire.

The richness of Lacan's formulation can be appreciated when his affirmation "The woman does not exist" is evaluated without prejudice. Women, considered one by one, all different, lack a universal. They are inscribed in an essential relation to the Phallus, yes, but they are there as "not-all," pursuing a signifier impossible to articulate, "something" that is not on this side, but beyond speech, S(A̸). That signifier takes them or could take them (it is not a question of creating another universal after doing away with it) into a world of values of lived experience beyond phallic imperialism and its universe of signification: this is the secret of those mystics that are not crazy and the subtleties of the feminine soul that disrupt, in the saying of lovers, phallophore arrogance. It is a ques-tion of a beyond whose motto is *encore*: the inverse (right to left) of the reverse (madness) or the reverse of the inverse (left to right) to madness without which all rights are abolished.

Freud (Lacan) or Foucault

In the fifteen years (1990–2006) since the first edition of *Jouissance*, queer theory emerged (coming after Gay and Lesbian Studies in the 1980s, which in turn came after the upheaval that feminism represented for thought in the 1970s), taking up and building on Michel Foucault's research (1926–1984) on the history of sexuality in Greece and Rome. It was Teresa de Lauretis who in 1990 coined the untranslatable expression "queer theory" in order to account for multiple phenomena and experiences, and their corresponding theories, regarding the modalities of *jouissance* that escape an imposed and dominant social normativity, now baptized with the presumptuous name of heteronormativity.

Heteronormativity is the social norm presented as the backbone of classical democratic societies. The norm speaks for itself and does not need to be approved by the judicial system. It corresponds to the ideology and prejudices of white men, adult, middle class, defined in their sexual orientation toward women, monogamous, and centered on the heterosexual couple as the paradigm of the love relation, marriage, and family: "It assumes that a complementary relation between the sexes is both a natural arrangement (the way things are) and a cultural idea (the way things should be)" (QT, 238). Heteronormativity is not only an ideological complex. At its most radical, it is the ideology that configures beings by classifying them and making them feel strange to themselves (queer) when they do not conform to a regulating system.

Queer are all those who do not adjust to that norm: women, inasmuch as they do not consider themselves the "complement" of men; racial and cultural minorities; the indigent and homeless; men and women who look for personal satisfaction in nonstandard relations or encounters (genital, heterosexual); those who are the object of segregation and distrust because their forms of *jouissance* are queer, alien, different from what is expected. What is expected is not statistically the majority because, given queer diversity, the majority of the population falls outside of heteronormativity. The official ideology imposes itself by the force of biopower (Foucault), which is the effect of the discourse of those who "well-*jouir* and well-think."[16] Discourse is the transindividual instrument that exercises its performative force independently of the instances of the subject, its agreement or desire.

Biopower manifests itself by creating and distributing signs of identity that, following a norm, pretend to establish what the other is in relation to what he should be. Classificatory systems (beginning with nineteenth-century psychopathology) are powerful discourses that create abnormal identities. Michel Foucault exhaustively studied the fascinating process of production of what is termed "queer" and opened new avenues for a refreshing and critical knowledge. Foucault did not use the term "queer" in the sense it acquired years after his death and that continues to the present. His courses in the Collège de France are exemplary investigations, continued now by many thinkers grouped together under the label of queer theory.[17]

The basic hypothesis of this theory is that sexual and gender identity, as well as those identities that receive their names from dominant ideology, are total or partial social constructions that categorize and segregate those who are "different." The political consequence of these critical studies is to challenge biopower and its dogmatic intention to limit the road to an "Other" *jouissance* thus defined.

In Lacanian terms, we could say that the Other is the one who aspires to *jouir*, beyond the unification that the phallic signifier wishes to monopolize. The *jouissance* of the Other is here of those who deviate from the norm; it is a suspicious *jouissance*, which must be limited and submitted to the Law. The Law has a perverse vocation because it does not recognize another *jouissance* than the one discovered by the light of a man's erectile organ, the phallus as *semblant*. The heteronormative motto is "everyone around the phallus and its substitute, the name-of-the-Father." As said years ago, "Outside the church there is no salvation"; today, with a false and archaic Lacanian banner, one might substitute "Outside the church" with "Outside the name-of-the-Father."

Queer theory is threatened by its own success. The publications multiply, its exponents present their positions in forums, bookstores have special sections dedicated to their books; the universities do not isolate its proponents, but offer them a prominent place. Its irreverent impulse fades due to the appearance of a new normativity and cooptation in the distribution of power, at least at the intellectual level. No one, or nearly no one, defends "straight" thought, which has become politically incorrect. Sexism, racism, and homophobia have not been done away with, but they are now more successfully concealed. The closet is now full of those who betray themselves in lapses and symptoms and thus reveal their rejection of these "minorities," who continue being objects of rejection. It is not because those who "well-*jouir* and well-think" have repressed their prejudices (in the psychoanalytic sense), they have just learned to suppress them from discourse.[18]

The proponents of this theoretical and political movement have been divided from the beginning regarding the place that psychoanalytic thought, particularly Lacan's, should have in its general conceptions. In the United States, many consider that beyond some questionable affirmations by Freud and Lacan, they cannot do without the contributions of psychoanalysis and value the usefulness that its theory and practice have for their objectives. Moreover, just as in the 1970s many feminist pioneers considered that Freud was a "male chauvinist pig," an advocate of women's misery, many authors now pounce against Lacan as if he were a proponent of heteronormativity, someone who wished to condemn perversions in name of patriarchical or discriminatory principles. They insist in opposing Foucault to Lacan, now demonized as the adversary. The battle regarding psychoanalysis in queer theory is passionate.

I will not discuss the positions at play. The most recent and resolute opponent of the theory and practice of psychoanalysis is Didier Eribon, whose book inspired the title of this section:

> We have to choose: Freud (Lacan) or Foucault. Foucault or psychoanalysis. The greatness of the Foucaultian project consists precisely in the fact that it looks to bury the psychoanalytic theory of the individual psyche and oppose it to a theory of individuation as the effect of the subjected body, the disciplined body. (EP, 86)

For Eribon, Foucault's biographer and intimate friend, "the psyche which concerns psychoanalysis is the product of disciplinary society and psychoanalysis is a cog in the disciplinary machine" (EP, 86). This extreme position is also accepted in certain Lacanian circles. For Jean Allouch:

> Psychoanalysts do not denounce the errors, they keep quiet and are shocked, as if Foucault had not implicated them, as if he had not publicly articulated a reasoned critique of psychoanalysis, something that corresponds to something like a prayer for the dead of psychoanalysis. (SM, 169)

If psychoanalysis is what Foucault says it is, Allouch continues, it is finished "even from before Lacan's death" (SM, 169). For that reason, and echoing a previous affirmation, he adds a definitive statement: "Psychoanalysis will be Foucaultian or it will cease to be; that means that we have the task of bringing Lacan and Foucault together (SM, 179) and

"Foucault has preceded us and we can do no better than to catch up with him, with Lacan" (SM, 173).

We thus see psychoanalysis confronted by those who wish to bury it and having to defend it from those who wish to save it, by following Foucault's lead. In the following pages we propose that these alternatives are based on an error of perspective and lack of awareness that psychoanalysis (Freud and Lacan) is the undeniable foundation and direct precedent from which queer theory derives, as a logical and necessary consequence. They are also unaware, in the sense of disavowal, of what Foucault lacks, the "one more effort" that would have allowed him to break off completely with the heteronormative system. As Tim Dean states:

> Indeed, while queer theory traces its intellectual genealogy to Michel Foucault, it can be argued that queer theory actually begins with Freud, specifically, with his theories of polymorphous perversity, infantile sexuality, and the unconscious. Lacan's "return to Freud" involves rediscovering all that is most strange and refractory—all that remains foreign to our normal, commonsensical ways of thinking—about human subjectivity. Thus from an Anglo-American perspective, Lacan makes psychoanalysis look rather queer. By virtue of its flouting norms of all kinds (including norms of intelligibility), Lacanian psychoanalysis may provide handy ammunition for queer theory's critique of what has come to be known as heteronormativity. (QT, 238)

That critique begins, historically, with the detailed note Freud adds to *Three Essays on the Theory of Sexuality* in 1915:

> Psycho-analytic research is most decidedly opposed to any attempt at separating off homosexuals from the rest of mankind as a group of a special character . . . it has found that all human beings are capable of making a homosexual object-choice and have in fact made one in their unconscious . . . psycho-analysis considers that a choice of an object independently of its sex— freedom to range equally over male and female objects—as it is found in childhood, in primitive states of society and early periods of history, is the original basis from which, as a result of restriction in one direction or the other, both the normal

and the inverted types develop. Thus from the point of view of psycho-analysis the exclusive sexual interest felt by men for women is also a problem that needs elucidating and not a self-evident fact. . . . (SE VII, 145–146)

Freud knew what he was referring to. It is well known that this theoretical position is the result of analyzing his own tendencies, as well as his relation with Fliess.

I will not tire the reader with quotes that may already be familiar. We know that when Freud was asked about the possibility of transforming someone's sexual orientation, he responded that it was just as difficult, through psychoanalysis, that someone pass from homosexuality to heterosexuality as to produce a change in the opposite direction. In a letter from 1935 to an American mother who was worried about her son's homosexuality, and whom he berated for not calling things by their name, Freud said in no uncertain terms that there was no reason to be ashamed of the condition since it did not suppose a vice or any sort of degradation and could not be classified as an illness, but rather a variation of the sexual function.[19] It is true that, as in the explanation on lay analysis, the majority of psychoanalysts pursued policies contrary to Freud's position, and it is also known that in 1956 his daughter Anna tried to block an English journalist from reprinting that letter in *The Observer*. Even today, psychoanalysts in many countries believe homosexuality is a disease and that homosexuals should be banned from practicing psychoanalysis.

Lacan, criticized for affirming in Seminars 1 (1953) and VIII (1960) that homosexuality was a modality of perversion, was an admirer of Foucault's work and someone who, in his institutional trajectory, opposed any attempt to segregate psychoanalysts based on their sexual preferences. The word "perversion" never entailed a moralizing description and was a clinical observation not tinged with value judgments that could damage the analyst's neutrality. Lacan was aware of the progress made by feminism in the struggle for equality, and it is evident that his theses on femininity in *Encore* (1972–1973) are a response to the critique of Freud's thesis made by the Women's Liberation Movement. I would even venture to say that Lacan's conceptions of the division between women and men *parlêtres* and his theses on surplus *jouissance* are the greatest contribution of psychoanalysis in the history of humanity to a feminine "jouissology." Since then the concept of perversion has changed, and for that reason we can say that perversion is the belief that there is only one (phallic) *jouissance*, while disavowing the possibility of an Other *jouissance*.

As with Freud, Lacan's positions have found detractors among his closest collaborators. Even today, it is possible to read that some of his followers, such as the reknown Charles Melman, discuss homosexuality in clearly homophobic terms, despite some incidental denials:

> It is true that the homosexual has not chosen his destiny [it is difficult for us to admit it and, even so, what a sad destiny!] and that the same forces that in others lead to heterosexuality reveal in them, sometimes to profound surprise for the subject and without being able to avoid it [such as he himself would have wanted to have been able to choose, of course] that he was on the other side [*sic*]. Only religion condemns through shame and exclusion [not us psychoanalysts, who are excluded from this privilege]. Having said this, it is possible to formulate an ethical judgment that emerges less from the general need for narcissistic certainty, induced by a different sexuality, which we can formulate through the following question: does homosexuality give the subject more freedom in reference to the order of language that determines him in the unconscious? [who said anything about more or less freedom within language in function of sexual preferences?] We can only respond in the negative. Perversion [here pejoratively assimilated to a homosexual condition] is a system of constraints and dependencies more rigid than what it refutes for insufficiency, a vulgar characteristic or stupidity [this is what we are on this side, but "on the other side" they are worse]. For this reason we cannot accept that homosexual perversion is emancipatory; it seems that an invasion of the phallic order has an essentially conservative nature, even when it is opposed to the established order.[20]

These are the final sentences of a long article on homosexuality that considers itself clinical and Lacanian. The author laments that in masculine and feminine homosexuality there is a merciless condemnation of the father in all the figures that represent him. This hate, Melman states, is commonly transmitted to her child by a mother seeking vengeance for her castration.

I have quoted extensively from Melman's article in order to show that Foucault's critique of psychoanalysis is not unfounded, but cannot be thought to refer to psychoanalysis in general, but to certain champions of the norm who distance themselves from Freudian and Lacanian discourse: the true successor in the first case is Anna Freud, and the frustrated one in the second is Charles Melman. However, this is just anecdotal. What is important is psychoanalysis' contribution to the topic and politics that its practice and theory make possible. I therefore agree with Tim Dean's thesis on the pioneering thought of Freud and Foucault for an authentic queer theory. It is not a question of psychoanalysis having to run after Foucault with the hopes of reaching him (Allouch); it is Foucault who, renouncing Freud's and Lacan's developments, falls prey to ambiguities that overshadow the convincing results of his substantial genealogical and historical research.

What am I referring to? A none-too-innocent ignorance and silence (Foucault can certainly be criticized, but not for ignorance and ingenuity) regarding Freud's death drive and the concept of *jouissance* in Lacan. What we discussed in chapter 1 of this book required rewriting the history of psychoanalysis given that it marks turning points and gives meaning to the preliminary steps of the Freudian discovery.

Starting with Freud, we also indicated: (1) his ideas on homosexuality, contrary to any heteronormativity; (2) the affirmation of polymorphous perversion at the origin of subjectivity and underlying all human beings throughout their lives; (3) the notion that all drives are partial, aspire to a satisfaction that is never reached, propelling them to aim forward in a new search; (4) the overcoming of all biological perspectives in the understanding of human sexuality; (5) the affirmation of the transgressive character of the drive that does not resign itself to the goals of the pleasure principle and breaches them in the subject's road to a "beyond"; (6) the thesis that the death drive is the essence of the drive, always more or less linked to the life drives; (7) the repetitive nature of the drive's insistence; (8) the disapproval of all possible complementarity through successful genitality (always the target of Lacan's sarcasm). In sum, Freud's theory goes against the grain of a normative reading and champions the essence of psychoanalysis: listen to what is said in each analysis, at each moment of the patient's discourse, renouncing and challenging all previous knowledge. The theory of the drives, with its transgressive, repetitive and, at bottom, masochistic specificity, is the basis for thinking a queer theory that opposes the identities that come from the Other.

Queer theory is threatened by its lack of psychoanalytic knowledge when it believes that gay, lesbian, sadomasochistic, or other identities can serve as barriers to heteronormativity, given that those identities derive from classifications and judgments established by the Other. It is not by inverting the sign of discrimination that discrimination is defeated. Psychoanalytic research is an essential tool for the deconstruction of normative categories. Why? Because it allows the singularity of desire to be revealed in each case: the basis for the formation of social movements where alliances can be formed and not blurred between subjects previously pigeonholed by a classificatory system, which is always the effect of the hostility of the other often disguised as objective, while pretending to make what is different something aberrant, crooked, or in need of correction.

What about Lacan? More than a demystifying and unconventional re-reading of Freud, Lacan contributed concepts that can serve as the basis for a theory not coopted by official discourse. Concretely, he challenged the aims of "genital maturity" that prevailed in analytic discourse when he began teaching and, more importantly, advanced the concept of *jouissance* to a central place in analytic reflection. *Jouissance* as the opposite pole to desire: between the two the whole of subjective experience is played out. In both cases, it is the question of a subject immersed in the network of language, split and separated from the object that is both cause of his desire and evocative of prohibited *jouissance*. Lacan's theses are the consequence of the omnipresence of the dimension of *jouissance* in human life; they function as insurmountable barriers to the phallic imperialism that characterizes our culture and leads subjects to live behind bars that channel *jouissance* through the ditches created by power.

The monolithic phallic system in Lacan's formulas of sexuation is the opposite of being prostrated before Priapus's altar. From that monolith emerges the thesis that a woman is "not-all" in relation to him (Him); he can only dream with organizing the world under his aegis and is also "not-all" because women (The Woman does not exist) exist and carry the message of surplus *jouissance*, irreducible to language, felt but unable to be explained in the arrogant and imperialistic terms that historically hold sway. That is why, in line with Freud, Lacan speaks of perversion in terms of its civilizing and innovative value, without implying the creation of a new ethics inversely opposite to the dominant official discourse, the discourse of the master.

Lacan's conclusion, a consequence of his invention of object @ (that the sexual relation does not exist) is (should be) the basis for all queer theory. There is no normal or natural relation between the sexes. Their *jouissance* is not complementary, and the only agreement possible between them begins with the recognition of a heterogeneity that is neither biological nor cultural. Cultural differences exist, no doubt, and are open to deconstruction; it is not, as some would suggest, "a binary relation that is a sexist production" (SF, 67), a construction that can collapse because it is the work of culture.[21] From the perspective of psychoanalysis, the rejection of the sexual division of men and women has a name: disavowal (*Verleugnung*) of the difference between the sexes ("I know, but all the same").

The political work to be done in this field is immense, and there are many who do so with success: legal equality, nondiscrimination of sexual minorities (including the Church and Army), reproductive rights, legal gay marriage, single families, changes in legislation regarding the names of children no longer requiring the patronymic, parity in the work force between men and women, the end of the culture of the closet for those who live outside the hetero norm, and many others. Psychoanalysis applauds this movement that is contrary to age-old social ideals of adaptation to repressive norms. Many have found in their own analysis the road to expressing themselves openly in this sense. However, the imperatives of psychoanalysis are more radical and go beyond these necessary gains that are bravely recognized in the individual and theoretical trajectory of Foucault as historiographer and deconstructor of segregationist categories, as well as accuser of biopower's abuse.

That is the value of the notion of *jouissance* that Foucault pretends not to know. Let us read a well-known and key excerpt from his work:

> Sexuality is a very real historical formation: it is what gave rise to the notion of sex, as a speculative element necessary to its operation. We must not think that by saying yes to sex, one says no to power; on the contrary, one tracks along the course laid out by the general deployment of sexuality. It is the agency of sex that we must break away from, if we aim—through a tactical reversal of the various mechanisms of sexuality—to counter the grips of power with the claims of bodies, pleasures, and knowledges, in their multiplicity and their possibility of resistance. *The rallying point for the counterattack against the deployment of sexuality ought not to be sex-desire, but bodies and pleasures.* (HS1, 157, my emphasis)

Foucault's text is from 1976. As we already noted, the quote from Lacan's seminar that announces the baptism of *jouissance* is dated 1958. We stated that Lacan's teaching until then had revolved around desire, but from that moment on *jouissance*, its "opposite pole," had to be considered. The contraposition between desire and *jouissance* had a decisive point of inflection when, in 1962, in his Seminar X on *angst*, Lacan introduced the notion of object @ as surplus *jouissance*. The "opposite pole" implies that desire is now considered a barrier on the road to *jouissance*. For this reason, since 1990 our own work has taken on Lacan's 1960 formulation, which affirmed that only love could make *jouissance* condescend to desire, and inverted the last line to read that only love can also make desire condescend to *jouissance*. Psychoanalysis is what allows the subject to confront himself with his desire, an experience that must be interrupted so that the subject can find the roads allowing his desire to open the way to *jouissance*. This is not Foucault counterattacking in the name of "bodies and pleasures," it is Lacan vigorously working in that direction for more than twenty years (1958–1981).

The problem is that Foucault calls sex into question as a road to *jouissance*, which commits him to a new ethics, unknown to the majority of Foucault followers, but which has not passed unnoticed for more astute readers: an ethics committed to asceticism and distrust, if not rejection, of sexuality ("one tracks along the course laid out by the general deployment of sexuality . . ."), considered to be a tool for biopower.

Foucault's affirmations should not be understood literally; they appear to say the opposite of what he wishes to say. How are we to know this? Are we prepared to admit with Foucault that sexuality (an "apparatus [*dispositif*] of . . .") is repressive, despotic, dedicated to distributing individuals into hierarchies? Shouldn't we be suspicious of the promotion of "the arts of existence" by which we must understand "those intentional and voluntary actions by which men not only set themselves rules of conduct, but also seek to transform themselves, to change themselves into their singular being, and to make their lives into an oeuvre that carries certain aesthetic values and meets certain stylistic criteria" (HS2, 10–11)? Are these arts (technologies of the self, "care of self," "aesthetic of existence"), a continuation and culmination of the aspirations of the master, which does not recognize the necessary servitude imposed by the drives and their *langagière* characteristic?[22] Is the weight of new ideals, which claim to be changed, but are actually maintained, being carried on the backs of subjects? One of Foucault's most authorized followers, Paul Veyne, states:

> We can guess at what might emerge from this diagnosis [of Fou-
> cault's]: the self (*moi*), taking itself as a work to be accomplished,
> could sustain an ethics that is no longer supported by either
> tradition or reason; as an artist of itself, the self would enjoy
> that autonomy that modernity can no longer do without . . . it
> is no longer necessary to wait for the revolution to begin to
> realize ourselves: the self is the new strategic possibility.[23]

Don't we flinch thinking a return to the illusory and outgrown realm of
the autonomous ego, master of itself? There is an emphasis on asceticism;
the insistence on "resisting sexuality;" the slogan to "liberate oneself from
the instance of sex;" the reference to de-sexualization (understood as
de-genitalization). The quotes are many. We have even heard Jean Allouch
claim that Lacan's favorite philosopher was Plotinus! This was after one
of his seminars in Mexico on the topic of love, in which *jouissance* was
not mentioned once.[24]

Perhaps now the heading for this section of the chapter can be
better understood. It is "Freud (Lacan) or Foucault" because of the latter's insistence in confusing the fundamental concepts of psychoanalysis
(transference, drive, unconscious, and repetition) in order to introduce
new ideals, to promote a new ethics that pretends to surpass an older one,
which lead to the liberation of sexuality from the toxic realms of official
science (Ferenczi), and made subjects attempt new roads through which
desire could condescend to *jouissance*.

It is also important not to close one's eyes to Foucault's great sco-
toma, with a dimension of blindness: feminine *jouissance*. In the work
of the historiographer and deconstructor, the different forms of pleasure
are undifferentiated and concrete references are only to the pleasure of
men, which they may access through men, women, or ephebes. An entire
chapter of Volume 3 of *The History of Sexuality* is titled "The Wife," with
no reference to women's sexuality. The discourse revolves around marriage
and the woman's place as the guardian of the man's home, obliged to
offer her fidelity: "We know that adultery was juridically condemned and
morally reproved on account of the injustice done by a man to the one
whose wife he led astray" (HS1, 171). No one finds anything regarding a
woman's relation to "pleasure" here, even less *jouissance*. They rarely appear
in Foucault's written texts or in the many interviews he gave, although
there are explicit references to the intellectual and political movements
that shook up society in the last fifteen years of his life. Why? Is it because

femininity as a category is a sexist invention? To avoid the pitfalls of the organization of sexuality that overvalues sex as a source of "pleasure" (although *jouissance* is not mentioned)? So as not to differentiate and thus be an accomplice of segregation? I am inclined to think, perhaps "badly," that Foucault could not accept anything other than a masculine sexual pleasure (homo or hetero, that is secondary). I do not know the reasons for this lack of awareness and will not incur in applied psychoanalysis. His hagiographer states:

> Foucault was not an antifeminist monster, as some of his detractors state. On the contrary, he worked enthusiastically with his female colleagues, supported the emergence of political organizations of marginal groups, including those of women [even that!] and had the intention of having *Libération* give voice to different emergent tendencies within the feminist movement. To a lesser extent, he also participated in the struggle for abortion rights in France. (SF, 182–183)

It is worthwhile mentioning the implicit disavowal in each one of these statements. The various biographies of Foucault contain blurry references to feminism, as well as silence regarding the specificity of feminine pleasures and an erotic practice of sex that was not his.

A critique of Foucault cannot ignore the capital importance of his studies, before and after *The History of Sexuality*. We sum up our discussion by adding to Tim Dean's own conclusions in the article already mentioned: the Lacanian concept of *jouissance* is a necessary tool in any attempt to modify the epistemological field of *parlêtres* and their lives as bodily realities. Unfortunately, the manner in which Foucault tackled the topic of "pleasures"—ignoring its difference and opposition to *jouissance*—has led many queer theorists, and some psychoanalysts, to see pleasure with optimism, as if it were not complicated by its "beyond" (the pleasure principle) and could be expanded without finding other cultural barriers that must be deconstructed.

In this Foucauldian utopia it appears as though the obstacles to the sexual happiness of bodies emerged from "outside," as if there were no "internal" barriers to pleasure, inherent in the drive's *langagière* apparatus. It is disingenuous to suppose that sex is only a question of pleasure and the affirmation of self, care, and control, instead of being the point where one finds oneself with negativity and *jouissance* as a search, not without masochistic edges, of an object of desire that eludes us. That is what Freud understood and Foucault and his followers reject: the death drive. No, we must not aspire to reach Foucault as what precedes psychoanalysis. Rather, we must understand that queer theory is Lacanian or it is not. The work to be completed is not arduous, but rather a question of incorporating the psychoanalytic concept of *jouissance*, beyond pleasure. It is what allows the theory to pass from impotence to impossibility. The price of renouncing psychoanalysis is messianism and soteriology.

Chapter 4

Deciphering *Jouissance*

Jouissance Is Ciphered

I will now address a crucial turning point in Lacan's teaching, which requires reviewing his previous developments and draw out its effects for analytical practice. I am referring to an expression that appears in *Television*:

> What Freud articulates as primary process in the unconscious—
> and this is me speaking here, but you can look it up and you'd
> see it—isn't something to be encoded [*se chiffre*], but to be
> deciphered [*se déchiffre*]. I mean: *jouissance* itself. In which
> case it doesn't comprise energy, and cannot be inscribed as
> such. (T, 18–19, translation modified)

The assertion is unequivocal and definitive. What it mobilizes and displaces in Lacanian theory is so imposing that its commentary requires re-reading Lacan's previous teaching and reflecting on Freud's text as a whole. Lacan's thesis condenses and concretizes a new theoretical conception of psychoanalysis, which goes hand in hand with other modifications noted in the restless and unsettling Lacanian revision of Freud at this time.

Please excuse the literality and exegetic insistence bordering on repetition: what is ciphered is *jouissance*, and that is why it can be deciphered. Who would decipher it? A good decipherer: the primary process (in the singular?) articulated by Freud, the pair condensation and displacement. It is a transparent expression, not open to misunderstandings: the primary process, the unconscious, is not cipher or concealment, but the start of an unveiling (*aletheia*). It is always already deciphering, the passage from what is ciphered, written, the letter, the codicil, or the score to another field: speech, discourse. It points to an Other that bestows signification, includes

145

it in the network of meaning, makes it possible to become imaginary, and relates it to the I (ego) of the statement. A passage is thus indicated from the unsayable S(Ⱥ) to signifying articulation s(A). The primary process thus functions as the passage from *jouissance* to discourse. In other words, the Freudian unconscious, which operates by condensation and displacement, is the process by which ciphered *jouissance* is deciphered and transferred to the social link, articulated speech directed to someone, ready to be filled with meaning by whoever listens. Ready for misunderstanding.

Jouissance is thus transplanted, exiled from the body to language: "To pass *jouissance* to the unconscious; that is, to what is countable, is in fact a cursed (*sacré*) displacement" (AE, 420). At the risk of being redundant: the unconscious is not the original site of *jouissance* that is *jouissance* of the body. It is from that homeland that *jouissance* must take the road into exile, go on to inhabit discourse and recover itself there: an impossible and eternal return. The subject constitutes itself as ostracized, going from the original One to the Other of speech. For Lacan, the possibility of dreaming with "empty speech and full speech in the psychoanalytic realization of the subject," the title of the first section of the Rome discourse, can no longer exist (E, 206). From then on, the words able to say the whole truth are missing. Truth of the One, *jouissance*, and truth of the Other, language and culture, absolute knowledge—the two truths carving up one another reciprocally. Between them, the subject of psychoanalysis: split, barred, swept up by a double belonging.

The point of departure in the experience of psychoanalysis is speech, the mansion of the said (*dit-mension*)—the reference to Heidegger is obvious—"a deciphering of pure signifying di-mention [*dit-mension*]" (T, 9). From the beginning, this is the phenomenological field recognized as operating in Lacan's first return to Freud: "verbalization." In this field, the creator of psychoanalysis stumbles with the invisible motor of articulation and signifying play, "something" hitherto unheard-of that bathes speech and manifests itself as torsions of wordy articulations: "a web of puns, metaphors, metonymies" (T, 9, translation modified). Freud gives it a mythical name, libido, and Lacan one that is also mythical: lamella (*lamelle*). Libido is a word to be thought in the language where love is called *Liebe*; it is the Freudian myth. Lacan's term refers to the discharge of slime that detaches itself from the body and covers the subject's vital space. Words revolve around this inconceivable thing that "Freud supposes on the border of the primary processes" (T), here in the plural, and is nothing other than *jouissance*. Signifying articulation, the work of the unconscious borders, delimits, demarcates the *jouissance* that was ciphered, ignored, buried in a body exterior to speech. This is the underlying, substantial *jouissance* supposed by analytic experience since Freud. To be deciphered.

Jouissance of exile and nostalgia for the (necessary) curse of living in language, out of Paradise. The *jouissance* whose absence would render the universe vain (E, 694); not reached, but evoked; circumscribed, demarcated, invoked, maintained at a prudent distance by metaphors that trap meaning and metonyms that postpone it. The relation between speech and *jouissance* is what makes psychoanalysis an ethics of well-saying.

A deciphering and cursed displacement of One to the Other. From *jouissance* to desire, which is always desire of the Other and also (in Lacan) lack in being, nostalgia for a mythical past to be recovered in a no less illusory future by means of a phantasm lived in the present. The unconscious is thus a saying that is said (enunciation) based on an inscribed *jouissance*, an inscription of writing that supports one and many readings. *Jouissance* slips through in the saying that deciphers it. But the subject does not want to know anything about it. As Lacan noted in 1973, "the unconscious is not the fact that being thinks . . . [it is] that being, by speaking, *jouit* and . . . wants to know nothing more about it" (S XX, 104–105, translation modified). In saying, *jouissance* "consists in the logical straits" (T, 9) that discourse crosses.

The primary processes do not fulfill desire (how can they if their result is hallucinatory?), but they satisfy a subject that unknowingly uses elements from her *lalangue* thinking it is the same language of linguists and grammarians. Each one has a particular way of emptying out the treasures of an original *lalangue, langagière, linguistérie* (do we dare to say or to write *linguystérie*?). The singular way of living on the margins of language is called "style." One more definition of the unconscious can be proposed then: it is each one's style in deciphering *jouissance*, filtered through the logical straits that regulate it and which analysis seeks to broaden. Speech is the diaphragm of *jouissance*, and neurosis exhibits an inflexible obstruction that prevents contact between *jouissance* and saying through statements.

Saying is *jouissance*, but *jouissance* disappears, forgotten in what is said. It is a lost remainder because it passes through the signifying battery of language that charges it with meaning: the meaning the other hears in what he understands (AE, 449). Between the event of saying (enunciation) and what is retrieved (statement) there is a constitutive forgetting that is the *jouissance* of the one who spoke, the irrecoverable real distorted in meaning. There is no said without saying. The statement says, without knowing, a loss. What is spoken in analysis is the model for what is said. The psychoanalyst works with a certain material: the difference between what is said and saying. In the experience of analysis there is an inevitable penalty imposed on the chain of signifiers, with the hope of having it condoned; the other of the utterance is an other who does not understand and questions the one who speaks regarding a *jouissance* ignored in the saying. Such are the functions of silence and the scansion of time and space in the analytic session, as well as that of the analyst, who takes care not to understand. An interpretation is an evocation of the *jouissance* lost in speaking. In that sense, it points to the real, even when the analyst, knowing nothing about this, ignores that it is in the real of *jouissance* that she intervenes.

Meaning preys on and displaces speech—an imaginary shadow that relentlessly pursues the signifiers linked in discourse: it is the function and field of speech and language. In *Radiophonie*, Lacan states that the signifier floats above the bar of the sign while the signified flows underneath . . . to which we should add that the referent escapes as the product of this operation: a remainder of the real that is forgotten. That remainder is the object @, cause of desire, surplus *jouissance* (and minus inasmuch as lost *jouissance* for the *parlêtre*) and *semblant* of the real that, by exclusion, makes itself present in what is said. The symbolic signifying articulation, the imaginary meaning, and the real evoked *jouissance* constitute an omnipresent trinity in speech: empty of fullness and full of emptiness.

What if the word is not said? The subject is eclipsed given there is no signifier to represent him before another signifier. The speaker mutes and in its place the symptom appears, which is a reversal: from discourse to *jouissance*, an ignored and repudiated *jouissance*. Freud had no qualms in defining the symptom as a "substitute sexual satisfaction." It was his way of saying that the symptom is non-sensed *jouissance*: without sense, disarticulated. The word that is not said, misspoken, withdrawn is a symptom and (non)sense *jouissance*: *jouis-sens*, writes Lacan (T, 10); only neologisms are possible for this untranslatable Lacanian *lalangue*. Some possibilities are "jouissancesense" (*jouissance*+sense), "Ihearjouissance" (*j'ouis*+*jouissance*), and "Iyeshearsense" (*j'*+*oui*+*jouis*+*sense*).

In any case, *jouissance* does not come first; it is constituted in the retroaction of speech, as the remainder impossible to reintegrate, produced and left behind in its path: the snail's slime is never recovered. The snail does not become anchored or stained in ink by its slime; it secretes it on the way: "Not that the signifier is anchored [*ancre*] or inked [*encre*] when being tickled . . . but that it allows it among other traits to signify *jouissance*, whose problem is knowing what is satisfied with it" (AE, 418). Through the passion of the signifier, the body becomes the place of the Other (S XX, AE). For this reason we can only speak of *jouissance* in reference to the animal that speaks and suppose a *jouissance* outside the language that constitutes it as a lost (real) remainder, @.

Freud's and Lacan's unconscious is decipherment. The truth that speaks through the primary process is the truth of an anti-economic *jouissance*, against the grain of the pleasure principle: the least tension, homeostasis, the prudent ethics of Aristotelic moderation and happy medium. Lacan distances himself from Freud on this point and corrects him: "What else is the famous lowering of tension with which Freud links pleasure, other than the ethics of Aristotle?" (T, 19). There is no thermodynamics whose principles could provide a posthumous explanation of the unconscious. Actually, neither meaning nor energetics interested Freud. He rejected both aspects in dreams, one for being nonessential, the other speculative. Only the dream-*work* remained properly psychoanalytic: what transformed desire in a determined manifest content, using the raw material of latent thoughts, and was revealed in the analytic session as "free" associations, Freud notes in the *New Introductory Lectures on Psychoanalysis* (1933) (SE XXII, 7). Whether Freud liked it or not, he "misunderstood even himself for wanting to make himself understood . . ." (AE, 407).

In the unconscious, what prevails is not ataraxic pleasure, but disconcerting *jouissance* deciphered in discourse. That discourse is, at the same time, ignorance of *jouissance* and alienation of *jouissance* in the field of the Other due to the shades of meaning it drags along. This being so, the possibility and range of psychoanalysis as an ethical praxis is delimited in reference to the (impossible?) recovery of the lost *jouissance*, or at least the thought of its recovery. Whoever finds echoes of Proust in these words hopefully will not be disappointed in what follows.

Jouir in the awakening crosses the barriers of meaning and posits the question of being for the thinker. How can this outcome be reached if there is nothing more than chatter (*bavardage*)? Ciphered *jouissance* on one end, recovered *jouissance* on the other. The psychoanalytic act is determined by *jouissance*, as well as the modalities required to guard oneself from it.[1] This description regarding the nature of the analytic act must be added and contrasted to the now classic articulations in "Function and Field of Speech and Language in Psychoanalysis" (E), which recognize that an analysis has no other recourse than speech. In and with the medium of speech, in the half said (*mi-dire*) of truth, determined by something that is not speech but *jouissance*: *jouissance* of the body, a tickling the signifier allows when it shakes and skims meaning, and that only appears so far as the subject is alienated from his *jouissance* by offering it to the Other of signification (AE, 526). This skimming of meaning points to the recovery of lost *jouissance* by the only means in reach of the *parlêtre*, the *jouissance* of deciphering (T). Lacan makes this *jouissance* of deciphering the definitive characteristic of a new relation between the subject and *savoir*, the gay science considered a virtue, albeit a sinful one. It is the ethical side of the theory of *jouissance* that will be developed in chapter 8.

At the end of this gay science there is nothing but the fall into sin, due to the reconciliation of *savoir* and prohibited *jouissance*: the evocation of *jouissance* in the intervals of speech when the specular surface of meaning is crossed. A *jouissance* that goes beyond impotence before the real, not in order to find it, but to demarcate that real as impossible. A *jouissance* that denounces the ego as an ally of exterior reality and the strait jackets it weaves, by convention and obedience to the demands of the Other. In sum, a *jouissance* of decipherment that refers to the essential reality of the subject: a real beyond the imaginary and the symbolic, touched and delimited by the primary processes that reign in the unconscious: the saying of metaphors and metonyms that link a *jouissance* impossible to articulate. *Jouir* at the border of the impossible, *jouir* from the decipher-ment of ciphered *jouissance*, numbered, countable—*jouir* a *savoir* that does not preexist saying and, therefore, is not discovered but invented. To reencounter the *jouissance* that underlies the act of speaking, but which the subject wishes to know nothing about; to affirm *jouissance* with the style (or stylus) of speech inscribed in the Other to whom it is directed. In the end, no plenitude, a fall into sin: "Oh, intelligence, solitude in flames . . . desert of mirrors," the poet exclaims.[2] Purgatory.

Letter 52

A brief summary is now in order. I will make use of a simple topological presentation: a straight line with two end points, with *jouissance* on each end. Between the two points are ciphering and deciphering processes that allow re-finding at the end what was there at the beginning: a *jouissance* that carries the marks and fatigue of transiting through the intermediary points of a succession of states, denaturalized first and recovered once transformed. I would venture to call this metamorphosis "sublimation": from lost *jouissance* to recovered, transmuted *jouissance*—from rejected jouissance to a reachable one. . . .

A return to the beginning shows that this exposition follows a path that is coherent with Lacan's own and not alien to Freud's metapsychology: "What Freud articulates as primary process in the unconscious . . . isn't something to be encoded [*se chiffre*], but to be deciphered [*se déchiffre*] . . . *jouissance* itself (T, 18–19, translation modified). If there is *jouissance* on the left side of the line, one must recognize that between *jouissance* and its deciphering by the unconscious there must be a state or intermediary moment, that of ciphered *jouissance*, converted into a group of inscriptions lacking meaning in themselves, but ready to be filled with meaning once they have been subjected to a deciphering process. There are, then, three delimited and successive ordered states: (1) primordial *jouissance*, (2) ciphering or writing, and (3) unconscious deciphering. This lineal construction is imposed by reason and experience; it is not discretionary, but imperative.

The unconscious (Freud's, Lacan's, psychoanalysis') is already discourse: the passage from *jouissance* to speech, where a signifier signifies only if articulated to another signifier. What is signified and represented by the signifier is the subject of the unconscious, an effect of the articulation. Lacan's unquestionable expression stands out: "The unconscious is articulated with what from being comes to saying" (AE, 426). Between the being of *jouissance* to the "I think" of the subject of science is the articulation of the unconscious: *ça parle*.

The unconscious is a manifestation of truth, the Id (*ça*) of being that comes into saying. The truth that speaks does not tell the truth. The primary processes produce a transposition; they transmit a distortion, an *Entstellung* of truth. *Jouissance* reaches saying filtered by the web of language. Once saying has been produced (the very telling of a dream proves it), a new process of deciphering is necessary to incorporate that discourse in the field of meaning. Freud gives this process a very precise name: *Deutung* (interpretation). To avoid confusion it is necessary to differentiate between the work done on writing that is deciphering (the model here is hieroglyphics) and the work done on speech by the analyst in the course of the analysis: interpretation. *Jouissance* is something deciphered; the primary processes are already decipherments and can be interpreted. The decipherment reveals writing that, as such, is nonsense (*pas-de-sens*); it does not call the Other as in speech. An interpretation entails reading that writing: "it is meaning and goes against signification" (AE, 475). This difference does not refer to a binary opposition in which one would have to choose between decipherment or interpretation, but rather to a complementary relation that shows that each of these operations falls on a different point on the straight line, which goes from ciphered *jouissance* to *jouissance* of decipherment.

It is necessary to insist on the complementarity of writing and reading, decipherment and interpretation, since it is not uncommon to see even the most lucid and loyal of Lacan's commentators get carried away with enthusiasm by his affirmation of "the instance of the letter in the unconscious." They thus produce explications that confront a "modern," textual reading of Lacan with one now considered "antiquated" and centered on the spoken word and the signifier. My aim here is to make evident and demonstrate the topological continuity and difference of the insertion points on the line proper to each of the two operations.

On that line the unconscious is an intermediate linking point of decipherment found between the system of inscriptions that precedes it and the dialogue with the permeation of meaning that follows it. As an intermediate state in the decipherment of *jouissance* it is already discourse, but one that appears to be placed before and at the margin of interlocution and sense. One must (always) return to Freud:

> If I were to continue the analysis on my own account, without any reference to other people (whom, indeed, an experience so personal as my dream cannot possibly have been intended to reach), I should eventually arrive at thoughts which would surprise me, whose presence in me I was unaware of, which were not only alien but also disagreeable to me, and which I should therefore feel inclined to dispute energetically, although the chain of thoughts running through the analysis insisted upon them remorselessly. (SE V, 672)

The situation Freud describes as paradigmatic of the dream is a sender without a receiver, a chain of signifiers linked by their own design, making the ego a witness: a simple scene in which a perturbing, disconcerting play is represented, neither understood nor appreciated by the spectator that wishes to dispute it energetically. This is the unconscious at work. An interpretation comes later and, overcoming resistances, introduces the

Other of dialogue that is initially alien in that personal and solipsistic experience. That Other is the subject supposed to know of the transference, invented by psychoanalytic discourse: absolutely unnecessary, contingent, the place of an unveiling, which the ego, animated by a passion for ignorance, wishes to know nothing about.

If I return to the fiction of the straight line ("truth has the structure of fiction"), I find that at the other end there is no sense ("now I understand"), but rather a recovered *jouissance* ("Ah!"). This end is only possible by traversing the complete line that goes from *jouissance* to *jouissance*, an Other *jouissance*. An interpretation leads to meaning, which we can consider equivalent to the Freudian system of perception-conscience and is linked to the coherence that reigns in "our official ego" (F, 208).

It is the secondary process, not the primary process, that is testimony to the ego. In dreams it is called secondary revision, an operation that serves to cover up truth, protect sleep and absorb the impact of the real on the ego of wakefulness that clings to reality: a reality made of meaning, in the knot between the symbolic and the imaginary, to the exclusion of the real (TR, see the Borromean knot, figure 2.4, in chapter 2).

One cannot speak without being flooded with meaning, commanded by the phantasm, the imaginary that flows underneath the floating chain of signifiers. Analytic experience does not aim to consolidate them, nor to rectify this phantasm by offering a new, more consistent one, but rather to displace and unsettle it, lift its dead weight, denounce its suspicious pretention of suturing the relation of the subject to the truth that speaks. An analysis aims at reintroducing the dimension of the real of *jouissance* that discourse excludes. Everything in analytic experience is organized around emptying out meaning to reach a single and final meaning: there is no sexual relation. It is nonsense, and discourse patches, stiches up what drowns out and overwhelms that limit before which speech fails, while the drive silently returns to claim its privileges: "The essence of psychoanalytic theory is a discourse without speech" (S XVI, 11/13/68).

It was necessary to identify the five points of the trajectory that is now complete: (1) original *jouissance*, (2) inscription or ciphering, (3) decipherment into a confusing and incoherent discourse that manifests the truth while concealing it, (4) an interpretation that restitutes coherence at the cost of increasing lack of knowledge, and finally, (5) the emptying out of superfluous meaning in order to recover the truth of the original inscription, now transformed into an invented *savoir* that consists in deciphering *jouissance*. Is it possible to say that it is a trajectory that goes from *jouissance* to sublimation? It is the formula I am proposing: from one point to the other of *jouissance*.

I realize I am not saying anything new, and neither am I making an unknown aspect of Lacan's thought clear. Rather, I am returning to the origins of psychoanalysis, armed with the arsenal of Lacan's later seminars. As I summarize what I've written regarding the line with the two end points and three intermediate states (ciphering, decipherment, interpretation) that produce meaning, I find the literal reproduction of the schema drawn by Freud in his famous Letter 52 from December 6, 1896, which we now also have in a nonedited version (SE I, 233, F).

The text is accessible and known by all psychoanalysts, but even so it needs to be quoted *in extenso* in order to show to what extent it is coherent with a theory of *jouissance*. Also, to clarify how the text distinguishes between the Id and the unconscious, making Letter 52 a stunning point of contact condensing Freud's two topics and two periods of Lacan's teaching. We can demonstrate this with accuracy by returning to the literality of the Freudian text and without forcing it in the least.

Freud proposes a successive stratification of the human psyche that supposes mental states and memory adhere to a *re-arrangement* responding to certain new circumstances. He has a clear conception of this new re-arrangement, which he calls a *re-transcription* (*Umschrift*). He underlines the two words in italics. *Umschrift* implies writing, concretely an inscription. What is "essentially new" in this theory is the thesis regarding the existence of the memory of an experience as a series of at least successive and coexistent inscriptions. These inscriptions are registered by "various species of indications" (*Zeichen*) (SE I, 233). To make the thought graphic, Freud draws the well-known schema with the five elements ordered in lineal form. The three in the middle are characterized, in addition to the initials of their name, by the Roman numerals I, II, and III. The notion that this system of inscriptions has neuronal support is recognized as convenient but not indispensable, provisionally admissible and therefore disposable.

At the extreme left of the line is the notation W (*Wahrnehmungen*), correctly translated as perceptions. The term can lend itself to misunderstanding if taken in its technical meaning in psychology. Freud says the "neurones W" is "where perceptions originate, to which consciousness attaches, but which in themselves retain no trace of what has happened.

For *consciousness and memory are mutually exclusive* (SE I, 234, Freud's emphasis).

	I		II		III		
W	→	W_z	→	Ubw	→	Vb	→	Bew
X X	→	X X	→	X X	→	X X	→	X X
impressions	→	id	→	unconscious	→	preconscious	→	fading $
lost *jouissance*	→	ciphering	→	deciphering	→	meaning	→	recovered *jouissance*

What is this schema about? A direct recording of experience. From *Wahrnehmungen*, which in German clearly implies the apprehension of truth: the real such as it befalls, impacts, and marks a being that receives the impact, but does not conserve traces or memories of what has occurred. To avoid ambiguities with the traditional, psychological notion of perception that supposes an already constituted subject that in turn constitutes his very own perceptions (the *percipiens* considered origin and source of the *perceptum*), it is best to turn to the term impression, in the double sense of what makes an impression (a plate or moving film) and what is printed, engraved. They are a-subjective impressions, headless, no one's: the matrix where a subject is to come.

The idea is clearly presented by Freud many years later in the analogy between the psyche and the *Wunderblock*, the magic pad. The inscription made with a stylus on a celluloid surface can be done without leaving a trace on the celluloid (once it is lifted), while leaving the impressions on a film of soft wax underneath. These impressions without memory that are on the extreme end of the apparatus and are recovered (or not) by later inscriptions are the unequivocal manifestation of the subject's original real, before symbolization, *jouissance* itself: the Thing in Freud and Lacan. The apparatus as a whole is organized starting from this founding moment in which a "protosubject" (if this Greco-Roman hybrid is allowed) is impressed by the Real. If one does not fear analogies, why not speak of imprinting—the printing of the matrix of the future *parlêtre* by an experience that precedes and is exterior to language. Of course, as in the case of ethology, language is not alien to the very experience to which researchers subject geese or monkeys, for example. Marks of *jouissance*, a-systematic hieroglyphics, the minting of coins on the surface of a body: impressions.

From these impressions it passes on to a first system (I): "indication of perceptions" or signs of perception, *Wahrnehmungenzeichen*, which is "the first registration" or the first transcription (*Niederschrift*) of the impressions. As can be seen, Freud emphasizes the idea of writing. Now he adds the notion of signs (*Zeichen*), so important for Lacan. The Freudian characterization of signs is precise: they are incapable of consciousness and arranged ("articulated" in the Spanish translation) "according to associations by simultaneity" (SE I, 234). Writing, which is pure sign, is thus produced, lacking meaning and temporal order. As in all writing, this system is not diachronic, in the same way that a book or a musical record stores all its content simultaneously. All the imprinted and recorded inscriptions do not represent anything for anyone if not subjected to a diachronic process that establishes succession, makes it audible or transfers its writing by means of decipherment, a reading. The system of the *Wahrnehmungenzeichen* is thus a ciphered register of the *jouissance* impressions that marked the flesh of the proto-subject. These impressions are not signifiers, they are signs (as Freud notes in Letter 52), marks before the word, that appear to prefigure what Lacan develops in *Television*, when he opposes the register of the sign to the register of meaning.

I hope it will not be considered precipitous to affirm that Freud's succinct description of the first register coincides exactly, in essence, with what he called the Id during the period of the "magic block." We must leave aside the surreptitious hypostasis of a discourse foreign to psycho-analytic experience ("the biological pole") to comprehend the reference to be dispensable and superfluous, as Freud himself indicates in Letter 52 regarding the neuronal support for the stratification of the human psyche. The biology in question is reduced—this is the case at bottom—given that these experiences, which I do not doubt in calling impressions of *jouissance*, are written marks on the body. Better yet, on the flesh that will become a body by the function and grace of that impression. There is no order or agreement, no meaning or time. This is how *jouissance* is ciphered. Lacan provides a clear image when he compares this synchronic disorder with the function of the lottery machine filled with balls inscribed with numbers that themselves mean nothing: disordered written marks ready to acquire meaning once the prize is drawn (E, 551). When the balls come out in a certain contingent or arbitrary sequence, they come in contact with a preexisting symbolic matrix (the distribution of prizes) that will give meaning to the numbers drawn. The machine full of inscriptions is "a cauldron full of seething excitations" (SE XXII, 73) of the Freudian Id.

Jouissance is ciphered there. Only the signifier is able to establish an order when unfolding those elements of writing diachronically. In summary, I am positing that the first system of inscription in Letter 52 is the Id of the second topic, and its characteristics are what allow us to distinguish it from the second system, the unconscious, which is already a decipherment and translation of that primary writing of the impressions of *jouissance*.

The number is the cipher, both in the image of the lottery as well as in everyday language. A cipher without meaning: language, but on the side of pure writing, hieroglyphics without words, where the elements are alien to the organization of discourse and there is no agent of speech directed to another enabling a social link. Outside meaning but ready to be charged with meaning. It is necessary then that the "draw" be initiated, a series established and the number, beyond its cardinal function, "ordered." It needs to be "one" in the series of numbers, "that" number in the relation between the ones drawn and the other series of numbers—in the case of the lottery, the order of the winning numbers.[3]

The Id is a set of graphic elements, *grammas* or *grammemes*, not subject to any organizational hierarchy, comparable or interchangeable, alien to logical or dialectical contradiction, a pure positivity knowing nothing of negation. It is the reign of *jouissance* (of being) before subjective organization, being the latter the effect of an order the paternal metaphor imposes in the realm of the signifier. We know the name-of-the-Father establishes the primacy of the phallic signifier and empties the body of a diffuse *jouissance*, making it pass through a strictly limited zone (phallic *jouissance*), subject to the Law.

This is essentially Lacanian, but is also affirmed in as many words by Freud in Letter 52, which outlines the rectilinear topology of *jouissance* and speech, its ciphering and decipherment:

> Behind this lies the idea of abandoned *erotogenic zones*. That is to say, during childhood sexual release would seem to be obtainable from very many parts of the body, which at a later time are only able to release the 28[-day] anxiety substance and not the others. In this differentiation and limitation [would thus lie] progress in culture, moral as well as individual development. (SE I, 239)

The system that in Letter 52 Freud calls signs of perception, *Wahrnehmungenzeichen* (Wz), is a passage from corporeal impressions (W) to disorganized writing, a ciphering that is disordered and synchronic. In this system there is no notion of time, contradiction, or order. The Id, which appears twenty-five years later, is prefigured here and constitutes the raw material on which the signifier operates, that is, the battery of differentiations and values that language introduces, the code of significations. The language of the linguists does not function in this chaos where lived experience is ciphered. Rather, it is psychoanalysis' linguistery *lalangue* whose signification is not meaning but *jouissance*.

In psychoanalysis it is a question of recovering the possibility of *jouissance* that is blocked, untranslated in the system of the Id, and for which speech is the only recourse possible. This was the first aspect of the Lacanian discovery in its return to Freud: the unconscious is structured like a language . . . to which one must add that it is only in analysis that its elements are ordered in discourse; *jouissance* condescends to being heard and organized in a temporal diachronic chain. In analytic experience, the writing (of *jouissance*) can be read and the letter lends itself to be spoken.

We can make use of a technical analogy, the compact disc: a slim metallic surface where numbers, calculations, and digits are registered; they coexist synchronically in a polished surface completely alien to the art of music. However, these inscriptions without meaning are set up to be decoded, deciphered by a laser that transforms them into electrical impulses. These are in turn sent to a system of transformations and translations of movements that affect a megaphone or loudspeaker, where those inscriptions are transformed into music. This analogy can be completed by recalling the previous states to the numeric transcription of the digital inscriptions: the composer's musical score that is also a synchronic and hieroglyphic writing to be decoded by an interpreter (yes, the one who produces an *interpretation*) and then on to digital ciphering, electronic deciphering, sound, and finally to a diachronic hearing where the listener is the one who will endow the music heard with meaning, in relation to her or his subjectivity (the vector $s(A) \rightarrow A$) from the signifier to the voice) and back, retroactively, from A to $\leftarrow s(A)$ in the lower half of the graph of desire (E, 684).

We can now return to the point of departure: the primary processes Freud discovers in the unconscious are not ciphered, but deciphered. In other words: from the chaos of the Id in which *jouissance* is ciphered there is a passage to a certain order (the drawing of the balls in our analogy), a diachronic succession of signs that have been transcribed to elements of another order, signifiers whose battery is in language, taken from the field of the Other (of speech). As a result, the primary processes produce discourse, which at first sight appears to be absurd and devoid of meaning, but capable of being imbued with meaning and transmitting it. In the discourse of the unconscious, what is deciphered is *jouissance*, which can be discerned as a palimpsest, appearing between the cracks and unexpected leaps and links in dreams.

This is how *Unbewusst* (Ubw), the unconscious, is defined in Letter 52: a second transcription ("registration") in which the simultaneous associations are not primary, but "arranged according to other (perhaps causal) relations" (SE I, 234). Causality implies succession in time, cause and effect, diachrony. As discourse (the said), the unconscious is something heard, material in which *jouissance* is forgotten; *L'Étourdit* (1973) speaks of that *reste oublié* (forgotten rest). The unconscious is speech organized according to connections that repel thought arranged by syntax and logic. Interpretation is the activity which, taking the formations of the unconscious as a point of departure, endows speech with meaning and expels it from the realm of the "absurd," setting up a new Carrollian logic.

The level of the third transcription described in Letter 52, which goes from Ubw to Vbw, from the unconscious to the preconscious (*Vorbewusst*) is "attached to word-presentations and corresponding to our official ego" (SE I, 234–235). This has all the characteristics of rational thought, where the signifying chain carries waves of meaning: "this secondary thought-consciousness is subsequent in time" (*nachtraglich*) (SE I, 235). Freud adds that these "neurones of consciousness" are also "perceptual neurones," which I have preferred to call "impressions." Such is the apparatus: a line in which the successive order implies the abolition of time at both ends. Atemporal *jouissance* figures in each of the two ends of the line traversed: (1) the ciphering, (2) the unconscious decipherment, and (3) the interpretation that provides meaning in the preconscious when lived experience is linked to the order of language verbalized into a sentence, articulated in the form of propositions submitted to the logic of the secondary processes and capable of being catalogued as true or false.

Freud completes his description of the apparatus thus constituted by affirming that between one system and the other there is an incompatibility of reading or code that makes it necessary for the inscriptions that characterize each be translated in order to pass from one modality of inscription to the next. This theory pertains to the normal psyche, as well as to the neuroses (conceived as the effects of repression), the impossibility of a "translation of the psychical material" (SE I, 235) and also to the cure, which is a process capable of making what has been retained in prior inscriptions transfer to new modes of reading, proper to the more advanced systems. The advance that a Lacanian reading brings, and which I propose for Letter 52, is that what is ciphered and deciphered is *jouissance* itself. The development of Freudian concepts allows us to return to Freud's work and unambiguously establish the continuity between the Id of the second topic and the unconscious of the first. These instances are not interchanged or substituted one for the other; they are two topologically differentiated systems and two different modes (through writing and speech) of treating forever irrecoverable original impressions.

In synthesis, the sequence is as follows: from "raw" *jouissance* (W) to the Id (Wz), from the Id to the Unconscious (Ub), from the unconscious to the Preconscious (Vb), and from the Preconscious to Consciousness (Bew). This is not a system of inscriptions, but a living moment that reprises the initial point of departure: "so that the neurones of consciousness would once again be perceptual neurones and in themselves without memory" (SE I, 235).

Psychoanalysis in Proust's Way: *Jouissance* and Time

Jouissance, jouissance of the impressed body, *jouissance* of the One without the Other, can only be recovered by means of a recourse to the Other, the Other of language and meaning that alienates, obstructs, and prohibits *jouissance*. The analytic experience aims to embody and abolish the Other of dialogue and resistance so that *jouissance*, blocked by systems of inscriptions that have not been deciphered, can be subjectified. The Other of language is a barrier to be crossed in the search of the impressions left by *jouissance*. The body is the empty plate or surface, the stage, book, or disc imprinted with ciphered inscriptions or recordings. An analysis is a process of reading with a stylus or laser to make audible what is inscribed and unknown to the subject: *jouissance* itself. There is no hidden code to discover, only a code or Rosetta stone to invent, the system of *lalangue* in which *jouissance* was ciphered, alien to the battery of signifiers with conventional signification. From impression, avoiding suppression and repression, on to expression: the production of a book, or letter which, as in Poe, is hidden, purloined, and exposed in each *parlêtre*.

Re-citing: "the unconscious, structured like a language . . . For it is in analysis that it is organised as discourse."[4] When organized as discourse, speech directed to an other, it is charged with unheard of meaning, revealed as a *savoir* underlying the subject. It shows itself as the bearer of *jouissance* traversing the now permeable diaphragm of speech that blocked it beforehand. It is a *jouissance* of decipherment, *joui-sense*, *j'oui sens*, *jouissance*, as we noted earlier: passing *jouissance* through the diaphragm of speech, articulating, translating, and accounting for it. To do so, it is important to disassemble discursive coherence, to go against grammar, play with logical and homophonic ambiguities, traverse the custom house of meaning and dislocate the Humpty Dumpty that controls it, the same one that in Letter 52 (1896) Freud called "our official ego."

One must resignify forward back in time the traces of memory and traverse the phantasms that lead, at each moment and each case, to the fixation of what is remembered. It is a question of unblocking and con-structing the original structuring phantasms of experience and personal history shown in the compulsion to repeat. Repetition? Yes, the particular ways each one misses the encounter with the object of desire and thus recovers the lost *jouissance*, given that desire does not point to the future. Desire is nostalgia, impressed memory on the flesh of language torn by the Other, for what One was as object for the desire of the Other, constituted at the price of an internal split: a barred, divided subject between the One and the Other, making the body Other and the Other the site and stage for re-establishing the One. This is what in psychoanalysis is called Ideal ego, between the One and the Other. Between neurosis, alienation in the Other and psychosis, alienation in the One. Between the Other without One of neurosis and the One without Other of psychosis. Between the letter without reading of the One (in psychosis) and a discourse subject to the codes of the Other, which does not know the writerly essence of *jouissance* (in neurosis). Subjectivity sails between Charybdis and Scylla, and its shipwreck is the substance of psychoanalysis.

The sub-ject as what sub-tends, the sub-stance sup-posed of discourse and con-jugated in its phrases: a cipher that must be deciphered. The I (*moi-Ich*) that must come to be in a space that is unknown, where *Ça* was a hieroglyphic in the desert, a book buried with its owner's corpse. With these objectives, the practice of psychoanalysis is organized and its instances decided: to trap *jouissance* as decipherment in the play of signifying linkages and substitutions, the joke (*Witz*) and surprise; the Heideggerian *aletheia* and Joycean epiphany; the unexpected evocation that outsmarts defenses; the acuity of style that tears open the dumb surface of discourse that does not say although "wanting to say."

This approach to the recovery of lost *jouissance* is at the origin of Freud's own reflections. Isn't the "identity of perception" what directs the activity of the psychic apparatus? Isn't the "identity of thought" what poses (by way of the secondary processes) a barrier to meaning, regulated for and by the ego, on the road to the recovery of original *jouissance*? Read this way, armed with Lacan's differentiation between pleasure and *jouissance*, it is difficult not to recognize in Freud, *from the beginning*, that the conception of the psyche is determined by *jouissance*, lost and recovered by means of a working-through that traverses intermediate systems. Here neurosis is defined as the impossibility of a recovery of *jouissance*, whereas psychosis is sometimes instated in *jouissance* and sometimes renounces its recovery. The function of the real is at play. The identity of perception can be short-circuited by hallucinations that preclude passing through the different stages that decipher *jouissance*. The unconscious is not a hallucination, but a written ciphered enigma blocked in its path to speech. The Freudian mechanism of analysis is an enactment conceived to deploy discourse.

The transference is based on supposing the Other, whom the subject addresses, possesses the code able to decipher his hieroglyphic or, in another analogy, that music exists in the machine that transforms it into sound and not on the disc. The strategy of analysis consists in passing the disc through an in-different, a-pathetic laser in order to make the inscriptions recorded audible, for the synchrony of the Id to be transformed into the diachrony of the unconscious and the latter, in turn, into *j'oui-sens*. The other of the transference is not the owner of meaning but its pretext for the text written in *lalangue* to become *j'oui-sens*.

The resignification of the past that converts a *parlêtre* into the subject of an anagnorisis to come; the unveiling of an original and unknown identity; a rebaptism based on a new relation of the subject of discourse with the *jouissance* that directs (him) but he ignores. It proposes passing from the speech of linguistics to the vocalized word of linguisterics (*lingu-hystérie, linguisterie*), where the voice is not the chain, but rather object surplus *jouissance* and cause of desire. The chain, the spoken word, is the indispensable instrument to receive the voice as an object that evokes and makes a *semblant* of *jouissance*. Going back from speech to impressions, the signifier to the letter, desire to the drive, communication to *jouissance*.

The book is written, the disc recorded. They must be made audible, converted into words and music. Retrieve, *retrouver, rencontrer*, the writing that marks the *parlêtre*. The "identity of perception" is the *parlêtre's* reencounter with a prohibited experience of satisfaction. It is the point where the two ends of Freud's apparatus in Letter 52 are knotted together: perception and consciousness, *W* and *Bew*. *Jouissance*, the *jouissance* of the object (object @), substitutes the subject split by the signifier; it substitutes the same signifier as well and cancels the temporal sequence of speech organized in discourse.

Well on the margins of psychoanalytic research, this is what Marcel Proust discovered and where he went astray, when he worked on material that is also the material of analysis: *jouissance*. *Remembrance of Things Past* (*À la recherche du temps perdu*, also translated as *In Search of Lost Time*) is the chronicle of an analysis without an analyst, outside transference. Its 3,200 pages are a detailed investigation (*recherche*) of the codes subjectivity obeys, transmitting an experience that is both paradigmatic and unrepeatable. One can discuss who is the Other in Proust's writing: his reader, posterity, and so on. It is difficult to affirm the Other is the subject supposed to know of analytic experience. However, the result of this *ricercare*, a voluminous work, calls for an interpretation, a deciphering of its decipherment, commentary. Proust produces an artistic object that displaces its author: a work that, much like Joyce's, is the object of specular reflection and speculation on the part of scholars and students for centuries to come, an object of scholarship.

What I am interested in showing here (it is enough to show and not demonstrate it) is that *In Search of Lost Time* is the model of an analysis, as well as the best example of the Freudian hypothesis in Letter 52 and the effects of the Lacanian theory of *jouissance* that emerges from analytic experience. With only one objection: Proust does not recover Time at the end of his long itinerary because it is not Time he has lost. On the contrary, it is in Time where it was lost: the time of watches and history, discourse, diachrony, and the organization of successive, serial moments. Instead, Proust finds *jouissance*, the annulment of Time, synchrony, the closure of the psychic apparatus' progressive movement. Yes, *jouissance* does not occur in Time but in the instant, which is the abolition of the course (dis-course) of time. The instant and eternity are outside the order that recognizes past, present, and future. Verbal tenses are also determined by discourse, in relation to the enunciation of speech that establishes a sequence that does not exist in the Real, an effect of the Symbolic. Proust's time, the "regained time" of the last volume of his work is, in fact, the time abolished by the return of the first impressions. A word with a noble philosophical lineage imposes itself here: *Aufhebung*. *In Search of*

Lost Time deals again and again with the epiphany of *jouissance* in the reencounter with the incunabula of its first edition. The topic, always the same, always varied, recurs in the multiple examples Proust gives: the taste of the madeleine dipped in tea, the sound of a brief musical phrase, stumbling on loose paving-stones, the stiffness of a table napkin, the sound of a spoon striking a plate, which refers to a train trip when a worker hit the car's wheel with a hammer, the book found in the library, the same book the mother reads the insomniac child, now an old man. Despite the temporal reference in the title, there is nothing to add to the text if we replace the idea of time with *jouissance*. We only have to read Proust's prose: the recurrence of *jouissance* is the resurrection of a being that was; and that being enjoyed "fragments of existence withdrawn from Time" (RTP, 908) in contemplation that "though it was of eternity, had been fugitive" (RTP, 908). In those moments in which time is abolished, the subject is abolished as well, unless he regains himself holding on to the sensations of outside reality of present time and surrounding space:

> And if the present scene had not very quickly been victorious, I believe that I should have lost consciousness; for so complete are these resurrections of the past, during the second that they last, that they not only oblige our eyes to cease to see the room which is near them in order to look instead at the railway bordered with trees or the rising tide, they even force our nostrils to breathe the air of places which are in fact a great distance away, and our will to choose between the various projects which those distant places suggest to us, they force our whole self to believe that it is surrounded by these places, or at least to waver doubtfully between them and the places where we are now, in a dazed uncertainty such as we feel sometimes when an ineffable vision presents itself to us at the moment of our falling asleep. (RTP, 908, translation modified)

Ineffable, when the word is not in play: those moments of "*extra-temporal* joy that I had been made to feel by the sound of the spoon or the taste of the madeleine" (RTP, 911, my emphasis). This is a time which is the abolition of time after having lived and forgotten, traversed forgetting, resurrected a "direct *jouissance*," where "the only way to savour them more fully was to try to get to know them more completely in the medium in which they existed, that is to say within myself, to try to make them

Deciphering *Jouissance* | 165

translucid even to their very depth" (RTP, 911). A time of *jouissance* that breaks with the social frames of shared time, the phenomenological frames of the time of things and the psychobiological frames of the time of one's own life. A time made of instants without dimension in the same manner in which the straight line is constructed with points without dimension.[5] In this sense, I repeat, Proust's time is the abolition of time. It is, as he notes, extra-temporal. Discourse is in time, *jouissance* is outside, implying and annulling it. It is time submitted to an *Aufhebung* that recovers while dissolving it. For this reason, the title of the last volume of *Remembrance of Things Past* should be *aufgehoben* time rather than *retrouvé*: time regained.

It is not the return of the past, but "very much more: something that, common both to the past and to the present, is much more essential than either of them" (RTP, 905). It is what allows overcoming the deception that inevitably accompanies the experiences and loves of reality, to overcome the gap between imagination, desire, and memory:

> But let a sound, a scent already heard and breathed in the past be heard and breathed anew, simultaneously in the present and in the past, real without being actual, ideal without being abstract, then instantly the permanent and characteristic essence hidden in things is freed and our true being which has for long seemed dead but was not so in other ways awakes and revives, thanks to this celestial nourishment. An instant liberated from the order of time has recreated in us man liberated from the same order, so that he should be conscious of it. And indeed we understand his faith in his happiness even if the mere taste of a madeleine does not logically seem to justify it; we understand that the name of death is meaningless to him for, placed beyond Time, how can he fear the future? (RTP, 906)

The two times in which existence virtually elapses, past and future, are determined and fixed as such from the present instant, which is the instant of the "I think" of actual discourse. Past and future do not exist in the real; they are dimensions introduced by the symbolic that carries its effects onto the imaginary, in the form of a memory "back" and a desire "forward," from which "ego sum," here and now. The Proustian subject emerges as such when it escapes from "the order of time, the order of a psychological life centered on the phantasmatic construction of the ego. The resurrection, the recovery of *jouissance* from the true ego that appeared dead because it was buried, is an epiphany of the ineffable real. It shows the departure from the order of discourse that sets up past time as dead and future time as the time of death. The present, taken out of time, is at the same time a fleeting instant and a vision of eternity. If the symbolic and the imaginary are hidden and annulled, only the glare of the pure real remains, which dissolves subjectivity: Freud and Lacan both called this "hallucination." The subject finds himself with the object cause of desire but without the mediation of the phantasm. This is the sense of the manhandled Lacanian formula "traversing the phantasm."

One lives. A body in language. The Other that is the body, not-I and Other that is language, also not-I. "I" is the imaginary representative of the subject that pretends to suture the division between two alien and strange substances. The impressions of lived experience are stamped on the body, an experience to be signified with the signs of the Other of language: the taste of the madeleines, Vinteuil's sonatas, the images of trees and bell-towers. For the subject inhabited by speech there are recourses: an evocation, memory, an ordered series, spatio-temporal references. These recourses provide pale images, blurred by thought's secondary processes. They are disappointing, lack vigor, are wilted and make us think about what they were when alive, before being sealed by difference and marked by the sign of negation. The real is what is lost. When it returns, it is called hallucination. Can original *jouissance* be recovered other than by the blurred forms of evocation and nostalgia? Proust responds in the affirmative. What Freud calls "identity of perception" can take place due to random, contingent, nonintentional encounters. In Proust's case, even stumbling on uneven paving-stones, which makes for the emergence of a delicious experience: "The happiness which I had just felt was undoubtedly the same as that which I had felt when I tasted the madeleine soaked in tea. But if on that occasion I had put off the task of searching for the profounder causes of my emotion, this time I determined not to resign myself to a failure to understand them" (RTP, 899).

"Where do we meet this real?" Lacan asks:

> For what we have in the discovery of psycho-analysis is an encounter, an essential encounter—an appointment to which we are always called with a real that eludes us . . . First, the *tuché*, which we have borrowed, as I told you last time from Aristotle, who uses it in his search for cause. We have translated it as *the encounter with the real*. The real is beyond the *automaton*, the

return, the coming-back, the insistence of the signs, by which we see ourselves governed by the pleasure principle. The real is that which always lies behind the automaton, and it is quite obvious, throughout Freud's research [*recherche*], that it is this that is the object of his concern. (S XI, 53–54)

Freud's and Proust's searches are one and the same. Lacan's as well. *Jouissance* lies in wait of "fortuitous" encounters, "as if by chance." It is not a question of happiness but of the moment in which the subject is overwhelmed by the real, when everyone's calming frames of reality break apart:

The function of the *tuché*, of the real as encounter—the encounter in so far as it may be missed, in so far as it is essentially the missed encounter—first presented itself in the history of psycho-analysis in a form that was in itself already enough to rouse our attention, that of the trauma (S XI, 55).

Traumatism as a limit with the real, which always returns to its place: the impossible eternal return, *ça*, the Id, always present as the background of experience. Traumatic is not so much what is pleasant or unpleasant, outside the register of the sensible for someone or the "pathological" (in the Kantian sense), but rather what is excessive, inassimilable, and produces the fading of the subject. In the reencounter with Proustian Time, Freudian "identity of perception" and Lacanian *jouissance*, we have a common denominator: the abolition of time and space that frames subjectivity.

At this point, it is difficult to resist the temptation to quote and gloss the experience Proust narrates in the Guermantes' library, which is the (mythical) point of departure for writing his book. After 3,200 pages, the author finds that everything had been a preparation for the moment in which he would stumble with the resurrection of sensations that, like signs from the origin, guided his life. In what I have been developing, it is the moment when the two extremes of the line drawn in Freud's Letter 52 come together.

Over all these thoughts I skimmed rapidly, for another inquiry summoned my attention more imperiously, the inquiry, which on previous occasions into the cause of this felicity which I had just experienced, into the character of the certitude with which it imposed itself. And this cause I began to divine as I compared these diverse happy impressions, diverse yet with this in common, that I experienced them at the present moment and at the same time in the context of a distant moment, so that the past was made to encroach upon the present and I was made to doubt whether I was in the one or the other. The truth surely was that the being within me which had enjoyed these impressions had enjoyed them because they had in them something that was common to a day long past and to the present, because in some way they were extra-temporal, and this being only made its appearance when, because of one of these identifications of the present with the past, it was likely to find itself in the one and only medium in which it could exist and enjoy the essence of things, that is to say: outside time. This explained why it was that my anxiety on the subject of my death had ceased from the moment when I had unconsciously recognised the taste of the little madeleine, since the being which at that moment I had been was an extra-temporal being and therefore unalarmed by the vicissitudes of the future. This being had only come to me, only manifested itself outside of activity and immediate enjoyment, on those rare occasions when the miracle of an analogy had made me escape from the present. And only this being had the power to perform that task which had always defeated the efforts of my memory and my intellect, the power to make me rediscover days that were long past, the Time that was Lost. (RTP, 904)

Proust's idea regarding time in his novel and his life is sufficiently clear; additional quotes from the text would only take away the pleasure of reading the fifty pages of the scene in the library. We must go on to the next point that summarizes our reading of Freud and Lacan via Proust. I am referring to *jouissance* as writing, as well as the possibilities and modes of reading the engraved signs that make up our real ego.

Throughout Lacan's teaching is an emphasis on the notion that there is only *jouissance* of the body. This affirmation is often met with incredulity by scholars because it seems to contradict the experience of a *jouissance* of the mind or knowledge—what could be rightly called *jouissance* of the signifier or phallic *jouissance*, developed in the last three chapters. Of course, one formulation does not negate another. The Lacanian proposition is that if the signifier carries *jouissance* it does so inasmuch as it evokes and mobilizes writing registered as *jouissance* prior and exterior to the signifier. Speech is the *parlêtre*'s opening to approach lost *jouissance*, which is *jouissance* of the body. Apart from psychosis, then, there is access to *jouissance* of the body only through signifying articulation. And there is another *jouissance*, beyond: *jouissance* of the Other (sex).

This implies the already-described succession of impressions: ciphering of the experiences in the Id in synchrony and permutation; deciphering of the inscriptions of the Id in an absurd word, nonsense, seeming to be more an accident than revelation; interpretation of unconscious nonsensical speech by a regulated system of significations, according to the battery of language; and, finally, traversal of the barrier of meaning in order to recover, after wordy wanderings, the truth of the object that expels the subject from *jouissance*:

> There is the Gay science [gay savoir], which is a virtue . . . it is not a question of picking at sense, but of hovering over it without binding it to this virtue, *jouir* deciphering, which implies that Gay science produces in the end nothing but the fall, the return to sin. (T, 22, translation modified)

In the library scene, Proust feels and lives a *jouissance* recovered, which is the abolition of time in the superposition of the past of memory, the present of the phantasm and the future of desire, in an instant of epiphany and immortality. The objects in his memories are charged with hidden meaning. They take on the character of hieroglyphics demanding to be deciphered. These decipherments "however faint its traces, is a criterion of truth" (RTP, 913) because "the ideas formed by the pure intelligence have no more than a logical, a possible truth, they are arbitrarily chosen. The book whose hieroglyphs are patterns not traced by us is the only book that really belongs to us" (RTP, 913). These impressions are composed in us as in a book, "a complex illuminated scroll" (*grimoire*, RTP, 913) filled with magic spells before which we do not have the liberty to choose. They present themselves to us as revelations of our true and hidden being.

Who can read for us the "book of unknown signs"? Who can say that we have truly read it when reading is an "act of creation"; that is, it retroactively (*nachträglich*) constitutes what is read, where writing is constituted as prior to reading? What is the order of reality in *Remembrance of Things Past* before its writing by Proust, the author? We can say of the book what Lacan says of the unconscious: it neither was nor was not, it belonged to the order of the nonrealized. His writing creates it, and by recreating it, projects it retroactively in time. It makes it appear in a past that never existed; what's more, it creates the past as what is recovered by writing.

Thus, the synchrony of the object, the created product, is the effect of the diachrony of its organization as reading and its transformation into a new writing, the book signed by Marcel Proust that today can be read by anyone, if she wishes and has the courage to do so. What happens now has no relation to Proust's experience. He deciphered his book of signs and transformed it into an object that is a work of art, offered to a reader who can use it (or not) for deciphering his own *lalangue*, the inscriptions of which he is the effect. In this sense, the object of sublimation is proposed as an ambassador of the real.

It is this that makes art the most real of all things, the most austere school in life, the true last judgment. This book, more laborious to decipher than any other, is also the only one that has been dictated to us by reality, the only one of which the "impression" has been printed in us by reality itself. (. . .) The book whose hieroglyphs are not traced by us is the only book that really belongs to us (RTP, 914).

It is not necessary to continue paraphrasing when the ideas are so clearly expressed. The interweaving of the signifiers make the relation between Proust's project and the function of an analysis transparent: "So that the essential, the only true book, though in the ordinary sense of the word it does not have to be 'invented' by a great writer—for it exists already in each one of us—has to be translated by him. The function and the task of a writer are those of a translator" (RTP, 926).

> This work of the artist, this struggle to discern beneath matter, beneath experience, beneath words, something that is different from them, is a process exactly the reverse of that which, in those everyday lives which we live with our gaze averted from ourselves, is at every moment being accomplished by vanity and passion and the intellect, and habit too, when they smother our true impressions so as entirely to conceal them from us, beneath a whole heap of verbal concepts and practical goals which we falsely call life. In short, this art that is so complicated is in fact the only living art. It alone expresses for others and renders visible to ourselves that life of ours that effectually cannot observe itself and of which the observable manifestations need to be translated and, often, to be read backward and laboriously deciphered. Our vanity, our passions, our spirit of

imitation, our abstract intelligence, our habits have long been at work, and it is the task of art to undo this work of theirs, making us travel back in the direction from which we have come to the depths where what has really existed lies unknown within us. (RTP, 932)

"This work of the artist" has an intimate relation with the practice of psychoanalysis insofar as it dismantles the illusions of the imaginary, the trap of vanity, the overlapping layers of names and conventional significations, the dismantling *per via di levare* in order to make the unconscious porous: the intermediary between the Id and dialogue. Along Proust's and Freud's way, one arrives at comparable results: the recovery of *jouissance* through the joy of decipherment. The supposition from the beginning is the same: the book is already written, the disc recorded, but these inscriptions are buried, much like hieroglyphs in the desert. One need not invent nor add; one must recover and translate the original text with fidelity. This requires differentiation in order not to distinguish what is identical and not to confuse what is different. Why? To arrive at a new writing so that deciphered *jouissance* can be inscribed in an act making the effect of the decipherment pass onto the real—there where the subject knows once and for all who he is, based on a certainty derived from an action that inscribes his proper name as the effect of that action. Historicizing himself.

> Acts are our symbol. Any destiny, however long or complicated it may be, in reality consists of a single moment: the moment in which a man knows forever who he is because one destiny is not better than the next, but every man must respond to the one he carries within.[6]

At the end of the journey, the subject's constitutive split, the division structurally imposed between the One of *jouissance* and the Other of language is not overcome—it can't be. There is no resignation, just the acknowledgment of the secondary place of subjectivity in relation to *savoir*: a *savoir* without a subject, an objectified writing of which the *parlêtre* is the effect, insofar as a "response from the real" (T).[7] In order to accomplish this effect one must traverse the barriers of comprehension, meaning, signification, clinging to consensual frames of reality, shared certainties, the ideology of totalizing knowledge, the effect of university discourse (due to "education" (*e-ducere*) and the uniformity of representations produced by the media industry). One must always remember that the *parlêtre jouit*, but his *jouissance* horrifies him and he wants to know nothing about it. The One slips through, but is unrecognized in the discourse of the Other; the constituted structures of the subject tend to seal up that dimension of *jouissance* as the unconscious matrix of the *parlêtre*.

As we reach the end of this chapter, we can rewrite the story: Freud's brilliant conception of the psychic structure in Letter 52 and his patient work of *recherche* makes him first focus on the interpretation (*Deutung*) of the formations of the unconscious. Dreams, lapses and symptoms, led him to catalogue the rhetorical strategies that imbue apparently absurd manifestations with meaning. Gradually, with some resistance, he admits the unconscious is already translation and passage through the mill of speech of a reality more fundamental, synchronic, and real, which he called the Id. More than a century later, Lacan retraced his steps: he began with analytic experience that is the phenomenological experience of speech. He erred when he confused the Id with the unconscious in his famously gnomic phrase—*Ça* speaks (*ça parle*)—and later distinguished the two planes: while the unconscious is speech and speaks, discourse (of the Other), the Id *jouit* and is made of signs (*signatura rerum*), not words. Presented in this way may seem schematic, and more precision is therefore needed. The unconscious is not only discourse of the Other but structured as a language. It thus has two faces and is double-sided: on the one hand it looks to the writing of the Id and deciphers it; on the other, it receives the Other's signifiers and with those signifiers realizes the task of reading. The unconscious is sustained in that uncomfortable straddling between the ineffable nucleus of our bodily being and the structures for the exchange of speech.

In synthesis, the unconscious is decipherment of *jouissance*, and its products can be interpreted. The praxis of analysis consists in intervening in discourse by disarming the web of significations so the *jouissance* of *savoir*'s decipherment can surface. This *savoir* is no one's, but someone, the subject, is the effect.

PART II

THE CLINIC

Chapter 5

Jouissance and Hysteria

The Psychoanalyst and the Hysteric

A certain tradition dictates that the analyst begin talking about hysteria and hysterics, praising them and manifesting their gratitude for having been the inventors of psychoanalysis, silencing Freud the doctor and teaching him to listen.[1] Once they invented the psychoanalyst and he was able to follow the suffering unfolded with benevolent ears, they fell in love with the invention, this admirable object that without fail was sustained by listening. Psychoanalysts ask only to be spoken to. Because hysterics make the detailed telling of their symptoms and missed encounters with the Other their mode of existence, the analyst registers all her misadventures with free-floating attention. And because they live these misadventures for the witness who listens with benevolent sympathy, the encounter between them is inscribed in the nature of things and, at first sight, seems to be the very paradigm of predestination.

It is not only the hysteric who invents the psychoanalyst. The psychoanalyst also invents the hysteric because the device invented between them reproduces the species that engendered them. This is so to such a degree that, Lacanians after all, we accept as established fact that a structural becoming-hysteric is the condition for all *parlêtres* to begin an analysis, whatever their subjective position may be. The formula for the hysteric's discourse is the formula for beginning an analysis. There must be a complaint, a symptom, transformed into a demand to know, which hides an unconditional demand for love and is directed to whoever supposedly possesses knowledge ignored about one's own self. The suffering, transformed into a question posed to the Other, is the ground on which an analysis is possible. The analytic device offers a space for discourse to become hysterical. There is no reason to be surprised if hysteria has changed how it presents itself since the inception of psychoanalysis. The link between hysteria and psychoanalysis is complete (link does not imply harmony). The hysterics invented the device that engendered the analyst; the latter asks for and produces hysterics who show their charm in a field where listening and not vision is key. If beforehand they showed themselves in a spectacle worthy of Charcot and then faded with hypnosis, it is for speaking that we recognize them today.

In the couple analyst/hysteric, it is impossible to say who came first. That is a fact. As Lacan noted, the analyst creates demand with his or her supply. The hysteric has no problems in recognizing that it is exactly what she always wanted, even before realizing it. Disposing of an Other on whom to unload symptoms and dissatisfaction, a support and a neutral witness, who does not blame her, as others had who had listened previously—someone capable of understanding the truth in her words, and not rejecting her as insubstantial or a liar. When she finds the analyst, she is cured rapidly and makes the Other a substitute for her symptoms. Freud called this "transference neurosis." Lacan does not follow that path, although he does not consider this Freudian expression in detail. I suppose because he considered the expression to be pleonastic, since transference is the necessary neurosis for an analysis to progress as such. Neurosis enters transference, and the subject of neurosis enters analysis. The symptom as a "substitute sexual satisfaction" is now displaced onto the figure of the analyst—the *jouissance* that was anchored to suffering changes mooring. It is no longer adrift because it has settled in discourse or, better, in the vocative drive, a modality of *Trieb* that was scarcely discerned (by Robert Fliess) before Lacan.

An analysis can be the stage and port of entry of this change in the localization of *jouissance*. Yes, there is *jouissance* in analysis. Complying with the fundamental rule of the analytic contract, the discretely eroticized frame in which "anything" can happen without anything happening, the exchange of discourses and interpretations, speaking and being spoken. It is one of the traps of analysis and, on occasion, one of the hardest to break due to the "web of satisfactions" (E, 503) that can envelop the analysand and an analyst who is not up to the task.

The hysteric and the analyst invent themselves reciprocally in relation to *jouissance*. The desire of the analyst must appear as a barrier and evacuation channel for that *jouissance*. If this cannot be achieved, stagnation is an inevitable consequence in the analysis. We can see here that a dimension of *jouissance* in the transference is a form of resistance, as Freud found, yet it is also the very motor of analysis. Transference of *jouissance*, the funds deposited in the bank of the unconscious, quantified capital, ciphered.

The hysteric wishes to be heard if the Other wishes to be spoken to. It is not a fortuitous encounter, but rather performs a structural requirement. She demands being heard and requires the Other's time to measure the desire of her word. Discourse, as opposed to the instant of the gaze, requires time to unfold; time thus becomes an object. Discourse also must come together with the recourses that allow the Other to be sustained as listener: interrupted sentences, faltering due to tears and sighs, deferred intimations of pleasant or painful accounts, the creation of suspense in a delayed revelation, apparently arbitrary detours and deviations, when the Other formulates a question, careful metering out of secrets, distorted approaches to scabrous details. Listening to them, how could Freud not think of the image of an onion, with its concentric layers of resistance as the discourse approaches the center, the "pathogenic nucleus" (SE II) that is the memory of trauma, a fortress that encloses the encounter of one's *jouissance* with the *jouissance* of the Other?

Thus structured, discourse seduces and leads inward, but only for whoever wishes and expects to be seduced. The seducer counts on the consent of the one wishing to be seduced, who is therefore not a victim, but an accomplice. Needless to say, the analytic act is determined by *jouissance* and the need to be safeguarded from it.

The hysteric is enthusiastic about an analysis, which is arduous and advances with great difficulties. She complains about it, but demands and recommends it to those around her. Thus begins an analysis, with a detailed presentation of suffering and the responsibility, treachery, and ingratitude of the Other. Attentive to possible signs of interest on the part of the analyst to adhere to her demand, she offers an abundance of information, dreams and transferential associations that are lived as demands made to her. These are what in the past doctors and hypnotists recognized as a character trait and baptized with the name of suggestion. That trait led to one of Freud's unforgettable chapters in *Group Psychology and the Analysis of the Ego* (1921).

Desperate to be loved and believing that she in turns loves . . . falling in love being the next step, searching for proof of the desire of the Other coming through as a demand, sacrificing herself to the point of martyrdom. This availability to the Other's demands appears as a certain "plasticity," which can be contrasted to the other neurotic pole, which is the obsessive's "rigidity." Let the Other say what he lacks, and she provides it; she devotes herself to the lack in the Other, identifies herself and comes to be in the desire of the Other. If the Other wishes to be a sculptor who represents human beings according to ideal forms, he finds the hysteric to be malleable clay to his Pygmalion.

If the Other devotes himself to a cause with a uniform, she falls in love with the uniform now invested as an object of desire. A doctor's white coat, a priest's robe, majestic togas, the beauty of attire and make-up, eloquence in saying and political power act as imaginary objects to which the subject becomes attached with an almost ethological dimension. The sweet enchantment of a fading ego in its identification with the ideal ego of the Other: salvation in the Cause.

It is often the case that the object the Other recognizes is a woman, the Other woman. The question regarding the attributes possessed by the Other (woman) appears, the secret of her attraction to a man, as well as the identification with the possible reason for the attraction between them. The role as intermediary and spy of the secrets of love fits her like a glove. She acts as "representative," judge and jury: the "invitee" (as the title of Simone de Beauvoir's novel suggests) who sustains the intrigue, identifying with and listening to the complaints of one and the other, much like Dora, playing the roles the plot inspires.

She wants to take charge of *jouissance* by extracting it from the field of the Other and finds no better way than to get inside its "pouch." *Jouissance* is an essence that escapes her and can be secured only if recognized and caught in the Other, an Other that must be constructed, sculpted, and defended at all costs. Beyond all disavowals, the hysteric insists in sustaining an Other of unlimited *jouisssance*, the ideal Father of the Freudian myth: primitive, always already dead, immortal and powerful, despite all disavowals to the contrary.[2]

The hysteric attempts to mime that alien and fugitive *jouissance* by making it a *semblant* ("artificiality," as scornful clinicians used to say). She puts little stock in her performance, unsure about experiencing what she represents: entering the intrigue as an actress, imagining what she could feel in the place of the Other, the effects produced on that Other (*sans foi*), depending on the different op(era)tions needed to interpret her role. The representation appears artificial, pretentious, and false even to her. Lacan alludes to the faithlessness of the hysteric's intrigue (E, 698); the split that simultaneously places her on stage and with the spectators, participating and evading the dramatic play, telling herself at each moment that it is "all lies" and soon they'll know who she really is; being there without being there; feeling the imposture of each gesture and the impost of the voice; offering the Other an anesthetized or dead body, observed from the outside by a gaze anxious to capture what the Other does with that body, abandoned and inert.

Her dedication is less feigned than she thinks. She mistakes identifying the demand of the Other, which she has solicited and taken as object of desire, with the desire of the Other. She lives to fulfill the Other, dedicated to satisfying what she supposes is the desire of the Other at the cost of sacrificing her own desire—a doubtful desire that is handed over enthusiastically and with relief. She chooses the road of self-denial, sacrifice, and renunciation, thus becoming the indispensable complement, the appendicular object of the Other, complaining bitterly that she is treated as an object. She imagines the Other wishes her to be perverse and phantasmatically represents that (innocent) perversion. She does so in order to secure that Other, according to Lacan's formula regarding the general characteristic of neurosis (E, 698), thus confirming Freud's own observations in his texts on the phantasm and hysterical attacks from 1908 and 1909 (SE IX).

She offers herself as the object that conceals the Other's castration, which appears thanks to this false appendage as fullness without lack: lord and master of *jouissance* in the inaccessible site of the *Urvater*. This is the formula for hysteria proposed by Lacan in his seminar on the transference and later forgotten (why?) (S VIII).

$$\frac{@ \quad \Diamond \quad A}{-\varphi}$$

The strategy is self-serving: to be the object that guarantees the *jouissance* of the *partenaire* of love in the phantasm in order to negate not the castration of the Other (as in perversion), but one's own. She thus comes to occupy a preferential position: to be indispensable in the phantasm of the Other, although with uncertainty. How can she be convinced that another woman will not remove her from the place of privilege? Up to what point is the Other appreciative and worthy of the sacrifice and tribute he receives? What would be the effect of her separation and loss? If the Other wants her, he must prove it. Up to what point he is willing to go? Is he capable of responding to the unlimited offerings received? The libidinal lamella that unites her with the uncertain Other is an elastic organ that must be continuously stretched in order to confirm its limits (E, 719).

Eventually, and almost fatally, the Other reveals himself to be unworthy of the sacrifices, incapable of responding with gratitude, a traitor, perverted, a sadist and unworthy of trust. The steps following the sacrificial offering ("everything for him") is reproach, accusation, self-pity, violent demands, and provocations able to produce tangible proof of the Other's treachery. The next step is the displacement to a new Other, person, or cause that appears to demand the passionate sacrifice needed to reinstate or reach plenitude, always in wait of the absolute definitive Other to whom she could offer Everything. Before the figure of an Ideal Father, all the others (lower-case others) are lacking, dis-abled.

The four characteristics of the hysteric's beautiful soul are the following: first, she is a complainer, a victim, a Hegelian *schönne Seele*: an object of humiliations, betrayals, incomprehension, and ingratitude, the undeserved recipient of ill treatment and misfortune. She offers herself as object to the gaze and ear of the Other: "see what I am reduced to?"; "listen to the tale of my misfortunes, if you can." Sade's scathing title, *Justine or the Misfortunes of Virtue*, prefigures this attribute. The beautiful soul's being is blurred into a continuous complaint, a prolonged lament, a series of symptoms and cruelties. *Jouissance* runs all throughout her narrative without ever being able to identify it as such: in the details of the lover's deceptions; the doctors' mistakes regarding her suffering, crippled body, marked by surgical scars; the lack of recognition by children and friends; the unjust treatment of bosses or teachers. There is suffering and tears when telling her story in another scene: the suffering of a heartbreaking experience is revived in the extension of the lamella, beyond what is tolerable. The tale of persecuted innocence, of being punished for following her heart, requires the dialectical investment indicated by Lacan at the beginning of his teaching (E, 179). The phantasm of being beaten, identified by Freud in "A Child Is Being Beaten," is the privileged stage of the beautiful soul.

The hysteric's second attribute is beautiful indifference (*belle indifférence*), traversing the whirlwinds and hurricanes of desperation generated around her, without a hair out of place. The Other is confronted with his own limits when faced with an experience, unpredictable in appearance, which spurs him to action, and for which he is later reproached. Every time the Other resolves to do something for or against the hysteric's demand in response to her offerings and dedication, she withdraws from the tribute or reaction to that response. It is not *that* she wanted. Her desire is an unsatisfied desire. Indifference or even disdain are responses to the Other's actions.

Her insensibility is first and foremost in relation to the body. The nourishment or the slap in the face, caresses or sex, ornaments or dress that enhance or detract from her beauty are "all the same." It is a problem for the desire of the Other, a desire she awakens or evokes but from which she is disengaged and undaunted; it does not concern her. It can reach the extreme of anorexia nervosa that places her life in jeopardy. She mobilizes the desperation of those around her, but it is not her concern. The Other's *angst* is the food that nourishes and calms a hunger that is beyond hunger, an insatiable necessity for nothing that elevates the phallic power of whoever (the hysteric in this instance) refuses the dominance of the phallic signifier. In withdrawing, she exhibits the futile vanity of desire; they reproach her for it.

The hysteric's third attribute corresponds to "sleeping beauty," who dreams with a future awakening in paradise, but in the meantime awaits the arrival of a desiring subject who may awaken her, although without any excitement. Desire does not concern her; she acts out the role of the absence of desire. Action is always suspended, and when it finally takes place, she distances herself from the consequences, or is swept away by the incomprehensible turbulence of the Other. To love, study, fight for a cause, have a child, work, be for or against certain rules, are things that she can do without feeling they are her own. She goes about them indifferently, lending (not giving) herself to them, satisfying external expectations dissociated from consequences. When not engaged in these activities, she is asleep; when engaged, she is a sleepwalker. Sometime in the future, the desire manifested by the prince's kiss (love) will rescue her from apathy. Desire does not emerge; she is enchanted.

The hysteric's fourth attribute confronts her with her alter ego, the beast: an encounter with a bloody tormentor who makes her the object of the most abject vileness. A brutal, coarse, violent, indelicate being that relegates and humiliates her, about whom she complains endlessly and appears to be the necessary realization of a masochist phantasm. Beauty and the beast appear frequently in the clinic. The story of the beautiful soul, beautiful indifference, and sleeping beauty require this complementary character at some point—someone who is responsible for the misfortunes of virtue and gives substance and depth to the complaints. The complaints regarding family members, priests, confidants, and therapists are repeated monotonously. As we can well imagine, they are the source of obscure *jouissance*, emerging not from masochism, but from the phantasm that accompanies the suffering: telling that suffering before an understanding ear that identifies with her in her claims and com-passion (*Mitleid*).

In their own circles, psychiatrists take revenge and repeat what books do not say. For them, there are two victims: the wife of the alcoholic and the husband of the hysteric. Sometimes they form a couple, and the result guarantees their *jouissance*. For psychoanalysts, all victims are suspicious of being complicit, if not the masterminds of the crime (books on jurisprudence are involuntarily comic). Even the insightful analyst L. Israël wrote an article titled "The Victim of the Hysteric."[3]

In Function of *Jouissance*

It is now time to abandon characterizations and move toward a structural conception of hysteria in order to consider what the concept of *jouissance* brings to the clinic of pithiatism, the former name for this venerable neurosis that even psychiatrists prefer to know nothing about. Flaunting her dissatisfaction, the hysteric champions a supreme, sublime *jouissance*. The solution offered to the *parlêtre* is sexual normalization, passing through castration, which revolves around the impossible signifier of *jouissance*: the phallus. The hysteric rejects it (this is one of the reasons, and not a minor one, for speaking of the hysteric as "she," independently of the documented sex). The phallus, the road to *jouissance* available to one and all, is not a signifier for her but an object that reveals itself to be insufficient, incapable of fulfilling its promise. The hysteric takes the structural feminine position (being unsatisfied by the phallus) to the extreme. Challenging the vector that goes from T̶h̶e̶ Woman (who does not exist) toward the phallus, she emphasizes the importance of another vector, the one that in the field of the feminine poses the enigma of what a woman is and wants.

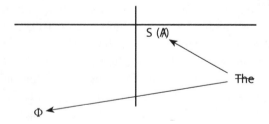

Not-all is a Lacanian formula, the woman not-all in phallic significaion, split between the man and the Other woman, alternately posing the question and always finding half-answers regarding the *jouissance* she experiences, but not knowing in what it consists. In the hysteric, the alternation is extreme. There is no half-measure to her passionate devotion. Her not-all is disavowed; an absolute dedication to the figure of a revived Ideal Father leads her to an "all-in." However, "all-in" leads only to deception, the announced shipwreck of the phallus and its arrogance. She thus passes from "all-in" to "all-no" in relation to the phallus, challenging all imaginary virility. It is the moment of identification with what is missing in the image, the moment in which she, as Lacan says, "plays the man." From "all-in" to "all-no" is the end result that, in both cases, centers on the phallus and its function. Deception encourages her questioning desire and leads, at a certain moment of the dialectic, to place herself "all-in" regarding the question of feminine *jouissance* posed to the Other woman: this is Dora's case when turning toward Mrs. K, mistakenly taken for homosexuality or perversion, especially when in 1923 Freud adds an Addendum that encourages such confusion. It is hysteria and nothing more than hysteria in Dora's relation to Mr. and Mrs. K.

Challenging the phallus while playing the man led to a dispensable text with the just title of *The Spontaneous Feminism of the Hysteric*.[4] The hysteric's question is inseparable from the question regarding femininity. The Lacanian response, "not-all," is not convincing for the hysteric, who plays an oscillating "all" or "nothing," always provisionally, longing for a definitive closure able to seal the status of "the woman." This is the reason the formula for the hysteric's discourse includes the repeated search for a master able to respond without ambiguity to the question regarding a woman's being.

$$\frac{\$}{@} \quad \overset{\rightarrow}{//} \quad \frac{S_1}{S_2}$$

This master is supposed to provide a response, offer knowledge (priests, doctors, teachers, psychoanalysts), a knowledge that always fails to say the truth and is in a relation of disjunction $(@//S_2)$ with the object cause of desire, surplus *jouissance*: the truth that moves her discourse. A master who, should the relation deepen and he come to believe he is master, will end up a beast.

The hysteric thus goes through life insecure about her identity, trying to define who she is, her proper name (that proper name that "inconveniences her" [E, 696]), miming different identities that are confused with roles (social, theatrical), searching for desire in the Other in order to identify with the object of that desire and thus reach a phantasmatic identity (the third attribute, hysterical identification, described by Freud in chapter 7 of *Group Psychology* [SE XVIII]). She repeats the question that is first of all directed at her mother: what is it like to be a woman, and how does she *jouit*? Disappointed with the response (feminine castration), it is also posed to the father: "what am I lacking?" This leads the daughter to identify with the phallus that, for the father, is a woman beyond woman (masculine castration).

Earlier I noted that for beauty and the beast, *jouissance* is guaranteed. In the neurotic couple whose desire is essentially unsatisfied desire, an exciting and challenging situation is produced: an incitement to *jouir* with the symptom, the privileged symptom of "every man," which is a woman (S XXIII, 19). To be the prince of the kiss that can awaken her is a masculine phantasm, which complements sleeping beauty's. He is the one who supposedly possesses the secrets of feminine *jouissance*, beyond other men (unconscious *partenaires* of the [homo]sexual act). Also, if she is the standard bearer of a doubtful *jouissance* beyond the phallus, he can be satisfied with what life as a couple provides: there is no other (phallic) *jouissance* than his. If she refuses the alibi and short-circuit of pleasure by prolonging and deferring satisfaction, he finds that inaccessibility sustains his erection and he can conduct every sexual missed encounter as a scene of violation and rape.

The absence and indifference toward desire elevates *jouissance* to the rank of unreachable absolute, where the feat of achieving *jouissance* to the nth degree is consummated by a *jouissance* of no *jouissance*. Desire is not lacking, but is unsatisfied because she cannot be fooled; she asks for the phallus and knows (too well) that the penis is only a disposable simulacrum, incapable of securing *jouissance*. Her *partenaire* is, beyond the male partner, the primitive Father, master of unlimited *jouissance* and not subject to castration: an unreachable exception that makes for the inevitable fallibility of all the others. Desire remains unsatisfied because she is not incautious; she confirms the Other's castration again and again and receives her own phallic value from that castration. Because she does not have it, she is (the phallus); she is *non dupe* because she knows the penis is only the metonym of the phallus (she doesn't want to talk to the clown, just to the circus owner). Of course, *non dupes errent*; that is the essence of neurosis. She often wants to be cured of her incapacity to be fooled, the cleverness that makes her desire an unsatisfied desire, her lasting inventiveness in cultivating dissatisfaction.

She wants to know, but even so maintains the dissatisfaction of her desire; the signifiers provided by the master, whether man of God or science, do little to please her. Beyond demand, her question points to desire. Like the child (the much denounced "infantilism"), responses to her many questions do little to appease her curiosity; they exacerbate it. An Other disposed to sate her hunger with responses will soon find her with "mental anorexia," a spitting out or vomiting of the signifiers demanded. Bulimia and anorexia: the questions "de-multiply;" she is an enigma, and knowledge breaks down due to its very presence. There is no signifier for ~~The~~ Woman; that is Lacan's answer to The question.

She addresses the Other with an insatiable demand (D). The Other, like the "why?" of the child, finally shows his lack; knowledge is lacking. The response obtained is the lack in being of the Other, an indispensable effect: $S(\bar{A})$. The demand reveals desire (d) as an inexhaustible undercurrent.

$$A \text{ (Other)} - D \text{ (demand [to know])} = S(\bar{A}), [d \text{ (desire)}]$$

The dissonance between D and d reveals the lack in the Other: the great A is $\bar{A}$. The demand made to the Other discloses the inevitable lack that is not in her but in him. The space of the unknown is thus displaced. Now, she is the enigma for that Other who does not know and is insufficient, especially when, seduced by the supposition of absolute knowledge, he strives to provide the answers. *Jouissance* comes about as the result of the master's lack, its impotence and castration. She puts him to work, but his words serve only to show his flaws (lack of the phallus). His knowledge is received with skepticism: "Fine, but it is not enough, although I don't know what's missing." The clinician is surprised to find that his words are often corrected, even when quoting what she has just said. No word can say her being; she clings to her difference, which she cannot yield, sensing that to be said by the Other is to recognize her castration. She supposes that her castration is what the Other wants and he will therefore *jouir* at her expense. In order to intervene, the analyst's starting point must be her or his necessary imperfection, renouncing what may be construed as knowledge: to reject the place of S_1, which is deceptively attributed, and put into play her or his ignorance. The hysteric invents the analyst with a dominating passion that is ignorance.

In the hysteric's discourse, words and knowledge can be learned, but they do not touch her body, cut and re-cut by symptoms, panic attacks, surgeries, eating and drinking binges, tantrums, cosmetics; the never-ending quest for unfading beauty and youth; the search in the mirror and the other woman for the secret of her unsatisfied desire. The *jouissance* of the symptom does not dissolve because of the phallic *jouissance* that runs through discursive articulation. It is phallic *jouissance* that has not traversed the diaphragm of the word and is retained, repressed. For this reason, Freud favored the hypothesis of a double inscription and the dissociation between two different *Vorstellungen*: the representation of the thing and the representation of the word, one separated from the other: consciousness and the unconscious, co-existing, but separate. Lacan gets around this question by saying that knowledge and truth do not bite on the same side of the Mobius strip (E, 732). No clever interpretation lifts repression, however irreproachable it may be in its logic and technique. Faced with the discourses of the master and the university, it is the hysteric who is right. That is why a psychoanalytic device and frame (*dispositif*) had to be invented, which is Freud's response to the enigma of hysteria.

What is essential to truth necessarily escapes the knowledge of interpretation, just as what is substantial, the sensibility of the body, escapes phallic *jouissance*. It remains untouched. That subtraction acts like a catalyst for the desire of the Other and, therefore, the place of what is lacking is invested with phallic value, signification and imaginary stature. By creating lack in being (desire) in the Other, she can construct an artificial desire. The lack in the Other functions like a mold and model for her identification: she will be what is lacking. In this way she acquires an identity and can aspire to be indispensable—inscribe herself in history by proxy, through the Other and whatever she can demand. This is how the fundamental deception she inflicts on herself functions: by confusing the demand (of the Other) with her (own) desire. To be the object of desire in a phantasm occupies the place of being a subject. It is necessary to create the hole, the Other's lack in being (as if it didn't already exist!) in order to be able to fill it herself. Hence, the creation of beauty and the beast and her great disposition for settling into the analytic device.

Reacting with emotion and becoming agitated by the lack of interest in the Other, berating his coldness as well as the passions she could arouse, responding with indifference and detachment, without reciprocity, always in the other direction. Cultivating the lack, asking to be seen, recognized, heard, admired, hypnotized—ordered by an Other that cannot possess her fully because there is always a subtracted remainder, given that the Other's response is not precisely what she expected. No father is The Father, to whom she addresses her demand.

An analysis suits and befits her; it is the source of *jouissance*, a resistance to desire, which has to be nourished and then thwarted by the function of the analyst. Thanks to that *jouissance*, the analysis can begin, but it can also stagnate in the swamp of a transference neurosis. Her passion requires a witness that is a subject of (com)passion, for whom she is disposed to continue suffering and making sacrificial donations. While complaining that she is taken for an object, she offers herself as an object to the Other's discretion. She attempts specularity, the reciprocal exchange of *i* (@), offering *i* for @, her image for the object, pulling off a bait-and-switch, a bluff where she is the first victim. Her idea, her phantasm, is a reciprocal shrouding of both desires. That is why she can function as a priestess of love. Her religion is the sexual relation, the one that does not exist. A supplement remains to make it exist, love, which could veil the triple lack in the symbolic, the imaginary, and the real.

The barred Other ($\mathbb{A}$) lacks @ to become A. The hysteric offers herself in the place of the object @. She is a restorer of completeness, hoping her own subjective division (castration) can be overcome in a relation of absolutes. If, thanks to her, the other can go from $\mathbb{A}$ to A, then indirectly and though identification, she can pass from $ to S in the completeness of unconquered love. She offers herself as surplus *jouissance*, the coffer holding the *agalma*: a guarantee of *jouissance* the Other lacks, causing his desire. However, the *agalma*'s secret must remain hidden, enclosed, and inaccessible. For desire to be sustained, it is necessary for its object to subtract itself, paying tribute to a *jouissance* of which this object "would like to be" absolute condition. Negating herself, she becomes the objectified and objective cause of the desire of the Other. In order for this to occur, she must subtract herself and dismiss all possibility of *Befriedigung* (satisfaction) by sowing and cultivating dissatisfaction.

The relation to knowledge in university discourse offers her a unique opportunity. She locates herself at @, in the place of ignorance offered to the discourse of knowledge (S_2), thus making herself a subject ($) which, at a certain moment, looks for a master. The hysteric's discourse is specular and the reverse of university discourse.

$$\frac{\$}{@} \longrightarrow \frac{S_1}{S_2} \qquad \frac{S_2}{S_1} \longrightarrow \frac{@}{\$}$$

hysteric's discourse   university discourse

She appeals to the primitive Father, the supposed master of *jouissance* and its knowledge: an Other who ignores castration and for whom she constructs an unsustainably exceptional place. Later, he stumbles, even if she is the one who provokes his falling apart. She reneges on that lack and identifies with what is missing, while thinking she can plug it up. "What I lack is to be lacking (for him)," someone once said, thus expressing desire as renounced and unsatisfied desire. Hence the difficult position of the analyst who cannot take refuge in the imposture of impassivity and lack of desire, but also cannot indicate the place of lack so that she may take shelter there. It is the moment for a calculated wavering of neutrality and showing necessary imperfection, which Lacan recommends to elude the dangers of indicating a space of identification that can later become the reason for an alibi, such as, "it is not for me but for you that I do this."

In Seminar XXII (1975) Lacan distinguished the three Freudian forms of identification and linked them to each of the rings of the Borromean knot. He referred to hysterical identification, the third type, as identification with the imaginary of the real Other. It is a real Other elevated to the category of absolute One, original Father, from which she later withdraws in order to reach the level of object cause of his desire.

Even so, the hysteric's desire is a desire without object and essentially unsatisfied: her object is the lack in the Other; it is what she asks for, consumes, and consummates insatiably. However, from the Other's lack she can have only doubtful manifestations, words that are as uncertain as the little assurance she takes in her own sincerity. The "faithless" side of her word is projected onto the word of the Other. Doubt requires proof of coherence and consistency, but only fosters mistrust due to the inconsistency of the Other: *Nobodaddy* (Millot).

To take the place of object @ in order to disavow the lack in A and immortalize the Other is what links her to, as well as differentiates her from, the pervert, as she imagines him to be. It is worthwhile to compare and contrast. The pervert takes the place of object @ in his relation to a subject, his *partenaire* in perversion, by proposing to make a subjective lack appear (\$), as well as pain, the curiosity of seeing, subjection to a contract he drafts and proclaims, fragmentation before his voyeur's gaze, the adoption of a transgressive creed that he inoculates with a proselytizing act. In practicing these perverse acts, he does not function on his own account, but on behalf of a third, the Other (the Mother), whose incompleteness is disavowed by this son-phallus who becomes a fetish or takes the fetish as an object of *jouissance* that denies the castration of the Other. In contrast, hysterics conceal their castration, undergone at the beginning, offering themselves to their *partenaire* in order to fulfill a desire they themselves provoke. The pervert solicits the conversion of the other; the hysteric is "of conversion": she makes and lends herself to the conversion she offers her *partenaire*. Lacan expressed this difference in *Écrits*: "To return to [the phantasm], let us say that the pervert imagines he is the Other in order to ensure his own *jouissance*, and that this is what the neurotic reveals when he imagines he is a pervert—in his case, to ensure [himself of] the Other" (E, 699, translation modified).

Thence the essential difference between the clinic with hysterics and perverts. While the hysteric abhors *jouissance*, the pervert devotes himself to cultivating it; the former represses and sends into exile, the latter promotes it . . . beauty and the beast may not make such a bad couple or worse (*ou pire*).

The pervert denies the mother's lack—she can only be phallic—and adores the object after elevating it to the dignity of a fetish: the magic instrument that he plays at disavowing, while transforming himself into a fetish. The hysteric does not fuel that hope. Her mother, like Dora's, is a deficient, scorned being at the negative extreme of her identifications, the place of unsalvageable contempt. "If being a woman is to be like her then I do not want to be a woman," is her motto and she devotes herself to establishing a difference (*vive la différence!*) that takes the form of a "bisexual phantasm" (Freud) or the negation of femininity. The father is worthy of sympathy for being with such an inadequate woman, and the hysteric is willing to identify with what the father lacks, an Other woman that could teach her what a "real" woman is, like Mrs. K. This is how the daughter becomes what fills the lack in A; she takes the place of Φ (not minus phi) and is thus covered with phallic value and signification. Her life is subject to the signifiers of the desire of the father, his castration. She lives to obey or repel this demand, oscillating in her identifications. Whether positive or negative, those are the signifiers that guide her life, although she may not want to know about her assimilating dependence. On the contrary, she affirms her singularity, pretending to be recognized as "herself" and describing herself (at least in Mexico) as "very special," downright melting if someone tells her she is "very sensitive."

To summarize: the pervert has the Mother and the hysteric the Father as objects of worship. The central difference lies in their stance toward the castration of the Other, which is what really matters. The pervert disavows it; the hysteric loathes and represses it. Therein lies their kinship and opposition, as well as their complementarity. The pervert "plays The woman," I would say, compared to what Lacan says of the hysteric, who "plays the man" (S XVI, 6/18/69).

Hysteria and *Savoir*

There is a particular relation between the hysteric and knowledge. She suffers from not knowing, her reminiscences, repressions, the lack of continuity in her discourse, "large gaps in memory" (SE VII, 17), a *jouissance* trapped in symptoms that speak without saying; she suffers because of the knowledge that remains unconscious. Her unknown *savoir* appears as a phantasm in the Other, the subject supposed to know with whom she can readily fall in love precisely for that reason. Her lack is filled in the imaginary as a discourse without gaps. The phallus, which distances from *jouissance*, has its equivalent in knowledge. Oh, if she only knew! Perhaps by knowing, the *jouissance* fastened onto the symptom could be reached in discursive articulation. However, the knowledge she lacks is an attribute of the Other, which, demanded and induced, gives only unsatisfactory responses and produces more questions. Bad faith? Contempt? He refuses to share the knowledge that he can't but have and thus sustains his domination, or employs it in aggressive, humiliating ways, much like a beast. In the phantasm, the Other of knowledge is sadistic; complicity is often established between beauty and the beast, who punishes her with his whip of words (CF 73–85). Sometimes the phantasm of knowledge as phallic power induces the hysteric to search for knowledge, awaken from her dreams, stir up the dormant curiosity, recover the lost body through knowledge of physiology, psychology, psychoanalysis, or literature, as a way of supplementing the inevitable lack in the Other, the response that inescapably escapes the enigma written as S(Ⱥ).

The dissatisfaction provoked by the phallus and its unfulfilled (*versagt*) promises are thus sustained. Since the Other cannot provide the knowledge she craves (it is always insufficient knowledge), she continues to question the Other woman, who holds the secret of what a woman is and wants. In a certain way, she produces the passage to the other side of the formulas of sexuation, inverting the direction of the vector: to possess knowledge as a phallus and thence proceed to respond to the question regarding ~~The~~ woman: $\Phi \leftarrow$ ~~The~~. The phantasm of being beaten reveals its well-known reversibility. The subject who was passive and *jouit* from interrogating the Other passes to being active and exerting sadistic knowledge on the *partenaire*, students, patients: those who suffer from not having that same knowledge. It is not unusual for the phantasm of sadistic/"savistic" knowledge to determine intellectual and professional inhibitions and thus new demands for knowledge, now addressed to the psychoanalyst. The phantasms of sadistic/"savistic" knowledge are thus present in the transference and as transference.

To address the Other until the lack appears, in order to offer herself as the plug for that lack: exasperate him, point out his inadequacies, propose him as a subject of analysis, when no demand exists on his part. To risk "healing" him of his symptom, which is a woman, tighten the libidinal lamella by testing his limits, speak incessantly about "the relationship," turning laments into accusations (*Klagen sind Anklagen*) (SE XIV, 248). She lives on the edge of break-ups and separations, tears and aggressive sacrifice: offerings carefully noted in the ledger as the Other's debts, a merciless memory for the faults, disloyalties, and inconsistencies of the Other.

The hysteric's sacrifice is one side of her love, the other being her accusations for the lack of reciprocity (not appreciating her sacrifice). Theatricality is a representation that points to a third, the future spectator and listener of the drama of ingratitude. That third can easily be swapped in the account book where the always-increasing damages suffered are noted and remembered in detail. In an article on aggressiveness, Lacan spoke of "the aggressive motives behind all so-called philanthropic activity (*charité*)" (E, 87). These motives constitute an essential aspect of the hysteric's intrigue: giving much more than is asked, she buys a debtor, someone who is supposedly obligated, an inseparable being bound to what he's received. It is the self-interest of her "maso-heroism" (C. Soler) and "civilizing function" (C. Millot) achieved by means of her sacrifice to either the idealized or perverse Father.

The specular relation and the phantasm of symmetry dominate hysteria. What she gives is what she demands; projection is a constant: "In your place I would have . . . ;" "If I were to do to him what he does . . . ;" "I can't imagine how I . . ." All this is experienced and duly acted out for a third—book, character, psychoanalyst—the witness of her passion who will take pity, blame the other, absolve her with the structure of a legalistic narrative where she is alternately victim, jury, judge, and hangman, sanctioning and applying the deserved punishment.

Her ego becomes the measure of all things. It is inconceivable that the other have different tastes or interests, love his family rather than hers, not share her spirituality or love of beauty. She needs, demands, and counts proofs of devotion and that she matters to the Other. The narcissistic jealousy she suffers because of a rival, job, the Other's use of time, all consume her, but also transform themselves into another way of affirming and complaining about the Other's increasing debt. She demands being the Other's everything regarding *jouissance*, the very condition of *jouissance* and that it be possible only with her. Her *jouissance* value must be equal to the *jouissance* lacking in the Other: she is a prisoner of the *jouisssance* of the Other, which she aspires to fulfill and enclose while playing at subtracting herself from that *jouissance* in order to confirm her value. It is because of what He lacks that she reaches phallic value, *jouissance* value, although she knows nothing of this except for the dissatisfaction that she can and does bring to desire.

The relation to the *jouissance* of the Other defines her. It is a difficult role in which she offers herself for satisfaction while also subtracting herself in mind and body. She is always evaluating her weight with the Other's scale so that unsatisfied desire can sustain her in the phallic-narcissistic space of plenitude that, in the imaginary, she can bring the Other. Thus, she remains dependent on the highs and lows of her exchange rate, exposed to unpredictable changes that are the cause and reason of frequent narcissistic lows that psychiatrists nowadays call "depression" and feed with medications.

It is enough for the Other to retreat, get "fed up" (in the double sense of the word), let her know he "no longer needs her," be overthrown from the phantasm of indispensability, put another (her equivalent) in her place, for her to be deprived of the reason for living: to be left without fundament or foundation, depth-less. That is how her identification with object @ as residue emerges. *Jouissance* manifests itself in reproaches and masochistic self-compassion, endlessly recounting the ingratitude where she is the first victim. She needs to speak out, find a soulmate who can sustain her "need for communication," beginning with the "nothing" she feels herself to be and generously hands over, ready to again become the Other's "everything."

Dissatisfaction is the promised goal of desire, and the result is resentment. With a well-deserved challenge to phallic infallibility, she imposes unreachable standards, creating an abyss between desire and *jouissance*. That distance is filled by the symptom. Unsatisfied desire becomes conversion *jouissance*, which she clings to and loves more than herself—as paranoiacs love their deliria—attached to resentment and showing her being through suffering. The symptom is made from unknown *jouissance* and knots together five types of resistances, such as Freud described them in 1926: the compulsion of the Id; the punishment of the Superego; and the narcissistic advantages derived from the transference, repression, and submission of the Other to the trials and tribulations of her own illness (SE XX, 149–150, translation modified). The stigmas or marks on the body are testimony to the complaints, resentment, and accusations hurled at the Other's failure to fulfill a relation with no lack and exempt her from being responsible for her own proper desire. She invokes and wagers on the sexual relation . . . that does not exist.

Without being too naive, we should ask why she, or any other neurotic for whom a symptom is *jouissance*, demands an analysis. If she does not want to give up her difference, what makes her "special," if her desire consists in sustaining her position as a dissatisfied demanding creditor. Or if she lacks faith in an analysis because it is based on a speech she distrusts and because she can never be certain of the place she occupies in the Other, including the analyst. These questions cannot be answered in a general way but are the backdrop of every analytic relation in its back-and-forth between the *jouissance* of the symptom, the *jouissance* of the analytic context, and the wished-for possibility of channeling *jouissance* through the flexible diaphragm of speech.

There is no general response for every hysteric, but it is important to point out that her situation is paradigmatic of every *parlêtre*; there is dissociation, as well as a distinct opposition between pleasure and *jouissance*. Herein is another fundamental difference between hysteria and perversion, as Carmen Gallano notes. The pervert seeks *jouissance*, but cannot distinguish it from pleasure. He realizes the feat of living pleasure as *jouissance*, while for the hysteric *jouissance* is unpleasant, painful, shameful, disgusting (IH, 115). If the pervert's dramatization of *jouissance* is monotonous (there are few books more boring than Sade's *The 120 Days of Sodom*, once the reader recognizes its mathematical structure), the hysteric's polymorphic *jouissance* (changeable and unable to be fixed) is surprising. We should not exaggerate: in hysteria, the compulsion to repeat and the fixed construction of the phantasm also operate by stealth. The "misfortune of virtue" is no more amusing than "vice amply rewarded."

While the pervert affirms a will to *jouissance* (this being the very name for pleasure), the hysteric obtains *jouissance* through rejection and indifference toward earthly *jouissance* in name of an absolute, impossible *jouissance*, beyond and against phallic *jouissance*, paying for pleasure with the dissatisfaction of desire. The symptom and disgust, pain and shame, fill the spaces of lost *jouissance*. Believing she is saying no to the Other's *jouissance*, she sustains this *jouissance* by distancing it from the possibilities made available through easily accommodating mental and bodily pleasures. She practices an ethical, apostolic stance in the ministry of difficulty.

Her body is offered as a set of disparate parts without unity, letting the Other's words and desire be the cement holding it together. In the words of Gallano, she rejects the consequences of the signifier in the real and lives as a subject in the separation (*la coupure*) between *jouissance* and the body (IH, 115). Much like the body in a dissecting room, as in Rembrandt's lesson where the learned speak, or the anesthetized body in the operating room: insensible to sex, rejected or lived with indifference. It is also the body offered to the scalpel that cuts segments or imaginary nerves of sensibility, representing (perhaps) a gain in spirituality: flesh for the surgeon, given to focal suicide and dismemberment.

She distrusts and rejects the *jouissance* of the Other she produces by means of the dissatisfaction that feeds desire. Thus, she alienates herself from *jouissance* by confining it to the symptom and appearing to say: "I do not *jouit* so that the Other of identification does not *jouit* me," "For [s]he figures that the Other demands [her] castration" (E, 700, translation modified). This measure is considered "castrating," representing the living image of castration—the modular parts that are cut and reconstitute themselves, like the lizard. By withdrawing, she demonstrates the universal value of castration in her devotion to the primitive Father of the formula $\exists X.\overline{\Phi X}$ and differs from the pervert who denies the not-all of women and affirms the absolute validity of $\forall X.\Phi X$, which Freud deemed a premise for the universality of the penis.

There is another clinical trait (difficult to differentiate from pejorative and disqualifying ones), regarding the inconsistent, fickle, and unpredictable characteristic and frequency of hysterical tantrums. These produce the Other's complaints as "victim of the hysteric," but ignores the *jouissance* he also derives from the tensive streching of the lamella;

in extreme speech, *jouissance* appears at the limit of what can be articulated: in insults, beatings, or fainting. The hysteric's *jouissance* (and her *partenaire*'s, of course) lies in her withdrawal from desire, proclaiming it to be beyond satisfaction and the reduction of tension.

C. Millot defines the hysteric as the guardian of a mystery: what is unreachable through phallic *jouissance*. However, dissatisfaction with phallic *jouissance* is not the patrimony of women, says. S. André. All *parlêtres* have this limitation for two reasons: there is no signifier for ~~The~~ woman, and the sexual relation does not exist. One may ask then: given that desire is the desire of the Other, is the hysteric a manifestation, effect, or product of masculine desire? Sor Juana Ines de La Cruz says it best: "You foolish men who accuse women, not seeing you're the cause of the very thing you blame . . . Why be outraged at the guilt of your own doing? Have them as you make them or make them what you will."[5]

In this chapter there are references to (feminine) hysterics that appear to ignore that some of Freud's first "discoveries" in the new clinic of the neuroses were cases of masculine hysteria, as well as not acknowledging the important book by L. Israël on this topic mentioned earlier. It is worthwhile repeating why. Although already well known, the differentiation is not based on the biology of sexuality, but on the unconscious election between two fields, men and women, delimited by the formulas of sexuation. In this sense, the not infrequent cases of masculine hysteria are also cases of ("feminine") hysteria, since what is decisive is the subjective position before the phallic signifier:

$$\frac{@ \quad \lozenge \quad A}{-\varphi}$$

If the hysteric negates phallic *jouissance* in function of a *jouissance* that goes beyond, it is obvious that no one embodies this protest more than the man who suffers from genital disorders and inhibitions, such as conversion symptoms, premature ejaculation, and impotence of various kinds. It is seen in cases where the direction of desire is inverted; the subject opts for passivity, making himself desirable instead of desiring, and defends himself against the *jouissance* of the Other (sex). He also figures that she wants his castration and protects himself with a symptom: not giving over his lack, or clinging to what he fears. He thus remains a "good boy" who does not confront the law of the prohibition of incest, which extends to "every woman" instead of "not-all" (FL, 173–190).

Last, we have to look for masculine hysteria on the side of the "beast," in the complementarity and complicity he establishes with the hysteric as his "victim." This is the meaning of Lacan's expression: "a woman is a *sinthome* for any man" (S XXIII, 84), a hysteric *sinthome*, one could say. The hysteric would not be able to sustain her discourse if not for the complicity of someone who takes the place of the unbarred Other, whom she addresses: someone who positions himself as a subject, makes her the object @ of his phantasm and is willing to give her the indispensable complement she demands. Nothing can be understood in psychoanalysis without assuming that desire is the desire of the Other and the unconscious is the discourse of the Other and, for these reasons, *jouissance* is prohibited to those who speak.

Chapter 6

Perversion, Disavowal of *Jouissance*

The "Positive" Side of Neurosis?

One must jump from neurosis, the refusal to put *jouissance* into words, a "negative," toward its "positive," perversion. We are once again before a photographic metaphor, Freud's this time: *"neuroses are, so to say, the negative of perversions* "(SE VII, 165, original emphasis). This formula or maxim is inverted in an article Lacan (should never have) signed with Granoff.[1] No, perversion is not neurosis' negative, but its positive. However, the inversion is not total: "the negative of perversions," Freud said in this formula that unified the perversions. But in the following sentence (that dates from 1905 to 1920) he added that in neurosis there was no indication of an inclination toward fetishism. In the 1920 edition of the *Three Essays on Sexuality*, this "particularity" of the neuroses was removed because it was observed that neurotics were not immune to the charms of the fetish. In this respect, which is essential for understanding the perverse phenomenon, a comfortable relation (for the author and the reader) cannot be established between positive perversion and negative neurosis. There is no incompatibility between neurosis and perversions.

The fact remains: *jouissance* is concealed in neurosis, and expressed only through suffering, complaints, and symptoms that say what the ego silences. The subject shows its division, ashamed of recognizing herself as someone who experiences *jouissance*. The neurotic is pleased to point out her lack in relation to *jouissance*, the one she recognizes and attributes so generously to others, those who live with ease and without any worries. All those who would be delighted by the spectacle of her suffering and subjective division, all unified in her phantasm: the tyrants, cruel and insensible parents, or castrating and possessive mothers. These are the others who experience *jouissance*, demand her castration, and whom the neurotic resists, thus concealing that the mutilation she repudiates has already taken place, and her suffering emerges from not knowing what to do about it, how to convert it to desire. The hysteric of the previous chapter and the obsessive of the chapter I decided not to write show the two poles of *jouissance* the neurotic rejects, the repression of the signifiers that evoke and possibly subjectify it. Thus, the neurotic experiences *jouissance* without knowing: ignoring, transposing, and disguising *jouissance* with the attributes of symptoms.

Her lack of knowledge is distressing and makes her the subject of analysis, a potential agent of the hysteric's discourse, which is essential for the experience to begin. In neurosis *jouissance* appears as a phantasmatic dramatization difficult to confess—a perverse imagery that could make her seem abnormal, contemptible, a pig that thinks only about nasty things. It is clear that this indecent inner theater allows her to play with the interest it may arouse in the Other, taking or being taken as an object of his phantasm. With a bathroom perversion (and not de Sade's bedroom), she makes herself desirable, lovable, a condition for *jouissance* . . . of the Other. She only wants to be loved. Perversion would make the job easier. The perverse plot on the phantasmatic stage is key in the hysteric's intrigue and the obsessive's strategy. What perversion? Any, all, whatever suits him or her.

However, this neurotic *jouissance* is unrealizable and condemned to the closet; it can be acted out from time to time, not always, not in all cases, but its staging is always a disappointment: forced, experienced as submission to the designs of a real pervert or a challenge to the feelings of guilt, shame, and disgust that surround and drown out an act that is fantasized more than acted out. What's more, her rejection of perverse acting in which she occasionally participates allows her to make her virtue self-evident. The neurotic's excursions in the field of perversion are not infrequent but are characterized by leaving the impression that they point more toward eventual guilt than present *jouissance*. It is not the acting that distinguishes neurosis from perversion, but the position of the subject in reference to this acting. It is not the phantasm either, because it exists in both cases and it is difficult to say who takes the lead. It is not the drive, whose catalogue is written by the neurotic, such as Freud did without having to recur to Kraft-Ebbing.

I have already signaled where the difference lies. It should surprise no one that it is in discourse, given that clinical structures are discursive facts, relations to the Other, subjective positions, as we prefer to say. They

are in fact relations to the unconscious, the instance that I translate literally from the German as the unknown: the unknown (*Unbewusst, l'insu,*
in French), knowledge (*savoir*) that one ignores (*l'insu qui sait*). Neurosis
and perversion (and psychosis, as well) are modalities of relations with
savoir materialized in discourse.

Except that the pervert's discourse is rarely heard by the analyst,
and for good reason. If the neurotic, as we've already said, comes to the
clinic to acquire knowledge allowing her to recover lost *jouissance,* complains about the Other who does experience *jouissance,* and shamefully
imagines him shameless, the pervert assumes the opposite position: the
positive of the neurotics' negative. He lives for *jouissance,* knowing how
much can be known of one's own and the other's *jouissance*: preaching
the gospel, affirming his rights to the body, flaunting his control. What
is lack and debt in one is possession and knowledge in the other. This
being the case, why would the pervert allow someone else to occupy the
place of the subject supposed to know? What could he possibly expect
(aside from advice and prescriptions that the analyst rejects in principle)
from the other's word?

Later I will discuss the relation between perversion and love, but
I can now say that in the pervert love gets confused with eroticism, the
ability and technique of the body: such is for him the dictionary definition
of the word "love." Is there space then for transference love, which ties
and unties the knots of an analysis? How should the techniques of the
body be inscribed in the experience of an analysis that relies on chatting
(*bavardage*)? There are substantial reasons here then for how rare and
difficult it is to analyze a real "pervert." From the start, there is a structural
missed encounter and noncorrespondence between the will to *jouissance*
and the desire of the analyst.

The reversal of positions regarding knowledge is also a reversal of
positions regarding psychoanalysis. The analyst is attracted to the evasive
discourse of perversion and watches over it, satisfied with pale substitutes:
literature (Sade and Masoch; Masoch and Sade; Gide, Genet, Mishima),
especially the perverse fantasies of the neurotic, or the accounts of neurotics at the hands of a pervert, which makes them live and relive infantile
sexual traumas and at the same time condemns them to silence.

The relation between the analyst and the pervert is uncertain,
precarious—always on the brink of interrupting the analysis, driven
to contradictory extremes regarding the place of the analyst, which is
complicity (with) and a challenge to perversion. If the pervert represents

the masquerade of approaching an analyst, as custodian of unconscious knowledge and the law of sexuality, the guarantor of proper conduct and arbiter of mental health, he lies in wait for the moment when he is able to defy those supposed ideals. The moment in which, seeing or believing the analyst to personify any one of those functions, is able to challenge him with the formula that defines him, defiance: "And why not?" Reason enough to maintain neutrality in those cases where hesitation, far from being advisable (like in hysteria and obsessive neurosis), leads to the fall of the analyst and any possible analysis. Inscription is only possible in this way for the pervert because passivity is proof of seduction and complicity, while activity is a challenge that reinforces his position.

In reference to the other, the pervert acts by gathering evidence of the subjective split at the very limit of fading, the recognition of a lack that, both as curiosity and desire to know, the pervert wishes to fill. Autoeroticism does not interest him, only the demand for participation (of the other, victim or public) or of the analyst, if the case presents itself. If the pervert provokes a "becoming neurotic" in the analyst, the latter's displacement to the hysteric's discourse, it is clear evidence of a perverse position.

It is not a question of attaining knowledge. The issue is how to disavow ignorance, among other things: the gap that condemns the sexual relation and its associated *savoir*. We are taking the first steps to progressively determine perversion's disavowal (*Verleugnung*). The pervert cannot invest the analyst as a subject supposed to know (beware the analyst who insists in occupying that place!) because the supposed knowledge is the subject's own ego. What he ignores with his knowledge is that one cannot know about sex, and what he considers truths are only "sexual theories," phantasms, chimeras that bring together things heard and seen, shreds of a variety of discourses: a collage of science, ideology, illusion, laws, and commands.

Faced with what cannot be known regarding sex, the pervert proclaims an imaginary control over the knowledge that is lacking; he fills in the gaps with rationalizations, projections, and wishful thinking. No surprise is possible. What is considered a successful interpretation quickly enters into one of two complementary categories: either "it is not so" or "I already knew that." Knowing all that can be known, the only possible remainder is the Other's error.

What does he know? He knows what he wants: to experience *jouissance*. While for the neurotic the place of desire is sealed off by the unknown and in the psychotic the question does not even exist, in the pervert desire is called "a will to *jouissance*," and the only problem he finds is the means to obtain it. He represents himself as knowing about desire and *jouissance*, unifying and thus resolving their original contradiction. This assurance makes him attractive and fascinating to the neurotic who aspires only to find someone able to solve the equation of desire, to convert her question into a demand for subjection. Being the negative of the pervert, the neurotic dreams with making herself positive, acquiring phallic value from someone who positions himself beyond castration and, at some point, becoming the object he lacks. The neurotic would like to learn from the pervert and shake off the burden of her inhibitions. The pervert seduces the neurotic with his phantasm of *savoirjouir* (*jouissance* know-how). This is a predominant clinical characteristic that prevails in the pervert's discourse: a preconscious phantasm of reaching *jouissance* through knowledge and power over an inanimate object, reduced to vile abjection or shackled by a contract.

To stage this phantasm, he must know-how in the Other: produce, seduce, or induce his complicity or terror. In order to reach this goal, he must apply himself and risk it all, show himself and hide, know how to handle reality: the *semblant*. It is a question of making the phantasm function and succeed where the neurotic always fails. The phantasm must be staged in order to make believe in a *jouissance* that castration orders should be renounced. This is another disavowal, the lack in *jouissance*, which gives new meaning to the *Verleugnung* Freud saw as an essential mechanism of perversion in fetishism as well as in psychosis.

The theater clearly represents reality; theater and reality, the phantasm and *semblant* mask the real, the impossible, the absence of the sexual relation. Reality is not the real, and verisimilitude is not verity (*veritas*); to make one stand for the other takes "consideration of the means of staging" (E, 425), figurability, *Rucksicht auf Darstellbarkeit*, the third aspect of the dreamwork for Freud. The blood must be very red; discourse must not present errors or lapses. The pervert disavows the unconscious, which is always ambiguous and equivocal. There is no room for chance; everything must be in its place. The ritual must be perfectly stipulated by the contract or edict; nothing of the real can be filtered into the montage.

The pervert is a conscientious *metteur en scène* (director)—contrary to the hysteric who observes what she does on stage from the balcony, or the obsessive who demands recognition from the balcony for his ridiculous exploits. With care for detail, the proscription of the unconscious, a premeditated play with the law and transgressions, the pervert is, of all the characters that pass through the analytic stage, the most adapted to reality. He is perfectly integrated in discourse, convincing and logical: not only an expert in the twists and turns of the laws, but also legalistic and a legislator. He teaches and preaches, catechizes and persuades. His kinship with the position of judge, teacher, priest, politician, and doctor is evident, as well as with the psychoanalyst; this link is structural, although later we will discuss the differences as well.

This is how we find him, set in reality, dedicated to making the latter a screen to hide what is lacking, proclaiming expertise, knowledge, law, fetish objects, philosophical systems, esoteric doctrines, meta-languages, promises of paradise on earth and beyond, idols and illusions—letting us know why we cannot know. He erects phalluses because castration exists and is intolerable: the Other's castration, that is. We find this in Freud since 1927 (SE XXI, 147), but it can even be read in the minutes of the Wednesday meetings in Vienna. On February 24, 1909, Freud presented the case of a clothes fetishist:

> The patient became a speculative philosopher, and names play for him an especially great role. In this patient something similar to what took place in the erotic domain occurred in the intellectual domain; he turned his interest away from things onto words, which are, so to speak, the clothes of ideas; this accounts for his interest in philosophy.[2]

Since Freud's discovery, this is the pervert's way of dealing with castration: disavowal, the imaginary conversion of himself, any object or ideal into the representative of a *jouissance* the Other lacks or the phallus that represents the lost *jouissance* as a signifier in the symbolic.

Perversion's civilizing function (sublimatory, auto-, alloplastic) is undeniable, even when it assumes a contesting, subversive or disintegrating stance. By constructing an ideal contrary to the dominant ideal (one law against another), he activates the Hegelian dialectic that ends with the cunning of reason.

The Perverse Phantasm: *Savoirjouir*

Disavowal would not be possible were the pervert to recognize what is disavowed from the beginning ("I know very well, but nevertheless"). Precisely because castration has been inscribed and he must face the desert of *jouissance*, his phantasm can be staged, sustained by a homogenous discourse that negates an irreparable difference between discourse (always *semblant*, reduced to what is plausible) and *jouissance*.

His phantasm is not hybrid and does not aimlessly roam between one side and the other (between the unconscious and preconscious) as Freud describes (SE XIV, 188). Horrified by the void, the pervert is a proprietor in the fortified fortress of the ego. This *horror vacui* makes the subject a collector of specular totalities: control of desire, discourse, the other—hence his very strong ego. Disavowal affects castration, the unconscious, and the lack in *jouissance*. What he wishes to hide is thus revealed. The bandage covers the cut at the price of signaling its presence and location. One must distrust a phantasm that is so substantial and arrogant or when a subject waves the flag of his phantasm, instead of being its effect. As Freud noted, the certainty the fetish and its by-products bring serves to emphasize the cracks: the castration of the mother, the desiring incompleteness of the Other, the dangers that threaten the throne and altar. For this reason we can affirm that a perverse phantasm is a screen phantasm of concealment: the specular construction of an ego that represents himself as a subject supposed to *savoirjouir*.

The pervert's position requires putting this supposition to the test. Desire is per-verted and deflected ever so slightly as a will to *jouissance* that barely stitches up the lack. The lack is intolerable, a veritable Medusa's head. By disavowing desire, he renounces and relinquishes it. Since desire is on the side of the Other, to desire is to exhibit lack and offer that lack to the Other's lack: in other words, to recognize that a reciprocal castration is the condition for its traversal.

Herein lie the difficulties when defining the pervert's relation to love. If, with Lacan, we accept that love is giving what one does not have (to give what one has is charity); if love is giving what lacks, castration, the gap in *jouissance* and if, as Lacan notes, we accept that love is the only thing that can make *jouissance* condescend to desire, we immediately recognize the difficult relation between love and perversion. A difficult relation does not imply absence or impossibility. Although frequently denied, we have always known that the word "love" has multiple meanings, depending on its use by a man or by a woman. We can develop this idea and say that the word "love" also has different meanings depending on the subjective position of the one who speaks (neurotic, psychotic, "normal" or pervert). It is not a question of deciding if perverts can "also" love, but of understanding the specificity of love when instead of acting as a pivot there is a disavowal of lack. Following Lacan's teaching, I posit this for now. At the end of this chapter I propose and develop that what is disavowed in perversion is not an absence, but something that actually *exists*.

Freud defined love as the (im)possible convergence between two opposing tendencies in erotic life: tenderness and sensuality. Neurosis and perversion are again presented here as negative and positive. The neurotic divides love by renouncing sensuality (repression) in favor of tenderness, thus inhibiting the drive's aim to *jouissance*. She gives up *jouissance* in favor of an equivocal and misplaced desire because it has been substituted by the demand of the Other, who now occupies the place of object in the phantasm. She complains about the emptying out of *jouissance* she provokes and is reluctantly consoled by restrained gestures of tenderness. This road is marked by impotence, submission, dissatisfaction, and justifications. The pervert, on the contrary, renounces impotence and impossibility, dreaming and affirming the possibility of *jouissance*. He dismisses tenderness in name of a sensuality that claims to be unbridled and lawless. Instead he announces another law: the lack of consideration and abuse of the other, beyond consent: a categorical and apathetic law ordered by *jouissance* as Supreme Good. Not without the other, for sure, given that his violation is needed to access the *jouissance* of the body—one's own, since one cannot experience *jouissance* in the body of the other.

This is the common measure that unifies what is phenomenologically diverse in the field of perversion: rape, pedophilia, necrophilia, voyeurism, exhibitionism, sadism, masochism, homosexual modalities in fleeting and anonymous encounters. Further, a love life characterized by dissociation and degradation is what allows us to distinguish between perversion and homosexuality as a modality of (love) object choice. The homosexual act is a behavior and the reason why it is an ethical choice, not a diagnostic category. The essence of a so-called "pervert's" love life resides in a disconnection that seeks *jouissance* without having to go through the desire of the Other, thus abolishing the dimension of tenderness. The consent and convergence with the desire of the *partenaire* restricts perverse satisfaction. For this reason there is no complementarity in the perversions. The sadist is not the masochist's couple; neither is the exhibitionist the *voyeur*'s. If there is a coincidence in *jouissance*, the subjective split of the *partenaire* is not produced, which is the preferred aim of the perverse act. That is why the neurotic is the pervert's ideal and destined partner.

He is also the one who informs the analyst regarding what occurs in the couple ("beauty and the beast").

We find another difficult relation between perversion and love. Desire is converted into will to *jouissance*; eros becomes learned doctrine, eroticism: expertise in the body, know-how, a search for the hidden sources of *jouissance*, a rejection of the monotonous channels for sexual encounters, invention and sampling, exploration, violation and stretching limits. "And why not?" In this sense, perverse discourse fulfills a civilizing function by making sexuality independent of the utilitarian functions of reproduction and satisfaction. It denounces a supposed sexual "necessity" by unlinking *jouissance* from the bonds of pleasure and, showing other horizons, challenges unifying short circuits and conventions in the organization of love, all at the risk of actually incurring in the sin of changing one master for another or by creating new gospels for obtaining a "good" or "better" *jouissance*. For a long time, eroticism has been considered the patrimony of perverse discourse, a form of the social link that affirms the fundamental right to *jouissance* and errs, due to what we've already discussed regarding the phantasm. It claims it possible to experience *jouissance* of the Other's body, an alien body from which we only receive signals, ambiguous information to interpret, signifying elements whose meaning escapes us. Eroticism has had formative value therefore by agreeing with psychoanalysis that there is no universal *jouissance*. It decentralized the monopoly on phallic *jouissance* and raised questions regarding each one's particular *jouissance*, ejecting the eye of God or the gaze of the police from the bedroom.

Displacing love for eroticism, the pervert "barely accentuates the function of desire in man" (E, 697). This "barely" leads us to a structural difference of capital importance. The phantasm that responds to desire includes castration, the $-\varphi$ that shadows object @, cause of desire, while the pervert shows himself as the owner of an autonomous phantasm, allowing him to short-circuit the road that makes one pass through the Other and his desire, the reciprocal castration of the *partenaires* in love.

The excessive "barely" places the "pervert" beyond desire, destined to exercise a will that acts like a universal imperative; this is what connects Sade and Kant. This will is neither free nor a whim, being instead the opposite of freedom: an a-critical submission, exasperated and apathetic to an absolute norm that ferociously commands and limits movement through alternative roads. In perversion there is a will to make *jouissance* a rational and unavoidable principle of action, placed in a dialectics of reciprocal opposition and subtraction of *jouissance* between participants in the perverse act. It is a will that is not born from decisions based on desire, but from coercion, which demands escaping the Oedipal law, castration, the division of *jouissance*(s)—a will that makes the pervert live for *jouissance*: control, organize, administer, anticipate, or defer it, regulate its rise and fall. This is why psychoanalysis can thank perversion (as well as hysteria, obsession and psychosis, and "mental health") for what it contributes to discourse, but not by idealizing perversion or any other "clinical structure." At the end of an analysis the subject does not find perversion, but freedom regarding the perverse act. The subject of an ethics of analysis will have a place, as the subject of *bien dire* who must decide if he wants what he desires (E, 571). The "barely" of Lacan's quote reveals that in perversion the lack in the Other is disavowed—maternal castration, said Freud, S(Ⱥ), wrote Lacan. In place of that lack, the object @ is converted into a fetish and plug, an object that does not include nor affirm castration, but disavows it instead, contrary to what occurs when the "barely" is missing.

Castration is at stake here: "*jouissance* has to be refused." If the refusal is refused, a possibility is affirmed: being the agent of a nonprohibited *jouissance*. However, this is precisely how to miss it, having to be refused "in order to be attained on the inverse scale of the Law of desire" (E, 700). Lacan's definition of castration opposes castration to *jouissance* (as is shown on the upper part of the graph of desire). I will return to this point in chapter 8 on ethics and *jouissance*, but it is clear that an ethics of analysis is centered on concordance between desire and *jouissance*: the questioning but not the pursuit of that small "surplus" that "barely" accents the function of desire (in men but not in women). Of course, centering ethics on desire as a road to approaching *jouissance* leads us to point out the difference with Hegel's philosophy of right, as we saw in chapter 1. Mentioning Hegel implies making reference to the master's discourse.

Perversion is the refusal, by disavowal, to convert the values of *jouissance* into the currency of desire. Freud called clinging to modes of primary, infantile *jouissance* "fixation": a refusal to convert and translate it into words, to articulate the @ by way of unstable signifiers of demand, with the inevitable loss. The conversion of *jouissance* to desire as a condition for re-finding *jouissance* is inconceivable in the perverse position, the object of another *Verleugnung*. The pervert loses when he refuses to lose because in this game the one who loses wins. It is by speaking, putting things into words, how one loses, fatally.

However, desire is not absent in perversion; it is barely perverted. As in other *parlêtres*, desire gives rise to the phantasm and, in his particular case, the renunciation of *jouissance* was already produced (the reason he is not psychotic); all disavowals and all the king's horses and all the king's men cannot place Humpty Dumpty back up on the high wall. The pervert knows very well that *jouissance* must be renounced, "but even so" he lives trying to reach it. Desire divides him, makes him a subject, $ (E, 700), and even though that desire is converted into a will to *jouissance*, it is still, as in anyone else, a mechanism of defense "against going beyond a limit in *jouissance*" (E, 699).

In his case, desire does not confirm the lack but is denied precisely where the prohibition to *jouir* appears: in the Other. The Other cannot and must not be castrated; the premise of the phallus (and its *jouissance*) must be sustained as universal (and exclusive). However, unable to ignore the castration of the Other, S(Ⱥ), and being inhabited by –φ, the pervert resolves the predicament by covering up –φ, making himself the instrument of the Other's *jouissance* (E, 697). He places himself in the imaginary, outside his own subjective division, as if he were that Other having to ensure her non-castration (E, 699). From then on he lives in relation to that mission, offering his services in order to secure the *jouissance* of the Other (the third on the scene), who is threatened by inescapable castration. His perverted desire leads him to become a tool for the *jouissance* of the Other. This is what gives form to the Sadian phantasm, whose structure Lacan provides in "Kant with Sade" (E, 653), drawing it as a broken vector.

We will not review the schema nor linger on the modification that accounts for the Sadian phantasm because it is not pertinent here, but it is worth pointing out its most prominent clinical application. The pervert who wishes to be seen and considers himself an absolute subject, both bearing and providing *jouissance* (an unbarred being), is led by the logic of the structure and his desire to turn himself into an object, an instrument and complement at the service of the Other. He is the fetish he reveres, the whip that flays his victim, the contract that enslaves the flogger; he is the gaze that comes and goes in the two scopic perversions (voyeurism and exhibitionism). In sum, he is @, which positivizes the phallus, negates the lack of the phallus, ensures that *jouissance* becomes phallic in the Other. This is what leads me to modify the Freudian and Lacanian conception of disavowal. The Other to whom the so-called pervert dedicates himself is not—although he may not want to acknowledge it—an absolute Other outside *jouissance*. The Other is the site of a *jouissance* that is proper to him but unknown to the pervert—a *jouissance* that is possible precisely because of the lack of the organ that, for him, imaginarizes the phallus. I will return to this point later in the chapter.

A subject is essentially unstable and vacillating. The place of the subject is uncertain because he is the effect of what is articulated in the signifying chain: at the mercy of the word to come, which will signify him (*a posteriori, après-coup*) and show his tenuous condition. The pervert refuses to identify himself in so precarious a manner, dependent on the response the Other gives to his words, his demands. He rejects the division imposed by making his demand for drive satisfaction become articulated with the desire of the Other. In this he is also the positive of the negative neurosis. While the neurotic lives by personifying the question posed to the Other regarding his desire and demanding the Other make a place for him, the pervert constitutes himself as a response; his demand is not a question but an imposition categorically forced on his *partenaire*. He is the cause for which the other divides himself. He thus suffers the metamorphosis that transforms him into an object and an instrument, but not a subject subjected to the fluctuations of the signifying chain.

He identifies with the real that makes *jouissance* accessible to the Other, with surplus *jouissance*, the cause of desire of the Other: he becomes object @. This identification cannot exist in a void; it needs a *partenaire*, an other, a subject that experiences subjective division and fading as an effect of perverse manipulation. The child who is raped or seduced, the exhibitionist's terrified spectator, the humiliated hysteric, the flogger who must act against his most intimate convictions in order to satisfy the masochist's contract—these are all examples of the forcing of the split to the point of fainting in a staging so atrocious it goes beyond the borders of consciousness, modesty, and disgust. That other is not good when he is complacent, but only when violated, resistant, supplicant. When the other consents, the perversion vanishes.

Thus considered, perversion is the opposite of what the pervert thinks he is and does. The phantasm that screens the ego and treats the other as an object of its actions, reveals, beyond the imaginary, that the opposite is true: the pervert is the object and the victim the subject of *jouissance*; the latter transcends the barriers to pleasure because of the pervert's manipulations and finds *jouissance* beyond it. The paradox is that the pervert, will to *jouissance*, who lives according to an imaginary *savoirjouir*, ends up revealing *jouissance* on two opposite sides: on the Other's whose lack is disavowed and the other's whose *jouissance* is reached through pain and suffering. Wishing and imagining himself the master of ceremonies, the pervert is actually the object of his passion. He loses the rewards promised and gives up what he wishes to take away. *Jouissance* slips away in the very accomplishment of the pervert's deliberate, conscientious, and willful act. The *jouissance*-like substance that escapes him is what surges in the one who suffers his exactions. The formula of the phantasm is thus inverted, expressed in Lacan's schema in the following way:

$$d \rightarrow @ \lozenge \$ \qquad \text{(E, 653)}$$

Desire (*d*) leads the pervert to identify with the object (@), placing him in relation to a cut, an impossible encounter with the subject (\$) in its division and possible *jouissance*. Contrary to what may be expected at the end of an analysis, the pervert does not carry out his desire and cannot decide if he wants what he desires. Desire has controlled him, submitting him to an imperative more inflexible than the Law, which he challenges. Is it surprising, then, that the one who demands an analysis is not the "pervert," but rather the real subject, his supposed victim? Why not justify perversion and propose it as a desirable goal? Due to the jealousy proper to neurotics distanced from *jouissance*, in order to defend traditional values? These are inevitable questions that complement and redouble the classic pervert's retort: "and why not?" The ethics of psychoanalysis is implicated in the response.

As we've already seen, the will to *jouissance* misses the mark because it is unaware that the premise of *jouissance* is castration and accepting the Law of desire; *savoirjouir* is only a phantasm that, like all phantasms, intervenes and presents a barrier to *jouissance*. The pervert insists and in so doing demonstrates his defense; he "also" interposes his desire on the road to *jouissance* instead of travelling down the road of desire in order to reach *jouissance* (E, 699). The ego is unaware of its own function in this lack of knowledge when it purports to place itself above the insuperable barrier between *savoir* and *jouissance*: more than in any other case, in perversion the ego is on the side of reality and the *semblant*. As Lacan notes: "there is only access to reality because the subject is an effect of *savoir*, but *savoir* is a phantasm made by *jouissance*. Still, because it is *savoir*, it necessarily misses reality" (CR1, 14).

Given that it is *savoir*, it must articulate the signifiers that constantly produce the real as impossible and escape the apprehension of truth; it also seeks to impose itself as a social link, a discourse that attempts to negate the lack on which it is necessarily based. The pervert makes the case because he is a pedagogue, a demonstrator, eternal proof of his thesis' justification: "It's a little too preachy" (E, 664). His discourse, centered on *jouissance*, thus emphasizes the lack in *jouissance* precisely because it is said and does not adhere to the now classic advice to keep silent regarding what cannot be said. With words of certainty, the categorical imposition of what he considers true, the pervert distances himself from the words that could question or modify his position. He cannot complain about his state because it emerges from a choice he considers reasoned and reasonable. His desire and will depend on a conjecture regarding the *jouissance* of the body: "a pure act of understanding that reasons in the silence of the passions about what man can demand of his fellow man and about what his fellow man can rightfully demand of him."[3] He lives for *jouissance*; it is his choice. Psychoanalysis cannot question it from the outside, and from inside it is unquestionable: putting it into question is incompatible with the position questioned. Such is the impasse and aporia of perversion for the psychoanalyst, not for the pervert.

His wager consists in always knowing more about bodily possibilities beyond the impossible sexual relation. In a phantasmatic scene, he dreams with replacing in the real what castration forced him to give up. He disappears as a subject in order to be, from the position of object, the master of *jouissance*, invulnerable to a division that he transfers to the other. He tirelessly attempts to make *jouisssance* pass through the gap in discourse and thus control it. Now we must draw the consequences of what we've discussed.

Perversion and Feminine *Jouissance*

As noted earlier, the pervert fears the void, the lack in knowledge. His plans materialize when *jouissance* becomes doctrine and the body an experimental field where knowledge pulls the strings of sexuality. He thus becomes (in the imaginary, at least) the nuclear physicist of libido who administers and governs its energy, deciding its use and economy. The horror of the void in knowledge means having all the answers, particularly (this is the stumbling block) being able to respond to the age-old question regarding what a woman wants. This question tormented Tiresias precisely because he claimed to have the answer . . . and Freud as well, even after so many vain attempts at a response.

If we return to Freud's (perverse?) thesis that there is only one (masculine) libido, and only one (male) genital that organizes infantile genitality around the alternative phallic/castrated; if we accept that in theory (as knowledge) the question regarding *jouissance* is answered by affirming the phallus as a signifier and its privileged function: to conjugate (put under a common yoke) logos and desire; if we adhere to the Freudian conception of human sexuality, we cannot fail to notice that at the heart of this theory there is a great hole through which a flow of *jouissance* that does not accept the common yoke of word and phallus escapes. In summary, on the side of women there is a supplemental *jouissance* in relation to phallic *jouissance*. Although we already discussed this in chapter 3, it is worthwhile to recall it and search for the essence of perversion around this point.

For *savoirjouir* to be possible it is necessary that all that is sexual be under the aegis of the phallic signifier and that women be "all" instead of "not-all": that The woman exist as a symmetrical equivalent, the opposite or negation of the man; and that feminine sexuality be reduced to the homogeneity of *jouissances*(s) through some sort of equation. Freud realized that he could not answer the question regarding what a woman wants; his response—the "phallus" (*Penisneid*)—did not resolve the issue: it just opened the space to a *beyond*. Lacan responded by saying that the question needed to always remain open because women are not absent from phallic *jouissance* but are also tributaries of another *jouissance*: an Other *jouissance*, supplemental, felt but ineffable, enigmatic, not exhausted in the discourse of knowledge, crazy (the man's is called "perverse"), and beyond the phallus (S XX). This *jouissance* that is not only different but also opposed and rival to phallic *jouissance*: "female sexuality appears, instead, as the effort of a jouissance enveloped in its own contiguity . . . in order to be *realized in competition* with the desire that castration liberates in the male giving him the phallus as its signifier (E, 619, original emphasis). Freud's acknowledged ignorance becomes a necessity in Lacan because it responds to a lack in the structure: the signifier of The woman as equivalent counterbalance of phallic *jouissance*. There is a lack in knowledge that refers to an impossible knowledge, beyond the phallus. What is ungraspable is not inexistent; it is not a lack, but rather an excess: a surplus *jouissance* that knowledge wants to delimit, enclose, localize, extirpate, making it an object of discourse and control.

The pervert's position regarding knowledge of feminine sexuality is as interesting as Freud's and Lacan's because it puts an end to a question they introduced and condenses the position congruent with the master's discourse as the other side, the reversal of psychoanalytic discourse. The pervert proclaims *savoirjouir*, disavows the lack in knowledge, the unconscious, and the phallus lacking in the Other; he sutures all the gaps. Up until now, following Freud, we maintained the essence of perversion to be a disavowal (in the past, *Verleugnung* was translated as denial or rejection) of castration that puts the phallus in danger, his throne and altar. Bound to his refusal of a part of reality, the subject thus removes himself from his uncertain place in order to recover the certainty the object provided, the becoming instrument of a *jouissance* he then ensures with his acts. Now, considering Lacan's formulas of sexuation and recent scholarship in what was earlier called the "dark continent" of femininity, we must put aside our previous conception of perversion.

Today many authors believe the word "perversion" should be eliminated from the vocabulary because it gives way to segregation. Personally, I feel disgust for psychiatric and psychopathological classifications, but think that psychoanalysis produces their reversal and shows their reactionary underpinnings. That is why the creators of the DSM-V and other monstrosities of the same kind wish to banish psychoanalysis' vocabulary and conceptions from their taxonomies. They are succeeding, but should we follow them?

With Freud and Lacan we have said there is a disavowal of lack in perversion. However, we can now say there is no such lack, but the presence of something that is beyond, not reached by the order of discourse that seeks to organize *jouissance* in reference to the phallic signifier and *semblant*. Perversion, which is clinically found on the masculine side (and gives rise to so many discussions regarding a possible "feminine perversion"), led Lacan to say that the masculine sex is the weak sex regarding perversion because its position is to make *jouissance* and the phallus equal (E, 697). Logically, if women are, they are unable to accept the equation *jouissance* = phallus. They can only be perverse if they take this position regarding knowledge. There are some cases, but not many. It is not uncommon to find this equation and feminine perversion when, in a homosexual couple, one of its members approaches an analyst with her demand, while the other sustains the perverse position in which only the phallus allows for *jouissance*. In these cases one wonders if it is pertinent to speak of "feminine perversion" given that man or woman is not an anatomical fact, but a subjective position, and our patient's *partenaire* is the one to occupy the masculine position. Her identification with the phallus and disavowal of feminine *jouissance* makes one woman encounter another woman, converting her into the object @ of her phantasm.

Perversion is on the masculine side and claims to know the price for disavowing truth. Truth, which is woman (Nietzsche with Lacan); the truth that unmasks the phallus as *semblant*, a displacement of the real through language, that reveals what speaks but does not say the truth, that disguises it with the attire of the *semblant* and the phantasm: truth is always half-said. The existence of another *jouissance* (that is not more or less) has always been recognized, but the unknown was covered over with circumlocutions regarding "the mystery of femininity," which concerns men and women. The function of knowledge has been to try to circumscribe and reduce that mystery by localizing feminine *jouissance* (even in Freud's clitoral and vaginal *jouissance*), conceiving it as equivalent to masculine *jouissance*, subjecting it to the model of the orgasm, positing imaginary cycles of erection and detumescence, experimenting with electrodes in the brain, counting the nerve endings in the anterior and posterior mucous membrane, measuring secretions and humidity, counting the days in a cycle and manipulating them with Fliess's calculations, regulating hormones and neurotransmitters, recommending massages and techniques of sexual gymnastics. There's more, but the solution does not come from knowledge; the discourse of the master here shows its most radical impotence.

A perverse response to the hysteric's question is found in master and university discourses, not in the analyst's. The former appeal to universality, reducing the enigma to a signifier (phallic, of course). What is disavowed is not castration but the *jouissance* of women, the Other sex. The perverse postulate is that women do not experience *jouissance* because they are at the disposal of the *jouissance* of the phallus-penis. If they can, it is because they are totally included in phallic *jouissance*, homogeneous with the man's. In both cases the only possible *jouissance* is phallic *jouissance*. Women are either nullified or disavowed in their particularity. We must again recognize that perversion "barely" accentuates the function of desire in a man. Its essence is the disavowal of feminine *jouissance*; this implies replacing an enigma with a phantasm: *savoirjouir*.

The hostile *jouissance* of the Other, *jouissance à l'envi* (defying) phallic *jouissance*, is unbearable: the Medusa's head that leads to the phantasm. The pervert's activity makes *semblant* of sexual being. Actually, sex is just the pretext to demonstrate that *jouissance* of the body can be completely subjected to a *langagière* articulation that organizes "positions." The pervert's discourse regarding *jouissance* is just that, a discourse, the substitution of *jouissance* with mental experiments that reveal their artifice: calculated modes for dominating and blocking the *jouissance* of the Other sex. It seems to be a search, but it is just a disguise. The theater of subjective division rejected and displaced onto the Other conceals an escape from the uncontrollable, materialized in the fetish, the victim, the gaze, or the contract. The underlying *angst* comes through in the repeated and dull dramatizations, the boringly crushing and inane sermons for victims and tormentors we've all read in Sade, Lacan included.

The pervert's limit is not the Other's castration, as Freud taught us, but the inconceivable *jouissance* of the Other, which the pervert both makes manifest in its disavowal and excludes for himself. It is not his particular misfortune because he was, like everyone else, always already excluded. His error lies in having presumed otherwise. He would like to be master of the Thing from which he is exiled. It is when "he adds overseer to the phantasms that govern reality" (AE, 423). Psychoanalysis can act (and often does) to reinforce perversion by repeating the idea of a servile Golem as "autonomous Ego." The strength of the ego that organizes and directs love life is the perverse phantasm of a master who wishes to reduce an ungovernable desire to a rational will, to master the drives, the "instincts" as some say, the Id, and subject them to laws and logical principles. We must listen to Cicero, speaking some two thousand years before Freud, in a speech that claims the opposite of the pervert's: "Volition is a reasonable desire; but whatever is incited too violently in opposition to reason, that is a lust, or an unbridled desire, which is discoverable in all fools."[4] The lack in knowledge (regarding the *jouissance* of the Other, the *jouissance* of women) is disavowed; in the place of the void, the pervert sets up the exercise of power as overseer.

To conclude: in essence, perversion is an attempt to cure the lack in the sexual relation and the irreparable heterogeneity of *jouissance*(s). It implies a decision to suture, which is the antinomy of psychoanalysis' own discourse and aim: to not conceal the gap. It is characteristic of perversion to wish to plug up what is derived from the subject's unknown. For the pervert, encountering the unconscious would reveal the unfathomable chasm that leads him to give up on desire and replace it with the will of a strong ego, to renounce tenderness by dissociating erotic life. His only chance, from a psychoanalytic perspective, is that in pursuing *jouissance* he find impotence, as Freud's case from 1914 indicates.[5] But like the case of the young homosexual, there is not much to hope for. It is difficult to replace the will to *jouissance* for desire when the "only" thing that can be offered for this necessary passage through impotence is the recognition of a real impossibility at the end of the road. Nonetheless . . . why not?

Chapter 7

@-Diction of *Jouissance*

Psychosis Is Not Chosen

Before, after, and instead of. This is how *jouissance*(s) are positioned in speech, diction, and the regulation of relations with the Other. Before the word, but not outside language: the psychotic's *jouissance*. After speech: in the *parlêtre*—not necessarily neurotic, psychotic, or perverse (is that possible?)—*jouissance* passes through the flexible diaphragm of speech that curtails and subjects it to phallic signification, diverting it through metonymic desire and making it a correlate of castration. Traversing the barriers of narcissism and the pleasure principle, the historicizing drive inscribes the subject's passage through the world, leaving a mark on the Other, taking on its burden and contributing to the discontent in culture.

Instead of, instead of speech, reverse of speech: this is how *jouissance* congeals in the neurotic symptom and perverse dramatization, with the emblems of the strong ego, as they say. There is also a *jouissance* that insists, an accursed *jouissance*, on this side of speech, pure being in being, before the lack produced in a being to be said. Without addressing us, psychotics speak of this incommunicable *jouissance* that disregards the Other, is lodged in the body and outside symbolization. They show us that speech does not function as a regulating diaphragm; the subject is flooded and displaced by a deleterious *jouissance* that rebels against exchange; it is proliferating, invasive, and does not allow for an Other word to limit and restrain it.

If Φ is the signifier of a *jouissance* prohibited to the *parlêtre* as such, we are led to conclude that in psychosis the Phallus has not been symbolized. Consequently, *jouissance* is not emptied from the body; lack in being is not established: the subject cannot become a desiring subject. Without this

217

productive lack, or the imaginary function of the $-\varphi$, there is nothing to look for in the field of the Other. As we already know, but it is worthwhile repeating, the Phallus does not fulfill its function as signifier per se, but only through another signifier (the name-of-the-Father) that establishes a fundamental core, the signifier one (S_1), master signifier, which can be articulated to every other signifier (S_2) of unconscious *savoir*. The Phallus bars the Thing, giving way to the emergence of a subject represented by the signifier of the name-of-the-Father, thus allowing phallic signification (see chapter 2). If this core (the name-of-the-Father) is missing in its place, the branches come loose and there is no tree. This brief image is Lacan's notion of foreclusion, key to psychosis. There is no limit to *jouissance*, no disposal site for the articulated word. In these patients, the obstacle in the structure makes it difficult to knot together knowledge and love, which is central for the transference. Interpretation is pointless here, if not persecutory and dangerous. It is a question preliminary to any possible treatment of psychosis.

This situation, the destiny of being that cannot be said as inter-diction, is not within anyone's reach. One is not mad just for wishing it so. Freud spoke of *Neurosenwahl*, choice of neurosis, but never of psychosis as a choice. I think the lesson of psychosis is that it is not chosen. This affirmation is conclusive, although debatable and much discussed. Lacan's 1967 statement, "the madman is the only free man" is not sufficient.[1] This was the year of his seminar on the four discourses, where he brilliantly synthesized discourse as a social link (*lien social*). *Lien*: link, connection, bond. In this sense, it is not appropriate to speak of the madman as free; he is the only one who lives outside discursive chains, making enunciated speech pass through the Other's "tribunal" and awaiting its verdict. In his own language, outside the constraints of discourse, the madman is free. To be in discourse implies forming a link and losing freedom. Madness creates an exception, and because of this exception (an exterior space) discourses (four in Lacan) constitute a set.

In 1968 Lacan returned to what twenty years earlier he stated in "Presentation on Psychical Causality": "Not only can man's being not be understood without madness, but it would not be man's being if it did not bear madness within himself as the limit of his freedom" (E, 144). His position is clear: freedom has a limit, and the name of that border (the borderline) is madness, at which point freedom ends. Lacan added: "The psychotic presents himself as a sign, a sign at an impasse, which justifies the reference to freedom" (AE, 363). An impasse is what cannot be traversed from one side to the other, separating freedom from its absence.

There is no place for psychotic discourse, where speech would not be *semblant*, but directly placed between truth and the real (which Julia Kristeva called "vreal").[2] All discourse is *semblant* because, although it presents itself as true, it is not; it speaks about entities that would not exist if not for discourse giving them a *langagière* status (S XVIII, CS). Finally, all discourse is *semblant* because its agent (who addresses the other) is the *semblant*, the one who occupies the place of truth while putting it at a respectable distance: master, university, analyst, hysteric. The psychotic cannot be or make *semblant*, living outside it even when not prohibited from crossing its border and being heard.

This does not mean that the mad are free to choose. In fact, if he is in a psychotic state, others choose for him. He is only free of *having* to choose, which is what discourse forces us all to do, knowing that one cannot choose without losing and renouncing some *jouissance*. Psychosis "saves" the subject from having to go through symbolic castration: forced to displace *jouissance* from the body, to use discourse whose object is constituted as lost, exposed to the barriers to *jouissance* that attaches subjectivity to phallic signification and the impossible sexual relation. The madman is a subject in direct contact with the object, precisely because his relation with the latter is not mediated by metaphors and metonyms in the signifying chain. Hallucinations (coming from an unspeakable *real*) replace the function of the phantasm (which is *imaginary*) for subjects linked by speech in the *symbolic* register.

Madness shows an image of freedom that is alien to those considered "normal," the more or less neurotic or pervert, who defend themselves from the real through the imaginary and the symbolic. They cling to the narcissistic image and settle into a supposed "reality" made up of links between signifiers and arbitrary signifieds (meanings). Such a "reality" is nothing more than a phantasmatic formation shared by the "well-meaning," allowing them (us) the illusion they are not mad. We live in the kingdom of sense, but we are not senseless, whether we like it or not.

Without realizing, the mad (schizophrenics in particular) denounce the presumption of reason that excludes them from exchange in our culture and restricts them to the field of medicine, especially psychiatry, shutting them away and controlling their bodies with drugs. Psychoanalysis is thus confronted with a dilemma: to idealize the mad and madness as a paradigm of freedom or to objectify it as an "illness," justifying manipulations and isolation. Our approach is to denounce the falseness of this dilemma and show a different road, one congruent with the never-disavowed determinism in Freud and Lacan.

The risk is twofold: on the one hand, to reduce madness to a condition of animality, and on the other, a Buñuel-like phantasm of freedom, where those of us chained to the function of the signifier that represents us before another signifier end up constructing the notion that "the mad are free," an imaginary compensation for our own lack of freedom, our alienation.[3] The problem is that the madman is not master of his body, but hands it over to the Other, who appropriates it, as also happens with the drug-dependent or suicidal. His freedom is contained within asylum walls or miserable hotel rooms, where he is often sent and filled with prescription drugs. If the last free man or woman were mad, we would certainly envy them, but is this the case?

How does one come to be psychotic? Is it the choice of a subjective position, for which we are responsible, as Lacan says in "Science and Truth?" Neurosis, addiction, suicide, and perversion surely are. In reference to what the clinic teaches us, is this also the case for psychosis? To choose does not imply selecting an object to experience *jouissance*. If this were the case, one would accept the crude psychologism of the autonomous conscience. To choose is to accept loss and give up *jouissance*. The paradigm of choice, forced choice, is Lacan's well-known "your money or your life" (S XI, 203). The choice imposed on the subject excludes their conjunction. The psychotic is someone who can respond to the impossible: money *and* life; he does not accept the loss of *jouissance*. To choose implies the loss of the object, and once the curtailment (*écornement*) of *jouissance* is accepted, one can then choose the modes of relating to the object as lost. That is the sense of Freud's *Neurosenwahl*, but it is not the case for psychosis.

We must follow Lacan's thought on psychosis and find the moment of inflection in his teaching. It is true that Lacan spoke of psychosis as the "unfathomable decision of being" (E, 145, translation modified). This expression appears in the article dedicated to psychical causality, written at the request of Henry Ey in 1946, where Lacan confronts the veterinarian-like aspirations of "organodynamic psychology." The "unfathomable decision" is imbued with a Sartrean spirit that was dominant at that time, and although one may wish to deny it, openly contradicts Lacan's conception produced some ten years later, which spans from Seminar III on psychosis up to "On a question preliminary to any possible treatment of psychosis" (1958) (E, 445). Here the question of psychosis is centered on the concept of foreclusion and opposed to the notion of an "unfathomable decision." The new thesis posits the non-intervention of the paternal metaphor. The determinism proper to psychosis must be looked for in the relation of the subject with language: the signifier that functions as the lynchpin for all the articulations in the chain is missing and therefore all the other signifiers wander off course. The superhighway is blocked, and the subject roams through secondary roads where all signs speak for themselves. The discursive link becomes unleashed, as well as the Borromean and generational chains. The noise of broken links deafens the psychotic.

When the signifier of the name-of-the-Father is missing in its place, as the clinic teaches us, what remains is not a subject in absolute indetermination and freedom, but a subject submerged in ineffable *jouissance*, subjugated to the arbitrariness of the Mother's desire. The paternal metaphor is the effect of the function of the Mother's absence, whose place is occupied by the name-of-the-Father. This failed function and foreclusion is only produced, says Lacan at a Conference on Psychosis in Children (AE), when there is a link between three generations: this is the necessary condition to produce a psychotic child. The thesis of the three generations contrasts with the "unfathomable decision" twenty-five years earlier, adding to the comprehension of psychosis as a noncompensated defect in the knot of the Borromean chain (RSI), which Lacan developed in his seminars between 1974 and 1977.

The Father curtails the worst. There is no question of his being an impostor: the subject's submission to discourse is the effect of that imposture. Due to the intervention of the name-of-the-Father, the subject is dislodged from *jouissance*, the burning bush of the Thing. However, the Mother's desire is not an imposture; that is very real, the core of what we know as primal repression (*Urverdrängung*). We know its effects when the imposture fails and the subject cannot enter the formations (discursive and unconscious) that are *semblant*. The worst ensues, which is what any treatment of psychosis must avoid in order not to "toil at the oars when one's ship is stuck in the sand" (E, 485). Between the master's plan to confine and restrict the mad and the idealist's appeal to an unfathomed and phantasmatic freedom, the challenge for psychoanalysts is to find a third way. Freudian determinism and Lacan's structural causality indicate the direction to take.

Psychosis and Discourse

There is no escape for the psychotic, no possibility for a manageable, operational entry and exit from language's exchanges. His separation from the chain of signifiers is an effect, the consequence of a defect in the subject's symbolic chain. The psychotic is placed and places himself outside the discursive ring.

Writing about the psychoses in a general way is always problematic. There is a tendency to present a comprehensive model that alludes to what the clinic shows about patients diagnosed as psychotic from a medical perspective, but not necessarily from a psychoanalytic one. Thus, "psychosis" and "the psychotic" become schematic labels that mislead the clinician and reader instead of guiding him in the subjective process to be understood. Freud knew this well at the end of his life when he wrote a text us Lacanians often forget, with good reason. "An Outline of Psychoanalysis" states:

> The problem of psychoses would be simple and perspicuous if the ego's detachment from reality could be carried through completely. But that seems to happen only rarely or perhaps never . . . We may probably take it as being generally true that what occurs in all these cases is a psychical split. Two psychical attitudes have been formed instead of a single one—one, the normal one, which takes account of reality, and another which under the influence of the instincts [drives] detaches the ego from reality. (SE XXIII, 202)

One must always keep this *Spaltung* in mind. To speak or write about "psychosis" and "the psychotic" is to restrict oneself to one of two "psychical attitudes": one that has distanced itself from reality, the Other of the signifier, and ignores the constant presence of the other attitude, which is still linked to the Other. In no singular psychotic will one find what one author or another writes about the inexistent ideal model of "psychosis." This consideration is essential in order to justify the affirmation made above that, because of the failure of the paternal metaphor and the foreclusion of the name-of-the-Father, the psychotic is located outside discourse unless a *sinthome* allows a link through discourse. The foreclosure of the name-of-the-Father probably does not serve as an absolute model for any psychotic, but does have a general clinical value in reference to "psychosis."

The Lacanian definition of discourse as social link, the link being between bodies inhabited by language, is the essential means to access the psychoanalytic conception of subjective positions in general and psychosis in particular. We begin with the definition of the signifier and its realization in the productive center of all discourse, the master's discourse: "a signifier is what represents the subject before (or for) another signifier" (E, 694, translation modified). This is an incomplete definition, if one does not add "that leaves as production the remainder @," an elusive real that escapes the discursive articulation of S_1 and S_2. The subject \$, in the position of truth in this subjective articulation, is represented by a first signifier before the second.

The definition of signifier is written as the matheme of the master's discourse:

$$\frac{\text{agent}}{\text{truth}} \xrightarrow{\hspace{1cm}} // \quad \frac{\text{other}}{\text{production}} \qquad \frac{S_1}{\$} \xrightarrow{\hspace{1cm}} // \quad \frac{S_2}{@}$$

With a double bar of separation, between the space of truth and production, a cut is inscribed that marks the disjunction, the necessary missed encounter between the two elements. In reference to their places in the master's discourse, it becomes evident that a relation of cut or disjunction exists between the subject and the object; the writing thus produced is the phantasm, where the cut is indicated by the *losange* ◊: \$◊@.

How can this formula be applied to an understanding of psychosis? In Seminar XI, years before he detailed the mathemes of the four discourses, Lacan proposed that the key was to be found in the link between the two signifiers and in the interval that separates them: the before (*auprès*) or for (*pour*) the other signifier in the definition above. In psychosis, the S_1 does not represent the subject for S_2, either because there is no differentiation between both signifiers or because the syntax that could articulate them is broken. Such is the effect of foreclusion.

Due to the function of speech or discourse, a fugitive remainder of *jouissance* is obtained, @, which by definition is inaccessible to the subject. In psychosis, this function of speech and discourse is radically disrupted. The sedimentation or disarticulation of the two signifiers (this is our thesis) provokes the effect of a structural fault line in the constitution of the phantasm and a disruption in the relation between the subject \$ and the object, cause of desire @. Psychosis may well be a process whereby the interval in the signifying process is affected, but its effect for the subject is the hole in the constitution of the phantasm, in the member that corresponds to the interval in the matheme of the phantasm: the *losange* ◊. Lacan articulated the writing of the *losange* in three ways: as (1) a cut, (2) the unconscious, and (3) desire. The relation of the subject with the object of the phantasm can be expressed in three ways, and this is precisely what fails in psychosis. The *losange* is either missing or broken, and for this reason there is no phantasm. If the expression "psychotic phantasm" had to be preserved, the phantasm would need to be defined differently.

The function of the phantasm is to distance the subject from the object cause of desire, which is also the object of *jouissance* or *jouissance* as object. Thanks to the phantasm, the subject is protected from *jouissance*, which is kept at a respectable distance. In Lacan's formula, the *losange* is similar to the graphic image of a shop window (or a mirror) that separates the subject from the desired, prohibited, or dangerous object. Psychosis is the crack in the window; the subject is thus exposed to an overflowing *jouissance*.

Returning to the matheme of the master's discourse, which is also the definition of the signifier, we have to mention the anomalous situation found in psychosis: (1) S_1 and S_2 are congealed, an indistinct mass, one equivalent to the other, what Lacan designated as a *holophrase* (S I, 225); S_1 is constantly iterated. According to Lacan, this fixation is not only responsible for psychosis, but other processes as well, such as mental deficiencies and psychosomatic conditions. (2) S_1 and S_2 are disarticulated; they lack syntax and are inevitably separated. In both cases, discourse as a social link does not exist. Taking the master's discourse as template, we can write the relation of the psychotic to speech in the following manner:

$$\frac{S_1}{\$} \quad \overset{\Diamond}{\cdot} \quad \frac{S_2}{@}$$

This writing shows that the relation of disjunction, or cut, indicated by the losange ◊, has been displaced to the relation between S_1 and S_2. This cut no longer operates between the subject and *jouissance*; the barrier that ensures their separation and encourages the search for its recovery disappears. This is the function of the phantasm ($\$◊@$) as a response to desire, illustrated by the graph in "The Subversion of the Subject and the Dialectic of Desire" (E, 692). There is a double break in the psychotic: the break linking one signifier with another, and the break of the phantasm as barrier to *jouissance*. There is also a double effect in the clinic: the interruption of an intersubjective dialectic and an unstoppable encroachment of the *jouissance* of the Other, not subject to phallic regulation and the law that organizes desire.

Either *jouissance* or discourse. We said that Lacan almost never spoke about a subject of *jouissance*, although he did make two references. The first was in Seminar X (March 13, 1963) in order to posit a mythical beginning that ends in subjective division (the formula for subjective division and causation). The second was in 1966, when Lacan presented the French publication of Schreber's memories (AE, 215). He then wrote of the polarity between a subject of *jouissance*, on the one hand, and the subject, which a signifier represents for another signifier, always other, on the other.

Foreclusion intervenes in the relation between the signifier of the name-of-the-Father and the rest of the chain. Unlinked, the *parlêtre* is thrown adrift from discourse, dependent on the Other's response and having to signify himself through the latter's speech, to ex-sistance. That is why for the psychotic, in a psychotic position, speech is not a symbol, an invitation, or an invention of exchange; it does not function as the diaphragm of *jouissance*.

The signifier represents the subject who is not psychotic. The subject is in the place of the signified; he is the signified for another signifier. Never completely, because a remainder is left over: @. The articulation with the second signifier is missing in psychosis. The signifier substitutes the subject completely; it does not (re)present it, and that signifier need not be conjugated with another: there is a coalescence of the signifier and the subject (signified). There is no inassimilable rest as residue of the operation. The psychotic is invaded by *jouissance*, from which one is usually excluded, due to the non-coalescence between signifier and signified. Words are things for the psychotic, not the fleeting remainder that forces us to give continuation to the discursive chain. There is a signifier S_1 that represents the subject absolutely, one blends into the other, without reference or remedy and without the gap being symbolized. This is why we speak of psychotic *jouissance*, but not of psychotic desire. In "absolute," paradigmatic psychosis there is no lack in being able to mobilize discourse.

The psychotic does not keep a distance from *jouissance*; he inhabits and is identified with his *jouissance*. He is *jouissance*. A hallucination is not someone's perception; there is no distinction between *perceptum* and *percipiens*. Because the *losange* that distances the subject from the *jouissance* of object @ is missing, condensation occurs between the two terms of the phantasm. We should think of speech as analogous to a holophrase, which designates the coalescence between $ and @, whose most conspicuous example is a hallucination. In perception, the subject has an object before him and can submit it to the Freudian "proof of reality;" in a hallucination, the subject is fused and confused with his object. They are not two, but one: there is no relation of reciprocal exteriority.

In psychosis, *jouissance* is not localized in a certain part of the body. It is not restrained and limited by the phallic signifier, representative of $-\varphi$, which is what the body lacks in the desired image. In psychosis, *jouissance* invades the entire body, now transformed into a screen, where frightening metamorphoses are projected, leaving the subject stunned, reduced to being the passive stage for transformations that obey the obscure will of an omniscient Other that governs and regulates organic changes. Hypochondria, hallucinations of mandates, influences, persecution, magnetism, irradiations, transexualism, negation, putrefaction, making the body a corpse, where the Other's will rules, the same one that controls President Schreber's flesh for years on end.

Another effect of the phallus' (castration) nonregulation of *jouissance* in psychosis is that the paternal, Freudian side of the superego, heir to the Oedipus complex, does not emerge to propel toward the other woman as promise and possibility. The obscene and ferocious order of an archaic *jouissance* subsists: unrestrained and out of control, maternal, Kleinian, commanding the impossible *Jouit!*, the Thing's unlimited *jouit!*, before and on this side of castration.

Due to the subject's deficient inclusion in the symbolic order, he is not able to distance himself from the real as impossible. Consequently, a complete disorganization of the body's imaginary is produced. Against this backdrop of fragmentation and a radical disorder of existence, the restorative function of delirium is deployed. The latter attempts to link the subject in a signifying chain, allowing for an account of lived experience. The whole of psychotic experience is the effect of the signifiers' dispersion: unstructured and detached from the social link. The metaphor of delirium attempts to remedy the lack in the paternal metaphor by conferring signification to what is missing in the Other, to reinstate the subject in the networks of the social link: the connection (*Bindung*) between *jouissance* and speech.

Drug @-Diction

Psychosis is not a choice, but there is another method for a subject to withdraw from symbolic exchange: by employing a chosen object. This is a real choice. It allows an almost experimental connection with *jouissance* and functions as a short-circuit in relation to the Other and its desire. This method provides the subject a certain way in and out, a more-or-less regulated production of separation in relation to the effects of signifying alienation. This separation can also be complete, meaning an absolute rejection of signifying alienation. It is paradoxical that the Other, from whom the subject wishes to separate, puts this method at his disposal. In fact, it is a product of commerce: trafficked, proposed, and offered by the Other in exchange to satisfy the demand of radical separation, the destruction of the "I think" in favor of an "I am," without mitigation and beyond all thought. I am sure it is clear by now that I am speaking about drugs and their permanent effect on the subject: drug addiction.[4] Attempts at separation (from the Other), understood to be a logical operation opposed to alienation (in the Other), is key for penetrating the wild jungle of drugs, a specific characteristic of our lives and world at present. It is a reality whose presence will become increasingly important, especially as we are not able to set limits to the creation of new substances that reach and modify the organism without having to pass through the filter of subjectivity.

The most tumultuous way of separating from the Other is undoubtedly suicide, which we will discuss shortly. Drugs offer an alternative: their clamor is barely a murmur, the banging of the door a mere slipping away; arrogance turns into humility; what was dramatic is now reserved; the arrogance of suicide is embarrassing. A difference is immediately noticeable; with intoxication there is no death, just being given for dead. Here, there is no vindicated body handed over to the Other with scornful disdain, like an offering—rather, a degraded body exhibited in the misery of its organic servitude.

Suicide highlights the proper name and makes it its own, not offered to the Other. On the contrary, alcoholics are anonymous, insofar as they are inebriated, of course. However, we must not speak lightly or flippantly about any sort of (drug) addict. The use of alcohol and other drugs configure a "behavior," not a clinical structure. Such behavior can appear in neurotic, perverse, or psychotic subjects, and the way to psychoanalytically approach each case does not depend on the use of drugs, but on structural defenses that determine the direction of the cure. When one encounters the use of drugs presented openly, it is wise for the analyst to go backward in reference to this concealing tactic the subject uses to show himself to the analyst. "I am a drug addict" is commonly said in order to escape the question of being: the name-of-the-Father, the father who names the subject, is a reference to the drug to which the subject clings (he is de-pendent). Drug addiction conceals and eludes this question by conferring a *semblant* of identity, a mask to be pulled off so that the subject's true questions can be heard.

What is interesting about this behavior is the way in which the subject approaches the particular object: drugs. One supposes that his addiction allows him a privileged, direct, and short-circuited access to *jouissance*, a way to challenge the demands of the Other and culture, which impose a renunciation of *jouissance*. Drugs become the object of an urgent need, accepting neither deferments nor differences from the satisfaction demanded. We therefore find a radical difference between the object of drug addiction and the object of the drive or the phantasm. Lack in being appears not to be provoked by an unnamed and irrecoverable object, but by a commodity bought in the marketplace. In this sense, drugs, as objects of need, mask or substitute unconscious desire, which remains unknown for being disguised as something the organism needs. It is a need posed in absolute terms: life or death; either there is chemical *jouissance* or there is nothing, nothingness. The subject is thus abolished, reduced to the condition of the remainder @. Drugs are not substitute sexual objects because they lack phallic value. On the contrary, they are a substitute for sexuality itself, a way of distancing oneself from the relational constraints imposed by the phallus. Drugs are related to the auto-eroticism of original prohibition: the subject administers himself a substance that connects him directly to a *jouissance* that does not pass through the filter of acquiescence or the forcing of the other's body. The destitution of sexuality is thus achieved.

What we find in Lacan's teaching on this topic is scarce, but toward the end of his life he left some valuable indications when he referred directly to drugs. Lacan noted that for us *parlêtres* the difficulty is how to derive *jouissance* from castration, to allow castration and desire to free us from *angst* and lead us to the investiture of the Other's body symbolizing the lack in ours. As the case of Little Hans shows, for young boys and girls *angst* emerges when they discover they are "married" to the penis.

The difficult issue is how to dissolve that ill-fated marriage by contracting another with the body of the Other or anything whatsoever. That is why escaping from this latter union is welcomed—"therein lies drugs' success." Lacan then concludes, "there is no other definition of drugs than this: it is what allows us to break up with the pee-pee."[5] Drugs are the couple that comes after the divorce of the man or the woman with the phallic order and the recognition of lack. They are the promise of paradise, "*Là tout n'est qu'ordre, beauté, calme, luxe et volupté*" (There all is order, beauty, luxury, peace, and pleasure),[6] where the Other is substituted by an object without desires or whims, an object whose only problem is how to procure it as merchandise, but which does not betray us.

The alcoholic and the drug addict challenge symbolic debt, an eternal and external debt they did not incur and do not wish to pay, since it is unpayable. Mexican *lalangue* says that to contract a debt is to "drug oneself" (*endrogarse*); the debt itself is called "drug." The relation between drugs and (symbolic) debt with the Father, the Other, the omnipotent debtor that demands exchange and a renunciation of *jouissance* needs to be stressed. Faced with the mark imposed by an Ideal, I(A) that absorbs whatever comes from the subject (the vector $\$ \rightarrow I(A)$ in the graph of desire), the subject hands over his will in the form of a body deprived of vital reactions: a metabolic machine without desire, a fantastical and phantasmatic denial of castration and the phallus as $-\varphi$.

Phenomenology exhibits the apparent differences between the impotence that affects male alcoholics and drug addicts and the sexual promiscuity and multiple sexual contacts of women in a similar condition. The contradiction is not structural. The phallic function fulfilled by men through the phallic investiture of a woman, who thus reaches *jouissance* value (and becomes a symptom), is something the alcoholic (a paradigmatic term for addicts) cannot fulfill. He locates himself outside, on this side of desire. The female alcoholic, for her part, refuses phallic signification: her body is not an object of narcissistic investiture; it is handed over, an object of little value that anyone can take and discard. The promiscuity of one has the same meaning as the impotence of the other. In both, castration has become real because it does not function to reach *jouissance* "on the inverse scale of the Law of desire." *Jouissance* has not been rejected, castration is not symbolized, *jouissance* is thus unreachable; the law of desire, which commands desire cannot function.

There is an Other. Oh, the Other! The Other who demands that one desire its desire and the subject be inscribed under its insignias of work, love, fatherhood or motherhood, descendants and condescension, decency and docency, production of objects as signifiers and signifiers as objects. Although barred and not in existence, there is an Other that imposes its Law and makes the subject responsible for his subjective position. The Other asks that the subject account for his passage through the world—explain and respond for the life given in the symbolic, when he was conferred a proper name that represents him before the set of signifiers.

The Other does not always demand; sometimes it is more destructive when it does not. A-d(d)iction is not only refusing to pronounce the words that represent the subject before the demanding Other. Life in late capitalism shows another way to command the capitulation of the *parlêtre*, the defeat of speech. It happens when the Other does not say, ask, or expect anything: when the Other is silent. I propose that in such cases we speak of A-d(d)iction: "Do what you wish, I don't care. I will not even hear or speak to you." The dogmatic function of a vertically transmitted message descending from on high has been abandoned: the function once fulfilled by God, an Emperor, the King, the State, the Party, or the Father in all its various historical forms. The Law is an object of derision, all these masks having faded in the present horizon. In appearance, freedom reigns. For many, the problem of the postmodern present is words that can be said, but lack effect. Subjects are counted but do not count; they are numbers to be used in statistics: their presence reduced to saying "yes" or "no" to questions in a survey. Politics becomes poll(itics).

The word said is a promise, invoking the comprehension and desire of the Other—actually, a lack it must inhabit so that someone's existence can have meaning. We could play with the double-sense of the Spanish *oración* (phrase or prayer). It comes from the mouth (*oris*) but is not simply exhalation; it is the demand for a response: the expectation of meaning given to the phrase/prayer in the grammatical and religious sense. The meaning depends on the response: it never inhabits the subject autonomously, but always comes from the one who hears, as the experience of analysis demonstrates. The subject's *jouissance* is constrained by the expectation of a response in dialogue, by desire. If the Other does not expect anything nor makes its desire known, if the Other is not desiring, why speak? The subject is annihilated by the deafness of the Other and chooses silence. The drugs that intoxicate and offer a shortcut to *jouissance* (although not through desire) reach the brain from outside the diaphragm of speech, making the compromises that link the body to culture come apart. The remains from the abolition of the subject is the body made object @. We shall call this @ddiction.

In *L'étourdit*, Lacan notes: "What is said remains forgotten behind what is said in what is heard" (AE, 449). We've said earlier that the subject's enunciation is forgotten in the statement by what is heard, which corresponds to the ear of the Other. And if the Other does not hear, what is the sense of saying? The subject of the enunciation is made null. Phallic *jouissance* (the blah, blah, blah), which could open the way to *jouissance* through desire, is obliterated. The roads that lead to *jouissance* beyond speech are impermeable, and so only the *jouissance* on this side remains, the original *jouissance* of being, before speech. Our three terms: a-diction, @ddiction, and A-(d)diction thus converge: all are modalities in which the subject no longer says and distances himself from *Kulturarbeit*, the work of culture that for Freud could make where the Id was, the Ego come to be. Political indifference, the renunciation of congregation (community), and the acceptance of segregation are visible manifestations in our world of a-@-A-d(d)iction. Psychoanalysis and analysts must engage this situation without becoming themselves part of this pervasive indifference.

In these forms of non-diction presented, the body becomes the place of a *jouissance* that displaces the subject, outside discourse as social link. Under the effect of drugs, the body is object @, not S(Å), as in suicide. In the latter, the body is pawned to pay off the debt, the pound of flesh handed over to the will of the Other. The payments come to an end: "do with me what you will." Throwing his body over the abyss, committing suicide, is a response to the insatiable demand of a usurious creditor.

To distance oneself from the Other, its demand (or silence), the ordered mediation of desires, is an operation that can be done loudly through a suicidal passage to the act. This is the most radical way to shut the door with the pretext of "not wanting to know" about life's conditions: the inevitably barred subject writes himself off the signifying chain. Paradoxically, this operation produces an indelible inscription. The suicidal act entails, along with distancing, a ferocious and merciless challenge to the Other and his *jouissance*. The subject who commits suicide kills; he is a "shy murderer," according to Cesare Pavese (who committed suicide). The self-immolating subject does not speak, but expels his cadaver as an object for organic decomposition. His tacit statement (*sentence*): "here are my rests (*corpse*)" is a decision which, far from giving the Other the object @ (the body as remainder), marks the Other by leaving a scar, the constant reminder of its inconsistency. Thus, the decomposing flesh is inscribed indelibly as S(Å), precisely because the rest is silence. By removing life from the body through his own choice, the Other of the Law is barred. That is why there is such fascination and horror, repulsion, secular condemnation, and guilt, eternal if that is still possible, that befalls the subject who commits suicide and his act.

There is an essential link between suicide and drug addiction. An early Lacan spoke of the "formation of the individual" and "family complexes" in 1938:

> This psychic tendency towards death . . . can be seen in those special kinds of suicide characterized as non-violent; while at the same time we can see in it the oral form of the complex: the hunger-strike of anorexia nervosa, the slow poisoning of certain oral addictions and the starvation diet of gastric neuroses. The analysis of these cases shows that by abandoning himself to death, the subject attempts to discover the imago of the mother. (AE, 35)

If the sexual relation does not exist, if love cannot supplement and thus fulfill its promise, if work, instead of liberating, extolls and affirms slavery, what is left? Despair, thirst, a pull toward the maelstrom, eloquently evoked by Poe, Lowry, Drieu la Rochelle (a character in *Will O' the Wisp*), and Rimbaud, who withdraws from the world after attempting, not in vain, to "fix the vertigo." What is left if not to binge on food the Other demands be eaten (bulimia), to later vomit and refuse to continue eating (anorexia)? The disorders of the oral drive are also clinical forms of a-@-A-d(d)iction.

What do a-d(d)icts ask without words? To be left in peace, not wanting anything the Other wants from them: a *jouissance* without desire that challenges the phallus and its unifying pretensions. The a-d(d)ict wants to remove himself from the game of giving and receiving (the exchange of words, objects, signs, creatures) in order to live out the perfect relationship between the alcoholic and his bottle, which Freud calls an enviable model for love with no flaws, betrayals, or reciprocal demands: to live ignoring the symbolic debt that the subject must pay.

I have said that a-@-A-d(d)diction shows the rejection of an e-diction, the edict promoted by the Other. The a-d(d)ict achieves this by a distancing movement (experimental, instrumental, operative) in relation to the Other, an oscillation where the subject (because there is a subject of a-d[d]iction) wishes to be master. As noted daily, all addictions begin by controlling the entrance and exit of *jouissance*. "I know very well how far I can go without losing myself." However, "I is an Other," and the Other, who pretends to act through the ego, to control that oscillation, is dragged away. *Jouissance* without diction overpowers and many times succeeds in destroying the diaphragm of speech. In the psychoanalytic clinic, the subject presents itself as the blink of an eye repeatedly made to the Other, *fort* and *da*—putting that Other in play, while not wanting to know anything about him. This Other often becomes the custodian and administrator of the subject's desperation. Alcohol and other drugs make the diaphragm of speech explode and open the floodgates to an artificial paradise. Drug ad-diction is artificial, but it is worth repeating that the situation of the subject labeled psychotic is not an artificial exit from responsibility.

Having reached this point, I can now point out other forms of addiction that I cannot consider in detail. I am referring to writing, especially that used as a form of separation (contrary to alienation) in relation to the Other and his demands. I am thinking of certain twentieth-century writers such as Kafka, Joyce, Beckett, Plath, Woolf, Pizarnik, Camus, Céline, Sebald, Roth, Musil, and Broch. Serge André's magnificent essay "Writing Begins Where Psychoanalysis Ends" studies the relation between psychoanalysis and literature and the presence of *jouissance* and desire in the finished work.[7] Besides writing, music and the plastic arts also show the creativity unleashed in certain artists that distance themselves from the social link and choose the sufferings of *jouissance* instead of the pleasures of recognition.[8] Finally, I should mention the many anonymous creators who make *art brut*, works by crackpots or ingénues, outside publishing houses and galleries, not directed to any other or Other. I mention this only to further explore addictive *jouissance*.

To summarize the general movement of this chapter, I have defined three distinct breaks in the link between the subject and discourse: psychosis, drug addiction, and suicide. In these cases, the relation is established by a separation from the function of discourse. In all three the field of language is at stake. The exit is chosen, in the Freudian sense (*Wahl*), in the last two, but not in psychosis. The relation with *jouissance* and the Other of the subjective dialectic is radically different for each of the three positions of a-d(d)iction. The challenge for the analyst is to restore the movement of desire that is at a standstill. Not having many possibilities, he can count on only one instrument: the transference, which focuses on whether the exit from discourse, which silences the subject and exiles him from the social link, is chosen or not. There are reasons why these three a-d(d)ictions are not the elective field of psychoanalysis. But, if not psychoanalysis, what else can be proposed?

Chapter 8

Jouissance and Ethics
in Psychoanalytic Experience

A *Langagière* Practice

The relation between *jouissance* and speech has been discussed repeatedly in previous chapters, perhaps excessively. Is a justification in order? No, but one is provided nevertheless. Our thesis is the following: the psychoanalytic clinic explores the modalities of a subject's relation to *jouissance* that passes through the active mediation of the diaphragm of speech. Clinical work is not based on anything other than what is said in an analysis. What is done there is to create the conditions for unfolding unconscious *savoir* by translating it into speech. Therefore, psychoanalytic experience moves completely within the subject's relation to *jouissance*. It is oriented toward a certain good, which is *jouissance* as possible, without which the universe would be vain, but which must be rejected in order to be reached. On the road to *jouissance*, the subject must necessarily make a stop at the port of desire.

This is the reason we find in the strict and exclusively *langagière* organization of the analytic experience. Truth is said after accepting that it can be only half-said (*mi-dite*), and must be filtered through the *semblant* by discourse. The words able to tell the whole truth are missing. We are in the world because of language, which gives us only a *semblant* of the world, something that seems to be (*par-aît, par-est*). An analysis is structured around the *jouissance* of being that language forecloses and therefore can only promise a deciphering of *jouissance*.

There is a basic supposition that experience reveals as false: truth can be told. The motto is to "say everything," but the injunction of this fundamental rule has no other goal than to confront the subject with

235

the impossibility of saying everything. It thus manifests the analysand's unconscious discursive strategy when faced with this impossibility. The initial "say everything" is followed by "even if it is unpleasant," a second injunction, the most superegoic imaginable because it conceals an order: *Jouis!* In other words, the experience of analysis consists in confronting the subject of the symptom with an impossible *jouissance*. In its place it offers gentle, ideal, and artificial conditions that in the analytic device of transference pave the way to love.

The symptom is a word that is lacking (at least in the early Lacan): "Having been unable to proffer this scrap of discourse from our throats, each of us is condemned to make himself into its living alphabet to trace out its fatal line" (E, 372). A word, yes, but if that word can be read in symptoms "it is because they themselves are already inscribed in a process of writing" (E, 371, translation modified)—a writing of *jouissance*, we should add, able to be deciphered, as our discussion of Letter 52 in chapter 4 showed. For this decipherment to take place, Freud invented a psychoanalytic device meant to *form* the unconscious, the Lacanian *langagière* unconscious.

"*Jouissance* has to be refused in order to be attained on the inverse scale of the Law of desire" (E, 700). As we know, the function of love is to make *jouissance* condescend to desire. In the experience of the transference, love is at stake; one loves the Other supposing the knowledge (the knowledge that is missing) that emerges from reading the symptom without fearing paradoxes and/or contradictory statements. The presumption of knowledge is not only on the analysand's part. The analyst also supposes (as an act of kindness) something that must be demonstrated: there is *savoir* in the Other, a productive unconscious ek-sists. The encounter between two supposed *savoirs* is the catalyst that allows speaking "truthfully" for the unconscious to be constituted and *jouissance* deciphered. It is not easy.

Analytic work is oriented toward making the diaphragm of speech more flexible and the passage of *jouissance* possible. This is the case in the original (historical) situation of the so-called neuroses Freud found in Charcot's Paris. Recognizing this orientation, one may also consider the specific function of the diaphragm of speech in so-called perversion and psychosis, when subjects provisionally assigned to "clinical structures" undergo the test of the analytic device.

"From *jouissance* to desire" does not mean that desire must be said. The nature of desire is, as we know, to bar and ban *jouissance*. Due to its fundamental function, disguised by the phantasm, there is "desire's incompatibility with speech" (E, 535). So, it is not that desire must be said; it must be read to the letter "since it is the letter's snare that determines, nay over-determines its place" (E, 536). Desire cannot be said, but taken to its real point of impossibility: the rejected *jouissance* from which it emerges.

One must go through speech (whose transmission is regulated by the conditions of the fundamental rule) in order to reach the letter, the original codicils of *jouissance* etched on the body: the forms in which the subject's relation to *jouissance* were originally inscribed. This history refers to libidinal migrations or renunciations of *jouissance*, the avatars of castration recalled when the compulsion to repeat appears in analysis. *Remembering, repetition, working through*: from the drive (*pulsion*) to compulsion and the failed encounters where desire stumbles in order to pass from one writing to the other, to the book we all carry with us.

The letter is written, and desire, the inarticulable remainder of demand, must be read to the letter. One must arrive at a point beyond demand to find what passes from desire to speech, since they are incompatible. This is the theory of the analytic device, and its function. The fundamental rule is comparable to the injunction to experience *jouissance* and transcends the function traditionally accorded to speech. The "normal" use of the word is to "ratify," "comprehend," and confirm, in the reciprocity of consensual meaning and the specular images exchanged by "communicators." In analysis, the aim is to cross the narcissistic barrier of the care of the ego or self, the phantasm that organizes every subject's relation to the world: the "plug" that protects from the real. Encouraged to associate freely, the subject is quickly displaced from the field of pleasure and forced to confront himself with what is traumatic or irreconcilable for the ego, the unnamable *ça*, nucleus of his being.

Starting with chapter 1, we noted that repression conceals but also preserves a sequestered *jouissance*, not readily available to the subject and painfully experienced as a symptom. It is *jouissance* of the Other, an Other *jouissance* of the body devoid of words. Neurosis is such a defense *of jouissance* (in the genitive and subjective sense): a protection against an excessive *jouissance*, and a *jouissance* protected, congealed, exempt from exchange in speech. The subject of neurosis defends himself by withdrawing from what is perceived as a danger in relation to the Other of the social link, the desire of the Other. That desire is denied by strategies of self-mastery essential to obsessives and sustained by

dissatisfaction in the hysteric's intrigue. The "neurotic" defense in relation to desire in these subjective positions shows that desire here does
not condescend to *jouissance*; the relation to the Other is thus a fenced
minefield of defense. It is understandable that the subject would draw
back from the supposed *jouissance* of an Other who demands his castration. Defending and justifying himself before the Other, living with
guilt, the subject of neurosis renounces placing a value on *his* desire by
confusing and confounding it with the demand of the Other. Whether
by subjection or insubordination, always depending on the demand of
the Other, he withdraws before the possibility of inscribing his proper
name, the name that bothers and pesters him, and instead opts for a
demand directed to the Other so that the latter may name him: "I will
do and be as you wish, or your worst enemy."

The analytic device consists in reanimating the movement of defenses
in relation to the Other, the demand for alienation guided by the phantasm
that protects and functions as a barrier to *jouissance*. Once re-animated,
operating in the transference, it is taken to a limit, an inevitable quag-
mire and point of impossibility. At this point, the subject is forced to go
beyond the phantasm, the *jouissance*-filled satisfactions the analytic setting
provides, and encouraged to identify with the cause of his desire, his lack.
This action, carried out by the timely cut in the discursive chain and
unexpected interpretive interventions, implies the spacing of narcissism
otherwise subdued by the complacent acquiescence of the Other (sympathy,
comprehension, reciprocity of feelings, and recognition).

The analytic setting is strange and difficult. In order to make possible
what runs counter to the accepted standards of dialogue, the discourse
of the analysand and its phantasmatic engine must collide, encounter a
desire that is, in turn, beyond narcissistic specularity, solidarity, confusion
of egos, benevolence, and shared ideals. It is necessary for this discourse
to find not another subject, but a void that confronts him with its own
void, instead of offering illusory plugs for his lack in being.

Pro(*pulsions*) and Their Vicissitudes

"To follow desire to the letter" is to recognize that the letter of desire
is the unconscious inscription of *jouissance* on the body. Psychoanalysis
is an attempt to read that letter and translate it as discourse, which is
always *semblant*. Subjectivity germinates and develops in the productive

gap that opens up between the writing of *jouissance* and the saying that runs up against its impossible (e)mission, the inaccessible and inanimate zone beyond the phantasm. Freud calls it "death" (the death drive), while for Lacan it is the "space" never tread on and where all drives lead: the impossible real.

The experience Freud founded is oriented toward touching the real with the signifier, knowing all the while that speech cannot fill up the void of the Thing (or at least in psychoanalysis where mysticism is kept at a distance); it can only circle the void, delimit the hole, recognize what is irremediably incomplete. The ocean in *Solaris* and the zone in *Stalker*, films by A. Tarkovsky, beautifully present the relation of the explorers with the unnamable, central, and extimate Thing, as well as the ways in which the inaccessible nucleus of our being is incessantly circled by an experience whose remainder is helplessness.

Faced with the unapproachable void of the central hole of the torus (see chapter 2), what can be done other than go round its soul, the peripheral empty space that circles the central hole through which air can pass, without ever penetrating it? In other words, there is nothing other than "pro*pulsion*" (*pulsionnner*), a neologism that translates the German *trieben* (propel, push, force) and its connection to Freud's *Trieb* (drive): an irrepressible and untamable propulsion, a force that spurs forward, skipping over earthly delights (*Erde Freuden*), pleasures, a characteristic of Faust's spirit in Mephistopheles's discourse that describes the drive for Freud (SE, XVIII, 42). What he conceived is congruent with what we are exploring here. The drive is Faustian because on the road to the Thing,

> the backward path that leads to complete satisfaction is as a rule obstructed . . . so there is no alternative but to advance in the direction in which growth is still free—though with no prospect of bringing the process to a conclusion or of being able to reach the goal. (SE, XVIII, 42)

From the Freudian backward and forward we pass on to the rich complexity of two spaces, internal and external, bordered by the empty, spherical surface of the torus. These interminable "pro*pulsions*" guide our lives with no end to their forward march other than death; they skip over the barriers of pleasure that, being so often denied, are affirmed, reluctant to compromise with life's dangers, and therefore written with prefixes: (com), (im-), (re-), (ex-) *pulsions*.

A question presents itself: what is the nature of the pro*pulsion* (the driving *élan*) if not the biological organism moved by needs and homeo-static tendencies, or the psychological subject incapable of distinguishing between desire and whim? It is not biological, cultural, or psychological. The nature of this pro*pulsion* is ethical: a movement in the field of the symbolic by which the subject inscribes himself, leaving memorable marks of his act, historicizing and enacting the negative and creative force of the Freudian death drive. This pro*pulsion* is therefore unrelated to the move-ment of energy tending toward the abolition of tension called "Nirvana Principle," which was a boorish, "low" point in Freud's reflections.

Pro*pulsions* circle the Zone, the Thing; before them, all illusions fail and lead to the moment proposed by Lacan in his seminar on ethics, when the subject confronts the reality of the human condition against a backdrop of *angst*, an irremissible and unfathomable helplessness. Confronted with his own death, the subject is shaken by a new certainty: he cannot and does not wait to be rescued by anyone; there is no protection or shield. This is how Lacan didactically defines the end of analysis: to place one-self beyond *angst* because *angst* signals and shields the subject from an unnamable danger. Desolation and helplessness appear when *angst* has been traversed, when there is no longer fear or danger and no demand directed at the Other (in the sense of nothing to ask for or responsibilities to impute). There is nothing uplifting here suggesting "we should make ourselves the guarantors of the bourgeois dream" (S VII, 303).

The ethics of psychoanalysis, linked to a Spinozian perseverance in being, to desire as a road to *jouissance* and a confrontation with lack, goes against widespread notions and reassuring strategies for achieving well-being. An analysis is therefore not therapy. On the contrary, it chal-lenges all forms of therapy and can expect only failure and disregard if it seeks to be equal to today's tranquilizers. Its aim is not the pleasure principle, complete well-being, such as "world" health organizations define it, but rather a beyond: the body experienced even in suffering, through tension without pause, *jouissance* that suffers the limits pleasure imposes.

Pro*pulsions*: driving, pushing, reanimating a search beyond the phantasm where objects @, imaginary elements of the phantasm, trick the subject by concealing the condemned place of the Thing, sustaining the lure of representations and ideals (S VII, 87). The symptom is sustained in the phantasm, an imaginary formation, a branch of the narcissistic tree of the ego, or the ego in the form of a self "in itself." Here *jouissance* remains at a standstill, unknown, renounced, unsaid (*versagt*), outside speech, charged with unknown meaning. From this stronghold of ignorance, the demand addressed to knowledge (the Other supposed to know) is founded and produced, allowing *jouissance* to be subjectified.

The transference is the first instance, the reason that informs the demand made to someone, to anyone (Sq, *signifiant quelconque*, is Lacan's proposed matheme for the transference [AE, 248]). It allows a subject to be produced in a signifying discourse (S_1–S_2) where he is the signified. The transference is the encounter with anyone who, being an analyst, rejects entering the field of significations and plugging up the demand with responses. Or to offer himself as an object of identification and the seat of knowledge ready to be applied at any moment to fill the space of ignorance or error. If the symptom is the short-circuit that distances the subject from his desire (the desire of a long and unending circuit), the analyst occupies the place of the symptom and reactivates the blocked *jouissance*. The analyst makes a film from a still photo and situates himself topologically as the soul of the torus, *agalma* of desire. All demands from then on turn 'round that space and find their limit.

This is the meaning that should be given to Freud's expression "transference neurosis." The psychoanalyst, as *semblant*, in the place of the *semblant* as agent of his discourse, takes the place of object cause of desire and surplus (also minus, lack) *jouissance*. The analyst puts into effect and sustains the movement of the drive around the object @, leaving the central space of the Thing forever empty.

The topology of the torus again comes to our aid to illustrate the place of the @-analyst. On the toric surface we can define the correct and incorrect placement of the analyst in relation to the demand received. Without blushing, one could say that the analyst tricks and defrauds the analysand (*l'escroquerie analytique* [S XXIV, 2/26/77]); he is a *semblant*, appears to be (*par-est, par-aît*), presenting himself as what he is not and concealing what he is. He is therefore a lure for desire, allowing the subject to emerge from the vanity of desire and beyond the vanity of plenitude. Placing himself at the margins in reference to the inarticulable center of desire, taking the place of @, not as knowledge that plugs up or inaccessible Thing, the analyst offers himself as fuel for the phantasm. He can even replace the symptom, dissolve it, pacify the conflict, and also be an obstacle in the process of the cure. This is sometimes a long-lasting moment when the analysis comes to a standstill in relation to "a web of satisfactions" (E, 503) emerging from the analysis itself. The analysis thus becomes resistance to analysis due to the (phallic) *jouissance* attained, which the analysand does not wish to give up. Or, it fails for making do with the subject's "adequate" functioning in the world, leading to a premature end to the experience of analysis.

The Charybdis and Scylla of *jouissance* inside and outside an analysis blocks the movement that sustains the question (in the form of a symptom) initially disguised as a response. If an analysis can begin once the preliminary interviews end, it is because the symptom, an unconscious response, becomes a question or enigma: the unknown embodied in a signifying chain of the subject's sayings. Having produced this displacement of the symptom's signifier to the signifier of the transference, there is a risk the analysis and the analyst be taken, not as the opportunity to keep the question open, but as a pretext for its detour (trans-ference) and closure.

The analyst, therefore, does not approach his patient as $, S_1, or even S_2, but as @ → $: an object that maintains an opening, the noncoalescence between two complementary discourses. The analyst represents the permanent requirement of saying and work around subjective lack. History, the endeavor Lacan so praised at the beginning of his teaching and vilified at the end, makes us believe it has meaning and is always ready to be filled with meaning. Lacan shows that history must be rewritten, penetrating the screens and disguises of meaning. If neurosis is an ahistorical impasse, the filling/drying up of desire (in the sense of filling up a hole or drying up a water source), an analysis should be the opening up of sources and uninterrupted pathways: the occasion to mobilize a symptomatic *jouissance*, the symbolization of a body that becomes the bastion of an Other *jouissance*. In chapter 2 we localized this Other *jouissance* with the schema found in "*La troisième*," at the intersection between the imaginary and the real, outside symbolic mediation.

In saying this, we do not suggest setting new ideal goals for the analytic experience, something the analyst refuses to do (or be) with good reason. To signal new goals implies the ominous shadow of the imaginary, a neo-phantasm, the prescription of the "right" road, even the promise of anticipating the demand. Or even the alienation of a "Good" that, if it does not emerge from the analysand's own indications, appears as the analyst's phantasm. Beyond these possible approaches, however, the analyst must recognize why an analysis exists (why it begins and continues) in order to also define when and why it ends. In other words, the analyst must avoid the pitfalls of attaching meaning (beware of understanding!) between the symbolic and the imaginary and outside the real, which is the field of psychotherapies (E, 384).

The Duty of Desire

Wo Es war soll Ich werden: where the Id, *jouissance* of being, synchrony of signifiers, (disordered balls of language in the immense lottery machine), the set of writings of *jouissance* that lie un-deciphered, like hieroglyphs in the desert, where *Ça* was, an order must be established: a discursive artic-ulation able to provoke unheard of and exhilarating effects, a diachronic link of signifiers that reveals the unconscious as knowledge organized by the name-of-the-Father in the place of S_1, making the rest of the signifiers (unconscious *savoir*) an S_2. The effect is a new S_1 (the product of the ana-lyst's discourse) that represents the subject. In another dimension, the aim of analysis, its prescriptive task due to the Freudian *sollen,* is to anticipate *jouissance* by way of well-saying (*bien-dire*) and the invention of *savoir*.

In order to produce this effect, the physical presence of the analyst is necessary. He should have breasts, like those *mamelles de Thirésias* Lacan mentions in his 1964 seminar (S XI, 270). He must lend his body for the investiture of love, occupying the place of cause of desire in order for transference love to function and for the subject to recognize his desire as lack in being. The analyst must provide not only his being and speech, but also his image. He presents himself as *i(a)*, the specular other: "the specular image is the channel taken by the transfusion of the body's libido toward the object" (E, 696). An analysis entails the encounter of bodies, and transference requires imaginary support, emphasized rather than effaced by the analytic device that subtracts the analyst's body from the visual field of the analysand. We should recall that if a subject ($) speaks in analysis, he directs his words to the image of the other, this being the initial unavoidable point in order to reach I(A), located on the other side of the graph of desire. This organization is clearly seen when we emphasize its movement in the graph of desire.

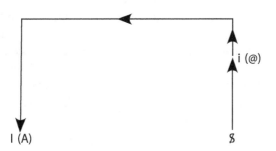

I (A)   i (@) $

The place I(A) is, more than a point of arrival, a suction, a vacuum machine of words that begins to operate once the subject accepts the fundamental rule of analysis and puts it in the place of superego: to experience *jouissance* in discursive articulation by saying it all, confronting the pain, indecency, disgust, and shame that resist the confession of the phantasm, the tabernacle of *jouissance*, linked to incest, perversion, and autoerotic libidinal satisfactions. It is evident that pleasure constitutes the main resistance in analysis for the analysand and the analyst; if the intention were to obey the pleasure principle, no one would undergo an analysis. An analysis exists due to a *jouissance* that points beyond narcissistic complacencies, always ready at hand.

I have so far outlined the triple function of the analyst: (1) *semblant* of @, a remainder that falls off from the real, impossible to symbolize; (2) the image of a specular other; and (3) support of the fundamental rule that makes the subject say (himself): the vacuum that suctions the analysand's sayings according to the law of analysis written as I(A). Real, imaginary, symbolic: this is the abc of psychoanalytic practice. As a device for constant invention and "psychoanalytic technique," this triple function does not organize "procedure codes" but the subjective position of the analyst in the *langagière* network created by Freud, of which the former is part. It is the "spider's stratagem" that condenses tactic, strategy, and the politics of analysis in function of ethics: "Let us say that . . . I relate technique to the primary aim (*fin première*)" (E, 725).

"Benevolent neutrality" always appears as an impossible ideal to someone who has not experienced a real analysis—even more so when the prescription of neutrality is reinforced with the Lacanian duty to "safeguard the imaginary dimension of his non-mastery and necessary imperfection for the other" (E, 699) and makes for the "calculated vacillation of the analyst's 'neutrality' " (E, 698), which can be more valuable for the hysteric than any interpretation. What is at stake in these formulations that may even appear to be contradictory? To ensure the real presence of the analyst and make her an active and acting force in function of *her* desire in order to preserve the horizon of *jouissance* at each moment of the discursive chain. But also to put a limit to *jouissance*, punctuate and channel it toward an unheard-of saying: to displace it from its enclosure in the symptom, crossing the barrier of *angst* that separates it from desire. *Jouissance* is thus summoned, diverted, provoked, expelled, and finally recovered, manifested, and denaturalized. The analyst's strategy always has this in mind; the time and fees for the sessions are regulated in terms of these indicators or apparently contradictory imperatives.

An analysis' ethical dimension is displayed in how it moves away from a universal code of moral or deontological indications and obligations, enabling it to search for the *particular* nucleus that in any and every *parlêtre* is the articulated relation between *jouissance* and desire. In each case the renewed ignorance of the analyst is upheld, following Freud's advice to renounce all previous acquired knowledge. The originality of every new experience makes it so the unconscious and sexual theories must be produced anew each time.

The analytic experience is not mandated by the commandments of the Other but by unconscious desire: it makes desire a duty and organizes one's duty in relation to unconscious desire; it distrusts, if not outright contradicts, suspicious moral rules. These moral rules are themselves derived from desire since they function as barriers interposed in its path, at the service of a presumed common and communal good—communitarian, even, as if they were all One, the unifying One of mass psychology, the master's uniform ideal, with its codes and legal censorship.

In psychoanalysis it is not a question of the laws, but the Law, which prohibits *jouissance* (of the Thing) in the real, displaces it to the field of the *semblant*, and orders it be reached through other discursive means. *Jouissance* thus becomes a *semblant* and occupies the place of agent in a new analytic discourse: inverse, an inversion, the reverse of the master's discourse. The Law orders desire while making the (absolute) object of desire, the Thing, unreachable. Led to desire in vain, circling the object @ as cause of desire, and only under the appearances of the *semblant* of an impossible *jouissance*, the Law elevates *jouissance* to the place of the Thing. This is how men and women inscribe themselves as historical beings by making themselves a name (the meaning of the "proper" name, the signifier given at birth) and record their path toward *jouissance*, by passing through desire.

This formulation seems to allow dreaming of overcoming the Law by means of a signifying articulation, implying the dimension of the promise, but it is nothing of the sort. There is no completion of the Other by or through the Other. We must therefore now return to the formulations of the three *jouissances*(s) we discussed earlier to avoid committing mistakes. Speech and the phallic order, led by the name-of-the-Father, put a limit to the *jouissance* of being, uproot the Thing's original homeland,

and produce a *langagière* exile. However, the Other limps. A signifier is missing in the Other, the signifier for The woman that would make the sexual relation possible. The phallic order does not guarantee completeness, and neither can the proper name. The name-of-the-Father, the representative of the Phallus as S_1, creates a gap of impossibility in the discursive register. That gap corresponds to the signifier of ~~The~~ woman, missing in the Other and beyond the Phallus. Semiotic, phallic *jouissance* stumbles with a limit, which is what lies beyond it and is inarticulable: the *jouissance* of the Other, feminine *jouissance*. Speech, subjected to the Law that prohibits *jouissance*, produces another *jouissance*, an unsayable surplus. After traversing analytic experience, the neurotic dimension of existence (produced by the cut of castration, appearing impotent for its inability to name the object of desire), does not end up with imaginary potency over an object under the power and control of the ego, but rather in an area of impossibility opened beyond the signifier.

Sexuality is linked to the phallic signifier, the signifier without equal. Beyond what the phallus covers and uncovers, the "dark continent" of femininity and enigmatic *jouissance* opens up: mad, ineffable, a true Other of the Other located outside language, which justifies repeating there is no metalanguage: no possibility of a "complete" analysis, if one clings dogmatically to a *langagière* practice. This refers to nothing other than the hard rock of castration against which the founder of psychoanalysis collided. There is indeed a hard rock if the analyst limits himself to the historicized function of speech able to say everything concerning *jouissance*, having to subsume all that pertains to the subject—that is, if the analyst allows himself to be caught by the imperialism of speech.

It is true that the Law commands desire. But desire in the neurotic register of experience is presented as transgression; desire for unlawfulness is the unlawfulness of desire in the neurotic impasse: "conscience makes us all guilty." Life and *jouissance* begin and prosper in the fertile soil of guilt, assuming the risk of going beyond the name-of-the-Father . . . on condition of making use of it (S XXIII, 136).

Inverting the Freudian formula, one can say the Oedipus complex (a Freudian dream, according to Lacan) is heir to the superego, the primitive and ferocious superego that proffers the unacceptable and impossible order to *jouir*. The well-known complex is a relief, mitigation and displacement of the triangular relation in the imaginary. It fulfills the function of staging and limiting guilt, while making the road to *jouissance* possible, even if limited and gradual for having taken the detour of castration: a phallic road with many limitations for both men and women. In this sense, Oedipus is the basis of existence and the central complex of neurosis: the absolute submission to the Phallus and the name-of-the-Father. As if having to be thankful for removing us from the *jouissance* of being and its accompanying psychosis, we remain forever subject to the impotence introduced by the complex: neurotic guilt.

To return to the point where Freud discovered his own limit is to reencounter Nietzsche's ethical proposal: to proudly accept that if we have killed God the Father it was not to remain subject to his word, because He is as castrated as anyone else, but to explore the zone extending beyond his domain, beyond good and evil. *Parlêtres*, one more effort is necessary! The ethical destiny of psychoanalysis is waged in relation to that effort, yet again. After 1972, Lacan reluctantly accepted "one more effort" to go beyond Oedipus and guilt: the thesis formulated by two of his most distinguished disciples, Deleuze and Guattari, in *Anti-Oedipus*.

The Act and Guilt

First the thundering voice of the Other: "*Jouis!*" Faced with the impossibility of this maddening commandment, the subject comes into ex-sistence through speech, proffered to the Other of language. This movement implies the phallic localization of *jouissance*, the emptying out of *jouissance* from the body and its submission to the Law of the symbolic. A mechanism is put into effect, either masculine identification with the real phallophorous father or feminine demand to the father (*père-version* in both cases). This passage through castration should not be confused with the end point of subjectivity. It is not submission to the father or accepting his conditions in order to be loved, but rather a point of access to desire, a dimension that is parricidal and transgressive, and inscribes signifiers different from the ones the father authorizes. It is the destiny of pro(*pulsions*), an Other duty, another duty.

In a stimulating text, Gérard Pommier writes: "The feeling of lack cannot be reduced to Oedipal guilt, it is inherent to existence. A subject must distinguish himself from the (superegoic) determinisms that awaited him even before birth."[1] In order words, he cannot live as a desiring subject if he does not distance himself from the desire of the Other and assume lack. Therefore, in the psychoanalytic sense, we can understand duty in two ways: to become Oedipal in order to transcend a maddening *jouissance* of being outside language, to later become trans-Oedipal, going beyond Oedipus in order not to be caught in the web of the phantasm, impotence, and suffering.

The ethics of analysis is affirmed beyond culpability, in the consubstantial relation of the subject with the guilt he or she necessarily finds as a desiring subject. The goal is not beatitude or absolution; each one must confront the guilt inherent in desire, and for this there are no rules or commandments regarding what should be done and how. On this road there are no enlightened fellow travelers, churches, parties, or teachers to guide the way, nor the possibility of renouncing the responsibility of choosing by merging with the interests of the group or institution. Each one of us is alone and cannot expect the help of the Other. The subject must play his hand in turn and cannot "pass," as in certain games. In chess it is called *Zugzwang*. To play one's hand according to desire and be subject to the consequences: a limit to *jouissance* that then leads it on different roads in the inverted scale of the Law of desire.

So-called neurosis, an ethical unease and not a disease to be categorized or medically treated, is impotence or renunciation to "play the hand" in coming to be. It is the refusal of a particular affirmative act in function of the acceptance of the signifiers of the Other's demand, either due to normative criteria or fear of abandonment and loss of love. The purpose of saying, the discursive experience organized by the analytic rule, is not comprehension or being satisfied with new knowledge or "intelligence." The purpose is to produce an act, as in Borges's "Tadeo Isidoro Cruz," whence the subject obeys the destiny he carries with him, writes the Proustian narrative, and, because of his act, knows forever who he is and not who he thought he was.

Analysis as a "treatment" for neurosis has an ethical purpose: to reopen the field of the singular choice, with no consideration for orders, ordinances, and orderings. Attention! It is not a question of re-discovering or going back to an ideology of freedom that goes hand in hand with an obscurantist psychology or the celebratory chants of individualism: "the ego is the theology of free enterprise" (E, 30n.11). That is why we mentioned the *Zugzwang* of chess: one plays the game; the remainder of the action taken is irreparable loss and inevitable error. The obsessive knows this well; in order not to lose, he always delays his act.

"To know forever who one is" is the retroactive remainder of the act, the wager that implicates the subject's being written as destiny and whose effect is abandonment and solitude. One can also speak of identification with the cause of desire, the unfillable lack that underlies all choices and acts. Psychoanalytically, that is destiny. It is not a real predestination, but reason constructed retroactively from the act. Because of his act and lack inscribed as the trace of his passage through the world, the subject "knows forever who he is." The new *savoir* is ambiguous: desolate and distressing on the one hand, but also "*gay savoir*": a source of enthusiasm and renewed contact with *jouissance*, an enhanced curiosity that displaces sadness and boredom, those states of the soul that blur differences and life's reliefs that some call "depression."

As Pommier points out, the analysand is analogous to the modern hero, defined not so much for his bravery but for confronting his *angst* and guilt. In analysis, he takes a paradoxical trajectory: having arrived in order to learn how to experience *jouissance* and avoid its barriers, he leaves knowing that *jouissance* is only possible through changes and exchanges, in the insistence of the lack in being that speaks in him, his desire. The ambiguity at the end of analysis is a mix of desolation and enthusiasm experienced psychologically as a "manic-depressive state," in the terms used by the English offspring of the Hungarian school of psychoanalysis. A desolate elation often accompanied by bad moods because things do not go as one wishes: things move with a rhythm that does not match that of desire, devourer of time. Desire, authentic desire, wants to know nothing of delays; it is in a rush to conclude.

In this ethics without ideals, beyond all ideals, one cannot *savoirjouir*, but one can know about desire, which points to *jouissance* as its always fleeting horizon, manifested in the interstices of the signifying chain and produced by the very fact of speaking: a signifier one represents the subject for a signifier two; this second signifier reverts back on the signifier one and gives birth to the subject of the unconscious. The process of signification is not sufficient unto itself; the remainder of the two signifiers' operation is the production of @, the object of surplus *jouissance* that escapes signifying articulation but functions as its motor: cause of desire.

The object @ that escapes with the trigger of the word cannot be encompassed by an "exact" expression able to recover and introduce it into discourse. The organizing real element of the discourse of science, a successor to religion, presumes to show the truth about the real in our present. The @ is an unsayable rest that falls off because all discourse is penetrated by *semblant*, something that even science has recognized in the form of only certain proper names: Heisenberg (uncertainty) and Gödel (incompleteness).

The illusion of a metalanguage: a supposed absolute knowledge, a discourse able to pronounce the truth of truth, an unbarred Other, an Other of the Other and guarantee of statements, is the prolific bedrock of the analytic setting. The phantasm of a guarantee and *jouissance* within the reach of discourse constitutes the Other of the transference, an Other that does not exist and is a mere supposition. The discourse of the unconscious, a transcription and decipherment of *jouissance* that cannot nor wishes to be known, addresses the Other in the transference. It is a *savoir* without a subject that "knows" us and makes the subject an effect of its saying—where the subject occupies the place of the signified in a relation of disjunction with object @, the writing of *jouissance* as lost, shining forth in the space of production.

$$\frac{S_1}{\$} \quad \overset{\longrightarrow}{//} \quad \frac{S_2}{@}$$

The subject of unconscious articulation leaves the darkness to which everyday discourse forces him because of the presence of the analyst, who embodies the analytic rule and compels saying. The interventions, punctuations, interpretations, and scansions in the discursive stuff (*etoffe*) make for the emergence of the master signifiers to which the *parlêtre's* being responds. In the cure, the analyst is the representative or *semblant* of object @ and with this function produces the master signifiers to which the subject's existence responds.

$$\frac{@}{S_2} \quad \overset{\longrightarrow}{//} \quad \frac{\$}{S_1}$$

It is thus necessary for the analyst to place himself at a distance from knowledge, to make the "I only know that I know nothing" operate (this is also the basis of Socratic teaching, Descartes's methodical doubt, Husserl's *epoché*, the Freudian prescription to begin each analysis by renouncing all referential knowledge learned in previous analyses, including one's own), to discover or invent anew that textual *savoir* that is unknown, the unconscious, a signifying articulation whose signified is that we do not know.

This is why there are no applicable prescriptions (in the normative, not temporal, sense of this word) for the analyst's interventions, which are always inventions, never recipes. The novelty of his saying cannot be an injection of knowledge, however acquired: "his lack of knowledge is not one of modesty, which implies placing oneself in relation to it; it is properly the production 'in reserve' of the structure of the only timely *savoir*" (AE, 249). Timely: there is opportunity and opportunism in the production of *savoir*, which is why there is a prescription in time. The "lion only springs once," at the right time, says Freud (SE XXIV).

Like the poetic word, an apophantic word (AE, 473) carries truth or falseness in itself, and a second or secondary judgment cannot decide if it is true or false: a self-validating true saying. It does not speak the truth, but produces it. The unconscious does not consist of propositions (such as demands), which a logical and linguistic analysis could qualify as having veridical value or not (truth or falsehood are inherent in propositions). The analyst's speech is or should be non-propositional (never of the kind "I propose you admit or reject my interpretation is true"). It is non-verifiable, non-falsifiable (despite and with Popper), acting, factual, phatic, located somewhere between citation and enigma, linked to a particular *jouissance* (the *jouissance* of decipherment), a continuation of the work of the unconscious, as we saw in chapter 4.[2]

The analyst's statement (the said) is non-sense, open to ambiguity, polysemic, equivocal, protean, reduced to its enunciation (the saying), lending itself to successive re-elaborations. According to Nasio, because of his interventions "the psychoanalyst is the one who evokes *jouissance*."[3] He evokes, but does not say, make, have, feel, transmit, or recover *jouissance*. He evokes it in the enunciation that is the ethical presence of the analyst at the center of the analysand's saying. This enunciation is not the cause, but the effect of the analyst's statement: "If it is placed beforehand, it is by retro-action, *après-coup*."[4]

Technique (the how, what, when, and how much to interpret) depends on the ethical imperative to evoke, as well as to signal an impossible *jouissance* through saying: an act of enunciation that is "a formation of the unconscious." The unconscious is thus formed (produced): what the analysand's speech "would have been," beginning with what was produced in him by the analyst's act (or the silence that he puts to work). *Jouissance* makes it so technique is subordinated to ethics, the statement to the enunciation, what is said to what cannot be said. In which case, as Wittgenstein famously said, "Whereof we cannot *speak*, thereof we must remain silent."

The fact that being comes to be in the retroaction of its act is something that concerns not only the analysand. The analyst is also implicated at the outset. Borges-like, he knows forever what and who he is. His desire is similar to an interpretation, a formula advanced by Lacan from Seminar VI on. The analyst's interpretation does not say being, but functions like a cut on a topological surface that modifies its properties and re-organizes what was there previously. It is not a phrase, but an act that knots together desire and *jouissance* passing through castration. Castration blocks the mad *jouissance* of being, is the condition for phallic *jouissance* and the signifying barrier interposed on the *jouissance* of the Other, according to what we established in chapter 2 regarding the three *jouissance*(s).

Interpretation leads to desire because it functions as a re-organizing signifier of subjectivity. It is, in fact, a name-of-the-Father that opens up the field of *jouissance* via well-saying, leaving the subject in condition to attempt the adventure of *jouissance*, unlinking him from the *langagière* chains that restrained him in a cage of symptoms. In other words, an interpretation tacitly leads, by its mere presence, to act beyond resignation and guilt.

Interpretation is oracular, presenting itself as something belonging to the real, beyond signifying articulation. It is not a discourse that is added to another discourse in order to confirm, deny, or deviate it, but an evocation of *jouissance* that lends itself to decipherment without telling the truth—forewarned that *jouissance* is not what is ciphered but what is deciphered. It is oracular because the unconscious, the discourse of the Other, is an oracle and interpretation its homology. An interpretation defines the being of the analyst and what is analytical, the Cartesian manifestation of the "I am" confirmed by the "I think" that follows the "I am" instead of preceding it. It is done through the symbolic, imaginary, and real presence of an analyst that does not separate from his saying in order to be represented by that saying. The analyst becomes in his saying. The said is an effect of the act and manifests an ethical position, the desire of the analyst. Its value is not the affirmation or the response that follows (master's discourse), judged on the plane of knowledge (university discourse), or response to the split in the subject (hysteric's discourse). An interpretation is a saying translated into a said that does not emerge from an analyst's subjectivity or develop from a "personal" countertransference masking the enigma of the analyst's desire.

The Immunological Analogy

The initial necessary condition for an interpretative enunciation to have effects is that the subject be in transference. Analysts agree on this point

universally even if they do not agree on the meaning of the words interpretation and transference. In Lacanian terms that are now commonplace,
the constitution of a subject supposed to know is necessary. Having reached
this point, I am tempted to make use of a parable (actually, an allegory)
to illustrate the relation between transference and *jouissance*. There are
Freudian precedents of course, but instead of using military analogies (as
Freud did), I use the comparison with immunology that sad circumstances
at present have made common knowledge. In sum, in an analysis the idea
is to provoke an immune deficiency.

The subject, with the exception of the so-called psychotic, is protected
by a defensive system of antibodies. An antibody, if we listen to what the
signifier allows us to hear, puts a break on and opposes *jouissance*, which
is the body's. We now propose an unlikely mix by putting together the
ignorance provoked, resistances, and repression to consider all three as
antibodies. Even before birth, the subject of the unconscious (*parlêtre*)
is bathed in words and discourses. Coming from the Other, these lead
the subject to label as improper and irreconcilable those signifiers that,
if articulated, could harmonize and resound with the body and with
jouissance. He rejects them for this reason.

A popularized immunology tells us that from the beginning the organism learns to recognize its protean components as its own, tolerating them
without adverse reactions. Lymphocytes circulate and carry information
to distinguish between what is proper or alien to the normal individual.
When an alien protein appears in the blood stream, it functions like an
antigen that provokes a rejection-reaction, a defensive process that ends in
assimilation or expulsion. When the alien proteins do not enter into the
blood stream but into the digestive system (it is the most common case),
they are scattered in elementary particles that are later used to reconstruct
other proteins, compatible with those of the organism.

Let us not lose sight of our analogy. The stable system for recognizing compatible components on the plane of the signifier is the ego, the
"official ego" found in Freud's correspondence with Fliess. The signifiers
coming from the outside (the Other) do not enter the subject unless they
pass through a "lymphocytic customs house" that decides whether they
are assimilated as one's own: the ego accepts them when deemed inof-
fensive or otherwise rejected. Their common destiny is to be analyzed by
isolating their elementary components and later reconstructed in complex
sets according to the ego's organization. All interventions coming from
the Other's knowledge that fall back on the subject activate the system of

immunological defenses already at hand. What is radically incompatible is rejected as a vile implant. These are the effects of what Freud called "wild analysis." The alien word is commonly assimilated and neutralized by an omnipresent protective system. It is a function of the thymus, doctors say, and, in a more vulgar sense, some analysts as well. The subject is tricked into not reacting when faced with the components he feels to be his own (egoic); he is induced to tolerate his own proteins because of the discursive and imaginary framework called the ego. The alien word is received and integrated into the defense apparatus. What's more, it can act as an "injection" that immunizes against a new, unpredictable, or devastating word. This "vaccine" must be equal to, as well as weakened in relation to, those "dangerous" signifiers that speak a truth the subject prefers to ignore.

From its beginnings, the analytic process was conceived to deactivate resistances to those signifiers, now assimilated to the ego, now rejected due to repression, ignorance, or bad faith and unrecognized as one's own. An analysis leads the subject to become a stranger to his own words. The dream, one's own speech heard as coming from the Other, is the royal road to producing this effect. The *faux pas* and what is produced by the scansions and punctuations of the analyst are not far behind.

The immunological system organized in each one of us that blocks what is properly one's own is the discourse of the Other that takes possession of the subject's body, his *jouissance*, by displacing and making it strange, converting it into an unapproachable interior zone, Id: an inveterate, irredeemable satisfaction of discourse. *Jouissance*, what is one's own, is treated as strange. "I is an Other" (Rimbaud: "*Je est un Autre*"), but he does not know. He does not wish to know anything about it, to "dissolve imaginary mirages," as Lacan says in the Rome discourse. That is, to make the "I" other, discover castration, hidden under the ego's mask, and denounce its imposture as a false monolithic whole in order to reveal the lack in being and the desire concealed therein.

I is Other, but thinks himself "One." Ignorance is not his sin; after all, ignorance is knowledge's only universal. The problem is when ignorance thinks it knows. Therefore, not the absence of knowledge but the resistance to truth on the basis of and in the name of knowledge: a referential knowledge allowing for localization in reality, active ignorance of truth and the *jouissance* it inscribes. This is the antibodies' action to which I am referring.

Now, back to our starting point: psychoanalysis seeks to provoke an immunological deficiency, to neutralize a supposedly protective system that is the set of all the barriers to *jouissance*. In this hopefully illustrative analogy, neurosis (a diagnostic label given to a universal subjective condition) appears as an autoimmune disease. In other words, the ego rejects the subject. The ego treats what is one's own, the drives that aspire to *jouissance*, as strange; it does not know the signifiers that represent them, but represses them, erects a system of defenses to protect itself, makes the intimate extimate, treats it as a strange body (a protein), turns it into a symptom, hidden and living as incomprehensible bodily suffering. The symptom presents itself as "most foreign to the ego"; like everything that has been repressed, it is "internal foreign territory" (SE XXII, 57). The symptom has never been better defined than with these words. One could also say it is an enclave of the discourse of the Other, a residue from the superego's initial order to experience *jouissance* that does not find the release offered by castration or a channel through the act as the practical effect of a well-said (*bien-dite*) signifying articulation.

One more time: *Wo Es war soll Ich werden*. Where the unnamed element in the symptom takes root, internal foreign territory, the ego must go, signify, make room for an unknown *savoir* found there. The resistances that reject what is authentic for considering them a menace must be dismantled. The relation between the subject and the Other is not reciprocal opposition or exclusion (in the polarity proper/strange), but the intersection of Eulerian circles where the lack in one is superposed and comes together with the lack in the other (see chapter 2). The result is the barred subject and the barred Other.

The ego's delusion at the heart of neurosis consists in ignoring that there is no possibility of completion between the subject ($) and the Other (Ⱥ); the reciprocal and complete superposition offered by the phantasm is a lure. The split is irremissible, and the remainder of the double cut is the object of *jouissance* (@), which is lost for both. In the current subjective position called "normality," there is identification between the subject and the ego, ignoring that the ego is the effect and ally of the Other. At the service of the ego (that is Other), desire is renounced under the Other's demand. It exchanges pro(*pulsions*) for satisfaction (to the Other), with the phantasmatic hope of being satisfied in turn.

Analytic treatment seeks to re-conquer the internal foreign territory by making it pass through the diaphragm of an unprecedented and unheard speech, able to invent a way out for desire through an act that declares subjective particularity. There were Id was. Limits must be placed on the pseudo-protective system of egoic antibodies, the Other's defense settled in the *parlêtre*, to enable the body for *jouissance*. How? By unmasking the antibodies, re-channeling the *jouissance* exiled after suffering a transubstantiation, and passing through the systems of speech: all detailed from one point to the other in Freud's Letter 52. After deciphering *jouissance* and *jouir* its decipherment, "I," comes to its proper place.

An interpretation has to be a statement that circumvents the system of defenses (assimilation or rejection). It cannot be foreign to the immunological system that rejects implants. Interventions based on the analyst's (referential) knowledge (an error Lacanian psychoanalysts are more aware of), consists in relying on signification, the meaning of the symptom or the transference treated as a symptom. A Lacanian interpretation, surprising and equivocal, acts on the signifier; it is non-propositional and bypasses the system of antibodies instead of stimulating them as antigens or integrating them in a process of assimilation. The analyst evokes *jouissance* and provokes it as well. His statement is closer to *Witz* than to a conference, it is non-con-fering (giving): an analytic act (S XVI).

The analyst's intervention is effective if and only if the immunological protections are deficient and the strong ego of revisionist metapsychology (the thymus) is weakened. The strategy consists in making the "I" other, an Other suspicious of complicity with the object of the complaint. The accuser is the first suspect, a fact not to be ignored even by the most inexperienced detective. He must be made to speak so the mask that conceals real motives and identity begin to fall. This identity is the same as the symptom's because it is structured as such. An interpretation falls on the analysand's discourse after deactivating common defensive processes, phantasmatic barriers. That is why I began this section by proposing that an "immunological deficiency" (an "analytic AIDS") be induced, making the subject pass through defenselessness, *Hilflosigkeit* (helplessness), in order to traverse life's phantasms and come in contact with the real that lies beyond it.

Allegories and parables captivate us, but after their presentation, the reader must be cautioned regarding their fictional structure: what is essential in their constitution is the difference between the two terms that joins them together, besides the imaginary kinship they establish. Immunology and psychoanalysis depend on different legalities. However, these rhetorical devices are productive; a discourse always deals with a reality that has been configured by another discourse, although the real cannot be captured by speech and can only be circumscribed. The shadow of the imaginary falls on all discourse because truth is structured like fiction.

Lacan carried out a portentous task by returning to Freud's statements and integrating them to his own enunciations. His positions must be constantly renewed. We must create an immunological deficiency in relation to Lacan's teaching and the protection many find in a discourse that reassuringly rejects innovations as dangerous implants. Lacan made "conventionalized" psychoanalysis strange to itself through the incorporation of other discourses (linguistics, philosophy, logic, topology), genuine antibodies that showed how the truth limped, worn down by a mishandled textual knowledge of the unconscious that only draws consistency in Freud's works. At the end of his life he said: "do as I do, but do not imitate me." His injunction is to avoid making his seminars and writings something definitive. He always avoided repeating his statements. This is how the object of psychoanalysis becomes difficult, strange, appetizing, desirable.

Letter to His Father

With his subject of analysis, the analyst submits to the ethical exigency of embarking on a journey through the lost roads of the phantasm, without being blinded by the illusions of physical and emotional comfort. He has already made the journey himself and attempts it with those who demand an analysis. At the end he finds the hurdle is not castration, as Freud thought, but the subjectivation of death.

What kind of ethical exigency is this? It is clearly not an ethics of universals, precepts, or morals. Neither is it one of indifference or apathy, complacency in death or disdain. An ethics announced by the title of a text that predates Freud, but which summarizes the ethical program of psychoanalysis: *Beyond Good and Evil*. Freud's oft-quoted *Beyond the Pleasure Principle* is its periphrasis and commentary, continuation or culmination. Lacan's seminar on ethics can be and should be read as the confirmation of a secret thread, invisible until now, that joins Nietzsche and Freud as two great immoralists who ask themselves: "Shouldn't moralists be—immoral?" (BGE, 119). Is not the underlying project of all moral principles known at present to restrain and order *jouissance*, subjecting it to norms and principles that are dead and resistant to the desires of the subjects that they regulate: codes proceeding from God, nature, coexistence, pleasure, reality? It may be the reason why "the whole of morality is a long, undismayed forgery which alone makes it at all possible to enjoy the sight of the soul."[5]

Psychoanalysis drives a nail into this panoply of morals: "An ethics arises, which is converted to silence, not by way of fear, but of desire; and the question is how analysis' pathways of chatter leads to it" (E, 573). Aspiring to the speech required from the analysand, emptying it of meaning until the drive's silent nucleus is found and *angst* overflows, to find in that beyond the productive lack in being. It is a beyond good and evil only in the sense that the objective is reached going beyond *angst*.

The originality of psychoanalysis is to put unconscious desire, not "the intention [that] is only a sign and symptom that first needs to be interpreted" (BGE, 33), at the center of ethics. A desire which chooses, decides, and acts, opposed to a lethal inertia. The subject cannot evade that desire by saying that someone else decided for him. It is a desire beyond all determinisms and ideals, where nothing is written beforehand, but if there is a decision, it can be written forever. A Freudian *Wunsch* that in Nietzsche is *Wille zur Macht*, will to power—a Nietzschean *Macht* that in Lacan is *jouissance*.

One must choose, decide; it is necessary. Not even sexuation is predetermined. Although some wish to call it terrorism, in "Science and Truth" Lacan said we are always responsible of our position as subjects. We need to respond for this position and the *jouissance* we accept or reject, to say if we wish or not what we desire. What follows is a clinical example of universal validity that has the discursive structure of the demand for analysis: a single man, thirty-four years old, who lives in his father's house and works in the profitable business his father owns, writes him a long letter: a violent recrimination for all the wrongs he has experienced in life and an accusation for his own incapacity to experience *jouissance*. Franz Kafka's letter is well known and holds great interest, not only because of its author, but also because of the identification the text provokes in "normal neurotics," whether they be analysands or not. The specular acknowledgment of someone else's text addressed to a father, far beneath his role as father, like any other, is possible only if the last page of the famous letter is ignored; until then, the complaint is one the analyst hears constantly. It is when Franz refers to making decisions and putting them into practice, when he can no longer justify himself for being seventeen years old. At that point, he interrupts his letter to suppose what his father could say to him (if "the unconscious is the discourse of the Other," what Kafka puts into his father's words is revealing):

If you look at the reasons I offer for the fear I have of you, you might answer: "You maintain I make things easy for myself by explaining my relation to you simply as being your fault, but I believe that despite your outward effort, you do not make things more difficult for yourself, but much more profitable. At first you too repudiate all guilt and responsibility; in this our methods are the same. But whereas I then attribute the sole guilt to you as frankly as I mean it, you want to be 'overly clever' and 'overly affectionate' at the same time and acquit me also of all guilt. Of course, in the latter you only seem to succeed (and more you do not even want), and what appears between the lines, in spite of all the 'turns of phrase' about character and nature and antagonism and helplessness, is that actually I have been the aggressor, while everything you were up to was self-defense. By now you would have achieved enough by your very insincerity, for you have proved three things: first, that you are not guilty; second, that I am the guilty one; and third, that out of sheer magnanimity you are ready not only to forgive me but (what is both more and less) also to prove and be willing to believe yourself that—contrary to the truth—I also am not guilty. That ought to be enough for you now, but it is still not . . . You have put it into your head to live entirely off me. I admit that we fight with each other, but there are two kinds of combat. The chivalrous combat, in which independent opponents pit their strength against each other, each on his own, each losing on his "own, each winning on his own. And there is the combat of vermin, which not only sting but, on top of it, suck your blood in order to sustain their own life. That's what the real professional soldier is, and that's what you are. You are unfit for life; to make life comfortable for yourself, without worries and without self-reproaches, you prove that I have taken your fitness away from you and put it in my own pocket. Why should it bother you that you are unfit for life, since I have the responsibility for it, while you calmly stretch out and let yourself be hauled through life, physically and mentally, by me. For example: when you recently wanted to marry, you wanted—and this you do, after all, admit in this letter—at the same time not to marry, but in order not to have to exert yourself you wanted me to help you with this not-marrying, by forbidding this marriage because of the 'disgrace' this union would bring upon my name. I did not dream of it. First, in this as in everything else I never wanted to be 'an obstacle to your happiness,' and second, I never want to have to hear such a reproach from my child. But did the self-restraint with which I left the marriage up to you do me any good? Not in the least. My aversion to your marriage would not have prevented it; on the contrary, it would have been an added incentive for you to marry the girl, for it would have made the 'attempt at escape,' as you put it, complete. And my consent to your marriage did not prevent your reproaches, for you prove that I am in any case to blame for your not marrying. Basically, however, in this as in everything else you have only proved to me that all my reproaches were justified, and that one especially justified charge was still missing: namely, the charge of insincerity, obsequiousness, and parasitism. If I am not very much mistaken, you are preying on me even with this letter itself."[6]

The letter's last lines are the reason it was never sent; the letter had already arrived at its destination: the author himself. The last paragraph superficially recognizes his father's reasons, while insisting on the son's own. However, the writer ends with the following: "in my opinion something has been achieved which so closely approximates the truth that it might reassure us both a little and make our living and our dying easier. Franz" (166). These are the words an analyst waits to hear when listening to the beautiful soul's account of his suffering. When the latter reaches the point in which a dialectical inversion of the complaint is produced, the analyst can determine that the preliminary interviews have concluded and the analysis can begin. This is the point where the subject reaches the limit of an accusing self-vindication and accepts responsibility for the *jouisssance* reached and/or rejected. The analysis takes him from then on in the direction of desire, in its double function as limit and road toward *jouissance*. The subject becomes, will have been, a mode of conjugating desire and *jouissance*, possible by and in language, in a different relation with unconscious *savoir*. The ethics of psychoanalysis is played out around desire, ceding it or not, as well as to a well-saying according to *jouissance*, now conjugated to desire.

This is the function assigned to the name-of-the-Father, to his *name*, a life-less authority in the symbolic world of words. Not the father who terrorizes the subject with an annihilating power, as Kafka details, but the one who can harmonize the law with desire, the signifier with *jouissance*. Desire and *jouissance*, the Other and the Thing. The experience of analysis begins and continues based on the dialectical articulation of the two pairs of concepts that split the subject ($). This is the reason why saying, the saying that deciphers, is the hinge and diaphragm that links them.

Two other historical and clinical examples not far behind Kafka's (in their celebrity and paradigmatic nature) come to mind, those of Freud and Lacan: subjects that construct themselves in saying and writing their desire, convoke desire and *jouissance* in a single act, which is called style, the stylus that leaves its mark in the Other with a historical inscription of desire. This desire is not a psychological variable, but constructed retroactively, starting with the fathers of psychoanalysis . . . and their analysts, disciples, institutions, dissolutions . . .

Give Up on Desire?

Jacques-Alain Miller has called attention to the errors committed when Lacan's seminar on ethics is read arbitrarily, when slogans, such as "do not give up on desire" are repeated, although Lacan never pronounced these words. This spurious slogan serves to justify perversion, tantrums, negativism, limitless egoism due to ignorance or the subjugation of the other. It is a perverse reading that confuses unconscious desire with the intention to *jouir*, by making *jouissance* pass through the affirmation of a sovereign ego. A Lacanian position stands against interpretations that advocate a "strong ego."

We must read the last class of Seminar VII attentively to notice his caution. Actually, one cannot compare the commonly apodictic Lacan with the one who notes: "It is in an experimental form that I advance the following propositions here. Let's formulate them as paradoxes. Let's see what they sound like to analysts' ears" (S VII, 319). He immediately adds, "I propose then that, from an analytical point of view, the only thing of which one can be guilty is of having given ground relative to one's desire" (S VII, 319).

The proposal states that giving ground on desire engenders guilt: this is a clinical fact, an irrefutable observation with ethical consequences.

The subject cedes his desire, and for this he has good reasons, the "best of motives": the Good, the Other's convenience and the subject's as well, given that his place is assigned in the Other by the Other. This entails betrayal and deception, either perpetrated by the subject to himself or what he accepts with the pretense of reciprocity (the Other would do the same: renounce his desire). However, this is not achieved, not because of the egoism of one or the other, but because each one's *jouissance* is incommensurable with the *jouissance* of the Other; the renunciations cannot be compared because loss and disadvantage are inherent to renunciation. *Jouissance* clamors and vindicates its offering. It does not accept exchanges or tradeoffs that tamper and betray it. The aim of desire is paid with a share of *jouissance*, the pound of flesh extracted from the body and claimed by the Other. It is the opposition between desire and *jouissance*: the two poles first presented in his May 5, 1958, seminar, where Lacan begins to reflect on *jouissance*, the unusual and inaccessible object of knowledge.

One does not give ground on desire without guilt because doing so implies putting it to sleep and nullifying its pro(*pulsion*), allowing for convenience, comfort, pleasure, the service of goods, the lesser evil, the calculated risk, submission to a manifested or supposed demand of the Other. It also implies conformity with the phantasm that renounces and realizes desire only in the imaginary, detains movement toward the inscription of the proper name and obedience to the Oedipal prohibition to not go beyond the father. Freud surely experienced sadness standing between the columns of the Acropolis, but his guilt would have been much greater had he not reached the observation tower and remained at the foot of the hill, not wanting to surpass his father (SE XXII). Sadness and solitude were the corollary of the achievement of his desire. Oedipus and his phantasms of crime and punishment function as sites of detention for unconscious desire, they protect from *jouissance* considered transgressive, incestuous, to be paid with blindness. For this reason, at the end of an analysis, having crossed the barbed wire of a law that orders apprehension and withdrawal before the possibility of achieving a *jouissance* that the Other (a subject of castration as well) had to renounce, what emerges is not awe but desire.

Freud could not reach Rome, climb the Acropolis, advance "such a long way": "there was something about it that was wrong, that from the earliest times had been forbidden . . . as though to excel one's father was still something forbidden" (SE XXII, 247). This is why in the letter to Romain Rolland, Freud mentions a previous text about those "wrecked by success." He finds that his incredulity and psychic refusal of having reached something fervently desired is the "universally valid motivation" of the Oedipus complex. In reference to desire it is safer to recoil, fade as a subject, suffer inhibitions, find refuge in neurotic symptoms, due to the antibodies that reject *jouissance* as alien or become paralyzed by *angst*, erected as a last barrier to disconnect desire from *jouissance*: inhibition, symptom, and *angst*. Neurosis, civilization and its discontents, derives from the Law that makes culture and the desiring subject possible, *jouissance* a transgression and crime and the desiring subject's ambitions damned, incomprehensible, mad. Culture is the discontent of a controlled *jouissance* that cannot be renounced.

It has been said that psychoanalysis is a practice not guided by ideals or prescriptions. However, the possibility of judgment is not excluded. The Freudian advancement of desire (in its relation to *jouissance*) to a central place in ethics allows for a critical revision of all the imposed detours of unconscious desire. Judgment (even the Final Judgment) before an ethics tribunal is therefore called for, where perjury is not permitted and an undisputable sentence is given, according to the subject's response to the question: "Have you acted in conformity with the desire that inhabits you?" (*Avez-vous agi conformément au désir qui vous habite?*, S VII, 314, translation modified). The question emphasizes the factual consequences of desire, and not desire itself: the action oriented by desire that is not someone's desire, but the desire that inhabits the subject. This is more nuanced and precise than Lacan's previous formula in that same class, regarding "giving ground on his desire" (*céder sur son désir*). Desire does not belong to the subject; desire is on the side of the Other and "inhabits" the subject. Lacan adds: "the standard of that reconsideration of ethics to which psychoanalysis leads us [is] the relationship between action and the desire that inhabits it" (S VII, 313); that action is inscribed in the tragi-comic dimension of life. Immediately following his question, Lacan insists that only in the analytic setting can it be posed in its purity. Just by being posed, he notes, it goes against Aristotle's traditional notion of ethics that celebrates temperance, restraint from extremes, and obedience to the master's enslaving and benevolent commands to defer desire. On this point, the ethics of psychoanalysis distances and challenges power.

Psychoanalytically, there is no innocent act. The act implies ethical consequences that make the actor guilty. The act is a creative irruption in the signifying order that entails transgression and parricide. The analytic hero is not innocent, but faces up to guilt. The aim is not beatitude or absolution. If God (the father) is dead and forms the basis of the unconscious order, it is because we have killed him. One is guilty for merely existing, separating (although impossible) from absolute alienation in the desire of the Other. One is guilty of affirming a word, traversing castration to explore the limits of phallic *jouissance*, filtered by the diaphragm of speech.

There are thus two types of guilt. One is experienced for giving ground on desire: imaginary, expressed in masochistic phantasms of punishment and redemption; the other is real, faced as the price of desire, assumed and proclaimed as an achievement of desire. This latter desire vindicates Nietzsche's madman in *The Gay Science*. Later, in *On the Genealogy of Morals*, he adds: "For cheerfulness-or in my own language gay science-is a reward: the reward of a long, brave, industrious, and subterranean seriousness, of which, to be sure, not everyone is capable."[7]

Jouissance, the measure and reason for the act, carries the shadow of parricide. Yes, "consciousness makes us guilty," but due to a guilt that is prior and unnamed. Oedipus, unconscious, is no less guilty than Antigone, who knows her crime. What's more, because Oedipus did not know his crime, the Other (the Chorus) is willing to pardon him, but he understands there is no possible absolution, and self-mutilation ensues. Antigone, his daughter and sister, accepts her guilt arrogantly and descends to the sepulcher to comply with the sentence pronounced by the Other of the Law. She has no regrets and does not punish herself. On the contrary, she defends her act and champions another law that commands her, a law higher than her political persecutors'. Analytic heroism distinguishes, in line with Hegel, between these two models of crime and punishment. It chooses between the one who acts in accordance with his desire and is able to designate himself as "I where Id was," confronting the responsibility of his subject position, and the one who unconsciously gives ground to the illusions of narcissism in the form of self-inflicted suffering and destruction.

"The only thing of which one can be guilty is of having given ground relative to his desire." This is the case for Oedipus, not for Antigone. Oedipus sacrifices himself for the service of goods, the well-being of the city; he abdicates and exiles himself. Antigone traverses the limits of her own comfort and other's, personified by her sister Ismene. Antigone vehemently refutes arguments regarding the advantages of political obedience, while Ismene speaks to her in name of the feminine condition that imposes submission to the dictates of the Other. Antigone responds from the perspective of a different idea of femininity, linked to the desire of the

Mother, which in Sophocles's text points to what has not been regulated by the name-of-the-Father. Antigone thus speaks from the space of not-all within the phallic function: a desire that points not to the phallus but beyond, to the signifier missing in the Other, the reason that The woman does not exist.

Beyond guilt and *angst*, accepting that castration is original and structural, the analytic hero makes his play, risks and loses, touches the limits of the (im)possible in function of desire and what flows beneath the signifying chain, unarticulated and inarticulable: *jouissance*, writing on the body's parchment. He puts himself beyond good and evil and the legal organization of daily life, which makes all creative acts a punishable crime by the persecuting superego. Or by the Other who polices and punishes the subject after traversing the internal chains of the superego, obeying its fundamental imperative to experience *jouissance*. Here it is a question of a prior guilt that reins back an act in conformity to desire, contraposed to castration as punishment. An analysis shows the futility of the threat of punishment already executed, although it is not truly punishment since only by traversing it does *jouissance* become possible.

The subject confronts the threat and reveals its innocuousness because of desire. Having passed the first and essential castration and received the inscription that makes phallic *jouissance* function, there is no castration but aphanisis, the fading of the subject, its disappearance due to the demand of the Other (neurosis). The neurotic gives ground on his desire, protects himself from it as if it were dangerous. The fulfillment of desire is worse than frustration, and that is why he renounces the former, "to put his desire in his pocket" (S VIII, 229). When it can be fulfilled, *angst* and inhibitions ensue. The phobic subject is the one who best illustrates this.

Phallic *jouissance*, the effect of the subject's passage through castration, evokes and circles around incest, but is also a precarious and always uncertain guarantee that there is no incest, that the subject is something more than object @, surplus *jouissance* of the Other, and subject to its demand. The access roads to sexuality are the exit roads from incest, while chastity is incestuous because the subject is chained to the incestuous *jouissance* of the Mother, representing a perverse maternal *jouissance* with his own body. The latter is the most generalized form of feminine perversion that disavows there is another *jouissance* other than phallic *jouissance*: through the possession of the child's sexuality (male or female), subject to her edicts, literally sub-jected (underneath), at her feet. Fetishism is etymologically sanctioned. It is worthwhile recalling Freud's astute clinical observation here: obedience to the superego, sacrificing phallic *jouissance* in order to satisfy its demands, does not result in peace of mind. On the contrary, the subject is besieged by scruples and guilt the more "virtuous" he is. The renunciation of the drives increases discontent in people and culture.

For Three *Jouissance*(s), Three Superegos

The Freudian superego is heir to the Oedipus complex, replacing the threat of castration as an external danger by an internal regulation of the drives.[8] The superego is conceived as a system for allowing and prohibiting *jouissance*. If obedient to the law and within certain limits, *jouissance* is permitted, although restrained, pruned by the scissors of castration.

The Lacanian superego cannot be confused with Freud's. Its imperative is not to obey, but to experience *jouissance*, while *jouissance* is precisely what the Freudian superego prohibits. *Jouissance* is transgressive and has little to do with obedience. Having earlier differentiated between the three *jouissance*(s), the question is what the commandment to experience *jouissance* means, given that the three *jouissance*(s) are so different from a clinical and topological consideration that makes them mutually exclusive. Is it a question of experiencing *jouissance* before, instead of, or after castration? Are we inclined toward *jouissance* of being, phallic *jouissance*, or *jouissance* of the Other? Do we choose the conception of an annihilating superego that organizes an irresponsible madness; a regulating superego that allows and prohibits, but is always subject to its neurotic demands; or a transgressive superego that orders recognition of a desire that inhabits the subject, making the latter a Law allowing the road to *jouissance*?

I propose that Lacan's rich formulation that the superego orders *jouissance* can be understood only by paying attention to the ambiguity of his statement, which acknowledges the polysemy and polyvalence of *jouissance*. In this proposal one recognizes a triple superego that includes the Freudian superego, stumbling on the live rock of castration, and the Lacanian superego for which symbolic castration is not an absolute limit. The latter acknowledges it as access to the field of language and discourse made possible by the function of the paternal metaphor. However, it traverses symbolic castration by inscribing desire in the real through acts that break with imaginary specularity and symbolic authorizations. These acts challenge normativity in their very realization.

The triple differentiation is made between (1) a primitive superego, ferocious and obscene, demanding unrestrained *jouissance*, alien and before language, which ignores the name-of-the-Father as the metaphoric function leading to desire, Kleinian, to distinguish it from; (2) a Freudian superego that follows from the first: pacifying (and not to be trusted, *pas si fiant*); it promises a reward for obedience to the Ideal ego (derived from identifications with the signifiers of the Other, admonishments, a voice), uses the force of guilt, recommends halting the path to desire, accepts "it cannot be done," and leads subjectivity down the road to impotence, inhibition, symptoms, and *angst*. The two superegos described above must be distinguished from (3), the Lacanian superego that fosters experiencing *jouissance*, like the other two, but with an essential difference. In this superego, *jouissance* must pass through discourse and the *semblant*, which aspires to recover the lost *jouissance* (*recherche*) beyond prescriptions and barriers, confronting the subject with a limit (*nec plus ultra*), the impossible against which the subject stumbles as the effect of the inexistence of the sexual relation (S XVIII and CS).

Because of its clinical implications, this third superego must be distinguished from perversion, which could be its outlet, just as the other two could result in psychosis and neurosis. The difference is subtle and important: the difference between making *semblant* of experiencing *jouissance*, proper to perversion, and experiencing *jouissance* from making *semblant*: a Dionysian gay science that goes beyond the failure to order knowledge and life according to the Apollinean goals of plenitude, integration, and harmony between man and world or between man and woman. Beyond guilt and ideals, beyond the pleasure principle, good and evil, the father and meaning, but not beyond the *semblant* or the mask.[9]

The relation between the Lacanian superego and the pervert's obedience to experience *jouissance* by providing it to the Other is subtle but substantial. It is not a relation of exclusion because, at the end of analysis, desire takes the place that a normative and Freudian superego (condemning the subject to impotence) previously occupied; the perverse act is not prohibited due to legal codes. The subject can now attempt it, having to decide only if he wants what he desires and consents to a desire he discovers inhabits him. There is no prior condemnation, only the possibility of deciding. Herein lies one of the differences with so-called "perversion." The latter obeys the imperative that "barely accentuates the function of desire in man" (E, 697). The difference is structural: while the analysand identifies with his lack and acts in function of that lack, in perversion the subject identifies with the lack in the Other, but disavows it, making himself the instrument of *jouissance* "missing" in a woman. In other words, he acts as though there were only phallic *jouissance* and disavows feminine *jouissance*.

The pervert takes the place of object @ to ensure the *jouissance* of the Other through a representation in which he is the *semblant* of *savoirjouir*. The analyst, as a result of his own analysis, is in the place of the *semblant* of @, the place of lack in knowledge and *jouissance*. From that place, the analyst questions the split subject: posing the question of desire to the Other, rejecting all pretense to do away with lack, making ignorance act, recognizing *jouissance* in its horizon of impossibility, and letting the subject venture down the roads of the signifiers: the *jouissance* of making *semblant*, inventing *savoir*, to become excited, but not agitated, acting in conformity with the desire that inhabits in him.

The superego we have called Freudian, which commands submitting oneself to the threats of castration, remainder or heir to the Oedipus complex, is the basis of a particular form of *jouissance*: the *jouissance* of the neurotic symptom and guilt. This *jouissance* emerges with the subject's retreat from castration. In this sense, it is a phallic *jouissance* not able to channel itself in discourse; it is retained in the body and therefore considered "pre-phallic" or, as doctrine establishes, "pregenital" (as if the only genital were the phallus). It is a *jouissance* of the signifier, yes, but subject to secondary repression. Its effect is registered in *lalangue* as the oral manifestation of remorse.

Guilt and the phantasm of punishment ("A Child is Being Beaten") are not foreign to *jouissance*. On the contrary, a twisted *jouissance* is woven around them in which the subject invokes and offers himself as sacrifice, at the mercy of the *jouissance* of the Other. This *jouissance* is the basis for the compulsion to repeat, which led some analysts to speak of "fate neurosis" to designate a perverse phantasm that imposes conforming to the supposed perverse phantasm of the Other and his *jouissance*. Self-punishment and paranoia, dispossession, recurring accidents, prisons, misfortunes, surgeries—these are not the signs of having acted according to one's desire. Rather, desire is alienated in the phantasm of the *jouissance* of the Other, an Other to which both castration and its failure are offered. Guilt and remorse are within the realm of phallic *jouissance*: masochistic and Oedipal phantasms, punishments imposed for retreating before unconscious desire.

Jouissance as an effect of the superego's punishment exists, and the subject is mortified to know this. Melancholy and obsessive-compulsive neurosis thus appear as the breeding grounds for *jouissance*. Freud spoke of the segregation (*Entmischung*) of the drives in such cases. In his fiction, Kafka showed this obscure *jouissance*, the subjective desert of *jouissance*, which corresponds to renouncing desire in order to submit oneself to the enigmatic *jouissance* of the Other. The feat of experiencing *jouissance* by not experiencing *jouissance* is not the hysteric's exclusive legacy. The superego is *jouissance* without desire, outside or instead of desire.

On Love in Psychoanalysis

In Seminar X, Lacan states that only love allows *jouissance* to condescend to desire. For this miracle of reconciliation of opposites to be possible, the subject must be a desiring subject, inhabited by a lack that closes off the path to the *jouissance* of being and opens access to an Other *jouissance*, "trans-castrational." It is necessary for the subject that the Other be @, undergo "@dentification," represent the cause of desire that allows challenging external obstacles, the barriers of internal impotence. Going down this road leads to an "@-morous" dis-encounter, to the a-*mur*, the impermeable wall of inaccessibility that surrounds the Thing. The encounter between desire and *jouissance* can take place only with the emblems of castration and supposes breaking loose from the corresponding *angst*. As we noted at the end of chapter 2, between desire and *jouissance* there is, if not love, *angst's* unbridled and dissolving scream.

Psychoanalysis has a close relation to love because only love can be the passageway for the awaited and defended "condescendence" to take place. In analysis, the good (we have to overcome a certain embarrassment in saying it in order not to be justifiably accused of a "pastoral tackiness," as Lacan was also well aware) is related to desire conjugated with *jouissance* and, therefore, with love. One cannot suppose here a new idealization of romantic love or a return to the pious praise found in the first pages of Plato's *The Banquet*, which reach their extreme in the *Phaedrus*. There love is enshrined as a "fatal destiny" toward which one can only assume a forced courage. It is not a question here of passionate love or grandfatherly love founded on the reciprocity of compassionate comprehension. Rather, it concerns love as an unavoidable misunderstanding, an equivocation that, good or bad, leads to the reproduction of bodies.

For "condescendence" to emerge, *jouissance* must be rejected, lost, renounced, separated from the body by the Other of the signifier and the Law. The condition for love is primary repression. Its backdrop and location is the unconscious. It grows out of the Law on the prohibition of incest that makes the primordial Mother a prohibited object for *jouissance* and induces desire through phallic inscription. This desire only finds objects that evoke what was lost and carry the mark of difference: particular objects that are and are not or are because they are not the Thing. Prohibiting it, the Law makes *jouissance*. All love has this guilty backdrop that circles transgression, wanting and requiring it.

From *jouissance* and auto-eroticism, passing through the Law to desire ordered by the Law. *Jouissance*, yes, but directed toward the other (the "extroversion of libido," if we recur to psychoanalysis' past) not inward. Consequently, there is an unconscious link between masturbation and incest and the corresponding guilt. Auto-eroticism leads to pleasure, which is the reason for a paradoxical *jouissance*: the *jouissance* of transgression, remorse, the punishment imposed by the Other, who keeps accounts on *jouissance*, worries about what the other experiences with his body, carries the whip, madness, or the flames of hell to justify his law.

Neurotically, the subject guarantees the Other by imagining he is a perverse transgressor. Pleasure thus serves *jouissance* by evoking guilt. When this guilt is lessened, the *jouissance* accessible to the neurotic is as well; sexuality becomes one more activity from which to get more or less gratification. Finally it is tainted by sensations of boredom, observed nowadays as the effect of the much-proclaimed "sexual revolution," which has not altered at all the neurotic condition of repression that preceded it. On the contrary, it has been fueled by sexuality, making it a motley mix of products that allows for a lucrative business without offending anyone.

The "wisdom" of the Judeo-Christian tradition consists in this neurotic strategy that allows the sexual to become the stronghold and paradigm of *jouissance*, displacing the rest of the body, limiting the male organ, subjecting it to a strict legislation and linked to the notion of sin. The counterpart is, logically, the localization, restriction, and exclusion (within limits) of feminine *jouissance*, earlier confined to maternity. This legislation condemns *jouissance* to asking forgiveness after being held accountable before the great Other, the final and generous beneficiary that concedes absolution to the self-incriminating and repentant sinner. The result of this operation, other than an increase in culture's discontent, has been the constitution of the erotic and the origin of a prolific mythology of love in the West. The legal institution of civil matrimony and its sacramental position schematically divided sexuality into opposing camps: obligatory and prohibited. To make sexuality an obligation, a subsection of deontology, a responsibility toward the *partenarire*, affects narcissism and creates an aggressive tension that justifies La Rochefoucauld's maxim regarding the incompatibility between marriage and delights (*Il y a des bon mariages, mais il n'y en a point des délicieux*), whose rigor is highlighted by Lacan (E, 97).

As we know, *jouissance* establishes itself in a concurrent relation to the *jouissance* of the Other. "You will not covet your neighbor's wife" is at once a pleonastic and impossible commandment. Pleonastic because any woman is the woman of an Other and impossible because it is precisely as the woman of an Other that she is desired. We have said from the beginning that the object can be possessed only on the imaginary stage of a dispossessed other. Only this dispossession makes it an object of desire; such is the case with the breast, a woman, and the phallus. The first woman is the father's woman, later the brother's, later the rival's. To desire her in the imaginary is to consummate the dispossession of the Other that demands his good. *Jouissance* is only possible at the price of sin. If the Other does not exist, it is necessary to invent him. That is, invent the being at the cash register who sees everything and demands payment. Omnipresent, the Judeo-Christian God goes inside the bedroom, observing and condemning, occupied and preoccupied by what one does with his phallus: with his *partenaire* (partner) or his hand. In this sense it is clear that the so-called sexual revolution has provoked a certain undermining of eroticism and even of pornography.

Neurosis, a universal suffering that is the effect of the primacy of the master's discourse, is the condemnation of desire and has various forms: forewarned, unsatisfied, or impossible. Such desire, beyond castration, is constructed as the only regulator in the ethics of psychoanalysis; it is the "incommensurable and infinite means" at the center of our experience as analysts and underlies the only valid question we can ask (ourselves): "Have you acted in conformity to the desire that inhabits you?"

It is important to clarify that desire cannot be confused with the phantasm, a shackle to *jouissance*, an imaginary construction that plugs up and maintains the subject at a distance from *jouissance* (neurosis) or acting on behalf of the *jouissance* of the Other (perversion), making *semblant* of not experiencing *jouissance* in the former and affirming *jouissance* in the latter. Because the Phallus (Φ) is a universal signifier, *jouissance* is prohibited to one who speaks. The *parlêtre* spends his life turning round it with his sayings and living his castration (-φ). The phantasm is the stage for *jouissance* as possible, presenting in the imaginary the fusion between subject and object, thinking and being, man and woman, phenomenon and noumenon, the rational and the real, the *semblant* and truth, all united without lack or loss. The phantasm is inspired by the desire it dulls and substitutes. It is the subjective response to lack in being, but also misleads the subject, presenting him with the mask of the real that is consensual reality, the ideological sphere of significations and meaning. The fundamental difference between psychotherapies and psychoanalysis has to do with the ethical choice between reviving and correcting the phantasm, on the one hand, or traversing it and thus placing oneself beyond its function to plug up desire, on the other.

Lacan's clinical observation regarding the relation between "giving ground on desire" and guilt is commonly read and transformed into an insistent and inexistent motto about "not giving up your desire." The desire that must not be given up is immediately confused with the phantasm of an imaginary realization of desire, supposing a fusion between the subject (\$) and the object @, ignoring what is essential about the formula of the phantasm, the *losange* ◊ that separates the two elements. This reading of Lacan's seminar leads to a perverse interpretation of psychoanalysis that supposes the subject stages the phantasm's realization and thus disavows castration, which orders the recognition of the real (the Thing) as impossible. The aim of analysis is certainly a freed desire, but freed from a phantasm of realized self-sufficiency, which anchors desire to the imaginary by proposing satisfactions that disregard the symbolic and exclude the real. The phantasm is the condemnation of a *jouissance* it pretends to represent.

In Pommier's book mentioned earlier in the chapter he points out what every psychoanalyst knows: the majority of analyses are interrupted after achieving a certain therapeutic effect and a certain staging of the phantasm, although the effects may well last forever. Must we lament that not all analyses can be taken to their logical conclusion? Or, perhaps we should ask what happens with analyses stopped at midpoint, when the subject reaches certain aims that resemble those of the pleasure principle?

The problem has an ethical dimension and concerns the good sought in analysis. If the cure does not coincide with the logical end of the analysis conceived as the construction and traversal of the fundamental phantasm, if there are "happy endings" without logic and final "logics" without cures, how to choose? The analyst does well to continue with the aim of making the diaphragm of speech flexible so that the subject may confront the truth of his being, a truth that borders death and the dismay of a deserted land filled with open junctions that ask why. But he may also recognize that the subject can, at a certain moment, show he is prepared to manage the suffering of existence. Lacan said that when this occurred in his clinic, he agreed they should leave: "An analysis does not have to be pushed too far. When the analysand thinks he is fortunate to be alive, it's enough" (Y, 15). The insistence in reaching the theoretical ideal of analysis can convert it into the imposition of a new ideal, a re-phan-tasmatization of the desire of the analyst, who after having traversed the imaginary formations that plugged up his desire, re-constructs it as a goal to be reached by the analysand, but where the analyst's ego is now involved. There must be space in analytic discourse for "the unfinished" instead of fragile formulations regarding the end of analysis according to always debatable criteria. Freud and Lacan knew this well.

Caution is needed when establishing criteria for the end of analy-sis because, whatever these criteria may be, they imply subjection to a new universal. There can only be criteria for the end of one (particular) analysis, infinitely variable according to each analysis. Better yet, criteria for the *denouement* of (one) analysis, as the title of Pommier's book sug-gests. Nothing allows assimilating the end of one analysis to another. One must also remember that the desire of the analyst, a desire without the phantasm, "is not a pure desire," but rather "a desire to obtain absolute difference . . . there only may the signification of a limitless love emerge, because it is outside the limits of the law, where alone it may live" (S XI, 276).

Since Freud, an analysis shows that a love without limits is a love that renounces its object, understanding that the object imposes limits on love and (pre)destines it to misfortune. This according to an errone-ously labeled pessimistic Freud, who transcends what he wrote regarding the unitive virtue of Eros. "Absolute difference" is found in *jouissance*, the traversal of *angst* and the phantasm, the dangers that prey on the indefinite and intransigent prosecution of desire. It is also a traversal of love as privileged space for reinforcing the narcissistic image through an encounter with a "soulmate." This absolute difference posits, if not a new art of love, at least a conception of love that goes beyond the specularity of identification, altruism, "mind your own business," "do unto others as you would have them do unto you," Kantian and Sadian categorical imperatives, reciprocity, oblativity, generosity, and other such forms under the rubric of "genital love." Yes, the end of analysis has to do with pure love, without object, absolute, without limits, without illusions of harmony or plenitude, at the margins of the law, starting from desire, where love and only love can make desire condescend to *jouissance*.

Notes

Notes to Introduction

1. Jorge Luis Borges, *Selected Non-Fictions*. E. Weinberger, ed. New York: Viking, 1999, 95.

2. See Jean Pierre Cléro, *Lacan et la langue anglaise*. Paris: Eres, 2012; José Attal, *La non-excommunication de Jacques Lacan, quand la psychanalyse a perdu Spinoza*. Paris: Cahiers de l'Unbévue, 2010; and Elizabeth Roudineco, *Jacques Lacan, esquisse d'une vie, histoire d'un système de pensée*. Paris: Fayard, 1993.

3. Attal (2010) notes that Lacan originally titled the seminar *Les fondements de la psychanalyse* (The Founding Principles of Psychoanalysis). In "The Non-Existent Seminar," J-A. Miller recounts that the circumstances of the interrupted seminar on the names-of-the-Father (in the plural) cannot be thought apart from why he was ejected from the list of teaching analysts. Lacan's teaching challenged the foundations of the psychoanalytic community: "to meddle with the Name-of-the-Father in psychoanalysis was still impossible . . . as if those who dare to interfere with the Name-of-the-Father were doomed to some act of vengeance." See *The Symptom* 12 (Fall 2011).

4. *Lalangue* is a neologism formed by *la* (feminine article) and *langue* (language). Lacan defines it in *Encore*: "*lalangue* serves purposes that are altogether different from that of communication. That is what the experience of the unconscious has shown us, insofar as it is made of *lalangue*, which as you know I write with two l's to designate what each of us deals with, our so-called mother tongue (*lalangue dite maternelle*), which isn't called that by accident" (S XX, 138, translation modified).

5. In keeping with the untranslatability of certain concepts and neologisms, we opted to maintain them in French, as they appear in Lacan's texts. Chapter 1 provides a detailed lexical analysis of *jouissance* and its verbal forms *jouir* (inf), *jouit* (third-person present), *jouissant* (participle), *jouirez* (second-person plural future). Other terms, concepts, or neologisms are translated in the body of the text or in chapter notes.

6. *parlêtre:* Lacan's neologism formed from the union of two verbs, *parler* (to speak) and *être* (being), often translated as speaking being or being that speaks. In order to avoid a translation that veers toward conferring an ontological status to the subject of the unconscious, we have opted to maintain the neologism in French.

7. N. Braunstein has published over twenty-five books and more than two hundred articles. Some of the more recent include *Psychanalyse et sculpture: trois essais.* J. Nassif, trans. Paris: Editions de Crepuscule, 2018; *Traduire la psychanalyse: interprétation, sens et transfe*rt. J. Nassif, trans. Paris: Eres, 2016; *A Cien Años de Totem y Tabú* (1913–2013). Mexico: Siglo XXI, 2013; *La memoria, La inventora.* Mexico, Siglo XXI, 2008; "Desire and Jouissance in the Teaching of Lacan," *The Cambridge Companion to Lacan.* M. Rabaté, ed. New York: Cambridge University Press, 2003.

8. Some examples of approaches to the concept of *jouissance* (in English): S. Zizek, *For They Know Not What They Do: Enjoyment as a Political Factor.* New York: Verso, 2008, and *The Metastases of Enjoyment: On Women and Causality.* New York: Verso, 2006; T. McGowan, *Enjoying What We Don't Have: The Political Project of Psychoanalysis.* Lincoln: Nebraska University Press, 2013; and A. Zupancic, *Ethics of the Real: Kant and Lacan.* New York: Verso, 2000.

9. *Langagière:* relative to the articulation of language.

10. Elizabeth Roudinesco, *Why Psychoanalysis?* Rachel Bowlby, trans. New York: Columbia University Press, 2001, xi.

11. Roudinesco, 44.

12. See Pura Cancina, "Concepto límite," *Acheronta: Revista de Psicoanálisis y Cultura* (Argentina), n° 14, 2001. Retrieved from www.acheronta.org.

13. Néstor Braunstein, "Gozología." Unpublished conference presented at the Argentine Psychoanalytic Association (APA), March 2018.

14. See Sara Glasman, "La satisfacción." *Conjetural, Revista Psicoanalítica,* n°. 7, August 1985, 86–103.

15. For a discussion of this debate, see A. Eidelsztein, *Las Estructuras Clínicas a Partir de Lacan II.* Buenos Aires: Letra Viva, 2017.

16. Néstor Braunstein, Untitled conference presented at Umbral (Barcelona, Spain) on February 4, 2017.

17. Braunstein notes that a theory of clinical structures can be found as of the 1950s in critics of Lacan, such as Serge Lebovici, Sacha Nacht, Maurice Bouvet Jean Laplanche, and André Green. J-A. Miller promotes this theory as early as 1981 and abandons it in 2008. See *La Cause Freudienne,* n° 71, 63–71.

18. J. Lacan, *Talking to Brick Walls.* A.R. Price, trans. Cambridge: Polity Press, 2017, 90–91, translation modified.

Notes to Chapter 1

1. In the 2001 edition, "to fornicate" was replaced with "to have intercourse."

2. See Georges Canguilhem, *On the Normal and the Pathological*, trans. C. Fawcett (Holland: Reidel, 1978).

3. See J. Clavreul, *L'ordre médical* (Paris: Seuil, 1979).

4. Translator's note: "Se-duction" and "to se-duce" here play on the third conjugation of the Latin *ducere* (to lead or command). The Other leads the child toward him or her.

5. See C. Soler, "Le corps dans l'enseignement de Jacques Lacan," *Quarto* 16 (Brussels), 59.

6. The reader may be surprised to find @ when referring to what Lacan considered his only invention. Lacan used the letter "a" in two ways: *a* in cursive indicated it was an imaginary object—the formula for the phantasm ($\$\Diamond a$) and the image of the other i(*a*) in the graph of desire—as well as "a" without the cursive, when he invented the *objet* a, belonging to the register of the real. I propose using @ when referring to this object: a lowercase "a" followed by a tail or spiral, *arobase* in French; the "a" is enclosed in the unfinished and not closed letter "o" of object. This typographical sign is now commonly used and appears in our "writing machines." It has no sound (it is @-phonic), a pure letter, thus avoiding the signifying ambiguities of "a" in different languages: the preposition "a" (in Spanish), the conjugation of the verb to have in French (*il/elle a*), the indefinite article in English, a definite feminine article in Portuguese, and so on. @ lacks a specular image because it is only a place, which in English is especially clear given that it is read as "at." The @ notation would have been unthinkable when Lacan invented the object "a" and up until 1990. It is advantageous to avoid ambiguities when discussing the four discourses. Whoever reads @ knows he is in the realm of the Lacanian algebra.

7. See M. Gerez, *Las voces del superyo*. Buenos Aires: Manantial, 1993. This is a detailed study of Freud's conception of the superego in the psychoanalytic clinic. Lacan's texts and teaching also provide an impressive account of this concept, which will be discussed in more detail in chapter 8.

8. E. Bergler, *The Basic Neurosis*, New York: Grune and Stratton, 1949.

9. J-A. Miller, *Recorrido de Lacan*. Buenos Aires: Manantial, 1986, 149–160.

Notes to Chapter 2

1. Diana Rabinovich, *Sexualidad y significante*. Buenos Aires: Manantial, 1986, 47.

2. See SE XIX and E ("Introduction to Jean Hyppolite's Commentary on Freud's 'Verneinung,'" "Response to Jean Hyppolite's Commentary on Freud's 'Verneinung,'" and Appendix 1: "A Spoken Commentary on Freud's 'Verneinung' by Jean Hyppolite").

3. If psychoanalysis is a "jouissology," as we claim, we must emphasize it is not an *érotologie*, as Lacan once proclaimed—rather an "erothanatism" that recognizes the omnipresent death drive.

4. Lacan corrected and re-elaborated this part of his teaching in his post-1970 seminars.

5. Translator's note: "La letra con sangre entra" is an expression commonly translated as "to spare the rod is to spoil the child." Here the author plays on the relation between the body and the word.

6. Translator's note: See E ("Psychoanalysis and its Teaching"). Lacan referred to Melanie Klein as a "tripière de génie" (gutsy genious, *tripera genial*). In an interview published in 1989 (*Cuadernos del Area Clínica*, No. 8, Agosto 1989, Monterrey, Mexico), Klein acknowledged she was labeled "La tripière" in France and deemed it was because she had guts.

7. See H. Kohut, *The Restoration of the Self*. Chicago: University of Chicago Press, 1977; L. Rangell, "The Object in Psychoanalytic Theory," *Journal of the American Psychoanalytic Association*, 33(2) 1985: 301–334; M. Gill and I.Z. Hoffman, *Analysis of Transference*. Vol. I and II. International Universities Press, 1982.

8. F. Nietzsche, "On Truth and Lies in an Extra-Moral Sense."

9. See J. Granon-Lafont, *La topologie ordinaire de Jacques Lacan*. Paris: Point Hors-Ligne, 1985, 45–67.

10. F. Scott Fitzgerald, *The Great Gatsby*. New York: Scribner's, 1953, 182.

11. See Derrida, *The Postcard*; L. Irigaray, *Speculum of the Other Woman*. G. Gill, trans. Ithaca, NY: Cornell, 1985; C. Soler, *What Lacan Said About Women*. J. Holland, trans. New York: Other Press, 2006; D. Luepnitz, "Beyond the Phallus," *Cambridge Companion to Lacan*. UK: Cambridge, 2003.

12. See NP as well as M. Tort, *Fin du dogme paternel*. Paris: Aubier, 2005.

13. In 1998, four years after the first French edition (based on the first Spanish version) of my book *Jouissance*, Patrick Valas published *Les dimensions de la jouissance* (Érès). This text relies on my work but does not provide any citations or references to my published text. On pages 78–80, Valas criticizes the position I am here presenting regarding the differences between the *jouissance* of being (pre-*langagière*) and the *jouissance* of the Other (post-*langagière*). I have no problems discussing this point, but wouldn't it be worthwhile to reference the author and text with which he disagrees? The same can be said of Marc-Leopold Levy's *Critique de la jouissance comme une* (Érès 2005). In pointing to these suspicious and flagrant omissions, I would also like to give my thanks to all those authors who recognize the existence of the first edition of this book.

14. After the publication of Gilles Deleuze and Félix Guattari's *Anti-Oedipus: Capitalism and Schizophrenia* (1972), Lacan criticized the centrality of Freud's Oedipus Complex much more.

15. C. Soler, "Abords du Nom-du-Pere," *Quarto* (Brussels) 8: 1982, 61.

16. Lacan's expression is not a happy one. Who can speak (psychoanalytically) of "normal" and "abnormal"? If we are all *parlêtres*, why use terms that are ideologically charged by normative discourse?

17. Lacan, "Court entretien à la R.T.B," *Quarto* (Brussels) 22 (1985): 31.

18. See Freud, *Beyond the Pleasure Principle* (SE XVIII) for a discussion of introversion and the withdrawal of libido.

19. Karl Polanyi, *The Great Transformation. The Political and Economic Origins of Our Time*. Boston: Beacon Press, 2001, 49.

20. Norman Brown, *Life against Death: The Psychoanalytical Meaning of History*. Hanover, NH: Wesleyan University Press, 1985, 267. Chapter 15 of this book can be considered a reflection on *jouissance*.

21. Aldous Huxley, *Point Counter Point: A Novel*. London: Chatto & Windus, 1954, 410–411.

22. The first to introduce the ethical consequences of these notions was G. Bataille, whom Lacan knew and quoted frequently: "the extension of economic growth itself requires the overturning of economic principles—the overturning of the ethics that grounds them. Changing from the perspectives of *restrictive* economy to those of general economy actually accomplishes a Copernican transformation: a reversal of thinking and of ethics. If a part of wealth (subject to a rough estimate) is doomed to destruction or at least to unproductive use without any possible profit, it is logical, even *inescapable*, to surrender commodities without return . . . The industrial development of the entire world demands of Americans that they lucidly grasp the necessity, for an economy such as theirs, of having a margin of profitless operations. An immense industrial network cannot be managed in the same way that one changes a tire . . . It expresses a circuit of cosmic energy on which it depends, which it cannot limit, and whose laws it cannot ignore without consequences. Woe to those who, to the very end, insist on regulating the movement that exceeds them with the narrow mind of the mechanic who changes a tire." See G. Bataille, *The Accursed Share*. Vol I. New York: Zone Books, 1991, 25–26.

23. "Structured *like* a language" means, according to Lacan's teaching from the 1970s, that it is not *a* language. To rename the Freudian unconscious, Lacan proposed several neologisms: *lalangue, le parlêtre, l'une-bévue*.

24. "Language is clarified, no doubt, by being posited as the device of jouissance. But, inversely, perhaps jouissance shows that in itself it is deficient (*en défaut*)—for, in order for it to be that way, something about it musn't be working" (S XX, 55, translation modified).

25. P. Julien, *L'étrange jouissance du prochain. Étique et psychanalyse*. Paris: Seuil, 1995.

26. J-A. Miller. Séminaire *Des réponses du réel*. November 18, 1983.

27. See Lacan, S III, X and "L'Etourdit": "The subject, as an effect of signification, is a response of the real" (AE).

28. Strachey's comment appears in a footnote on the same page.

29. Jean Laplanche and Jean Bertrand Pontalis, *The Language of Psychoanalysis*. D. Nicholson-Smith, trans. London: Hogarth Press, 1973, 321, my emphasis.

30. See Seminar X (class 13), Seminar XVI (Classes 9 and 20) and "Présentation des Mémoires d'un névropathe" (AE).

31. See Seminar X and "Position of the Unconscious," *Écrits*.

32. Translator's note: curiously, this neologism is missing from the *789 néologismes de Jacques Lacan* (Paris: Epel, 2002), so let there be 790. The *Littré* lists "causative" but not "causation." It does appear in the *Oxford English Dictionary*.

Notes to Chapter 3

1. P. Bruckner and A. Finkielkraut, *Le nouveau désordre amoureux*. Paris: Seuil 1997.

2. Translator's note: "phaultic" is a play on the words "phallic" and "fault" (*faute*).

3. H. Marcuse. *Eros and Civilization. A Philosophical Inquiry into Freud.* Boston: Beacon Press, 1974.

4. R. Graves and R. Patai, *Hebrew Myths*. New York: Greenwich House, 1983, 69.

5. In Spanish there is a marvelous ambiguity in the word *ablación*. (Translator's note: the author here plays with the meaning of *ablación*, which refers to a cut and is also homophonic with "*habla(ción)*," referring to speech, the activity of *parlêtres*.)

6. See A. Koedt, "The Myth of the Vaginal Orgasm" in *Notes from the Second Year*: Women's Liberation (New York), 1968, 37–41. This was a landmark text in feminist thought despite being clumsy and phallocentric. See a very good commentary by J. Gerhard, "Revisiting 'The Myth of the Vaginal Orgasm': The Female Orgasm in American Sexual Thought and Second Wave Feminism," *Feminist Studies* 26(2) 2000: 449–476.

7. See J. Allouch, *La psychanalyse. Une érotologie de passage*. Paris: Epel, 1998.

8. J. Allouch, "Lacan et les minorités sexuelles," *Cités* (Paris) 16 (2003): 72.

9. See CF for a discussion of the difference between the phallus as signifier, organ, or *semblant*.

10. "What, from the point of view of *jouissance*, differentiates both *partenaires* fundamentally, puts an abyss between them which I indicate by making two references: that for the man is the erection, from the point of view of *jouissance* and for the woman, for which I can find no better term . . . what they call 'the blow of the elevator' " (S XIV, 6/21/67).

11. See S. André, *Que veut une femme?* Paris: Navarin, 1987.

12. See E, 610, and F. Perrier and W. Granoff, *Le désir et le féminin*. Paris: Aubier, 1979.

13. See S. André, *Que veut une femme?* and C. Millot, *Horsexe: essai sur le transexualisme*. Paris: Point Hors-Ligne, 1983.

14. See S. André and G. Pommier, *L'exception féminine*. Paris: Point Hors Ligne, 1985; and C. Soler, *Ce que Lacan disait des femmes*. Paris: Editions du champ lacanien, 1997.

15. Lacan, S XVII (2/17/69). The names in brackets were added to what was said by Lacan. The mistaken reference appears in the official edition of this seminar, S XVII, 80.

16. Translator's note: Braunstein here plays on the expressions Lacan uses to distinguish between well-saying (sometimes translated as well-stated) and saying well.

17. See M. Foucault, *Psychiatric Power* (1973–1974); *Abnormal* (1974–1975); *Society Must be Defended* (1975–1976); *The Birth of Biopolitics* (1978–1979); and *The Hermeneutics of the Subject* (1981–1982). This series of texts constitute a unified and transcendent body of work whose interest for psychoanalysis is evident, although the consideration it deserves is not always "just" for the author. Also see J. Derrida, "To Do Justice to Freud: The History of Madness in the Age of Psychoanalysis" (1992), a text that highlights Foucault's "injustice" in his assessment of Freud.

18. In May 2005, then-President of Mexico Vicente Fox declared, "the Mexicans in the United States accept jobs that not even blacks want." The scandal grew to international proportions, although the arrogant statesman never apologized, claiming he had been misinterpreted.

19. S. Freud, "A Letter from Freud." *The American Journal of Psychiatry:* 107 (1951): 786–787.

20. C. Melman, "Homosexualité" in *Dictionnaire de la Psychanalyse*. Paris: Albin Michel, 1997, 276–282. Translator's note: brackets within the quotation are Braunstein's ironic comments on Melman's definition of homosexuality. Symptomatically, in the second edition of this same dictionary (2001), Charles Melman's entry was removed, and he is no longer listed as a contributor.

21. See also J. Copjec, *Read my Desire. Lacan against the Historicists*. Cambridge, MA: MIT Press, 1994, especially Chapter 8: "Sex and the Euthanasia of Reason," 201–236.

22. See L. Martin, ed. *Technologies of the Self. A Seminar with Michel Foucault*. Amherst: Massachusetts University Press, 1988.

23. P. Veyne, "The Final Foucault and his Ethics." C. Porter and A. Davidson, trans. *Critical Inquiry* 20(1) (Autumn 1993): 1–9.

24. In a friendly conversation after his seminar, Allouch said he preferred not to speak about *jouissance* because J-A. Miller's circle had coopted the term.

Curious epistemological criteria! Not to be unfair to our friend, in his book *Le sexe du maître* there is an astute and appropriate exposition of object *a* as surplus *jouissance* and the masochistic characteristic of every *jouissance*, which agrees with the spirit and letter of our own formulations of 1990.

Notes to Chapter 4

1. J. Lacan, "Comptes rendus d'enseignement (1964–1968)" in *Ornicar?* 29 (1984): 7.

2. J. Gorostiza, *Muerte sin fin* (*Death without End*). Mexico: Fondo de Cultura Económica, 2000.

3. See J-A. Miller, seminars of 12/19/84 and 4/1/87 (unpublished).

4. J. Lacan, *L'étourdit*. C. Gallagher, trans. *The Letter* 41 (2009): 31–80.

5. See G. Bachelard, *L'intuition de l'instant*. Paris: Éditions Gonthier, 1932.

6. Jorge Luis Borges, "Biografía de Tadeo Isidoro Cruz" (Biography of Tadeo Isidoro Cruz) in *Obras Completas*. Buenos Aires: Emecé, 2004 (Trans.)

7. See also J-A. Miller, *Des réponses du reel* (Seminar 1983–1984).

Notes to Chapter 5

1. L. Israël, *La jouissance de l'hystérique*. Paris: Arcanes, 1996. This book appeared in French years after the publication of our original Spanish version of *Jouissance*. Other than the title, it has various points of contact with this chapter. Israël's book is the product of his 1974 seminars, but responds to ideas circulating at the time. Israël passed away in 1996, when his book was in print. It begins with "In Praise of the Hysteric," 43.

2. See C. Millot, *Nobodaddy*. Paris: Hors Ligne, 1988.

3. L. Israël, *L'hystérique, le sexe et le médecin*. Paris: Masson, 1976.

4. E.D. Bleichmar, *El feminismo espontáneo de la histeria*. España: Siglo XXI, 1998.

5. Sor Juana Inez de la Cruz, "Hombres necios que acusáis" in *Obras completas de Sor Juan Inés de la Cruz*. México: Porrúa, 2007, my translation.

Notes to Chapter 6

1. J. Lacan and W. Granoff, "Fetishism: The Symbolic, The Imaginary and the Real" in *Perversions: Psychodynamics and Therapy*. New York: Random House, 1956, 265–276.

2. Louise Rose, ed., "Freud and Fetishism: Previously Unpublished Minutes of the Vienna Psychoanalytic Society," *The Psychoanalytic Quarterly* 57(2) 1988: 147–166.

3. D. Diderot, "Natural Rights," in *The Encyclopedia: Selections*. Vol. 5 (1755). S. Gendzier, trans. New York: Harper and Row, 1967, 115–116.

4. Cicero, *Tusculan Disputations*. C.D. Yonge, trans. New York: Harper and Brothers, 1877, 133.

5. H. Nunberg and P. Federn, eds. "A Case of Foot Fetishism (#225)," in *Minutes of the Vienna Psychoanalytic Society*, Vol. IV, 1912–1918. New York: International University Press, 1967, 243.

Notes to Chapter 7

1. Jacques Lacan, *Petit discours de Jacques Lacan aux psychiatres*. Cercle Psychiatrique H. Ey, Sainte Anne. November 10, 1967.

2. Julia Kristeva and Jean-Michel Ribelles, *Folie Verité. Verité et vraisemblance du texte psychotique*. Paris: Seuil, 1979.

3. Christian Fierens, *Comment penser la folie*. Ramonville: Érés, 2005.

4. Aníbal Lenis B., "Interpelar la droga-dicción" in *Boletín de Estudios Psicoanalíticos* 2 (Cali, Colombia). The hyphen in the title encouraged our reflections in this section, as well as the author's affirmation that "without needing others that make demands on him, the drug addict is someone who 'creates' or 'administers' his own *jouissance*."

5. J. Lacan, "Séance de Clausure de la Journée des Cartels de l'École Freudienne," *Lettres de l'École Freudienne* 18, 1976.

6. Charles Baudelaire, *Les fleurs du mal*. Paris: Pléiade, 1975.

7. See Serge André, *Flac: A Narrative*. S. Faifield, trans. New York: Other Press, 2001.

8. See George Steiner, *Grammars of Creation*. New Haven, CT: Yale University Press, 2001.

Notes to Chapter 8

1. G. Pommier, *Le dénouement d'un analyse*. Paris: Point Hors-Ligne, 1987, 197.

2. N. Braunstein, "Los enunciados del analista," *El psicoanálisis y el lenguaje freudiano*. Mexico: Siglo XXI, 1982.

3. J.D. Nasio, *L'inconscient à venir*. Paris: Christian Bourgois, 1980, 19.

4. J-A. Miller, *Le neveu de Lacan*. Paris: Verbier, 2003, 180.

5. F. Nietzsche, *Beyond Good and Evil*. W. Kaufmann, trans. New York: Vintage Books, 1966, 230.

6. F. Kafka, *Letter to his Father*. E. Kaiser and E. Wilkins, trans. New York: Shocken Books, 1966, 128–132.

7. F. Nietzsche, *On the Genealogy of Morals*. W. Kauffman and R.J. Hollingdale, trans. New York: Vintage Books, 1989, 21.

8. G. Gerez Ambertín, *Las voces del superyo*. Buenos Aires: Manantial, 1993; and *Imperativos del superyo. Testimonios clínicos*. Buenos Aires: Lugar, 1999. These two works summarize the essential elements for psychoanalysis on this topic.

9. G. Vattimo, *Il soggetto e la maschera*. Rome: Bompiani, 2003.

Index

alienation, 16, 36, 63, 78, 95–98, 127, 149, 161, 220, 227, 233, 238, 242, 264

addiction, 46, 67, 84, 220, 227–33

Allouch, J., 119, 130, 133, 137, 141, 281n24

angst, 25, 83, 89, 92–100, 140, 181, 214, 228, 240, 244, 249, 258, 263–69, 273

body, 16–34, 36–45, 51–57, 62–68, 76–100, 107–12, 116–29, 133, 146–50, 155–61, 166–69, 179–81, 186–94, 199–270

Brown, N., 101, 293

Canguilhem, G., 19

castration, 6–9, 22–32, 38–41, 61–65, 73–90, 95–136, 169, 179–272

Das ding (the Thing), 4, 6–9, 25, 29, 32–38, 45–46, 51, 56–64, 67–95, 106, 110, 120, 125–28, 155, 214, 218, 221, 226, 239–45, 261, 269–72

Derrida, J., 5, 74, 278n11, 281n17

Dean, T., 134–42

Descartes, R., 19, 65–66, 250

desire, 1–9, 16–274

discourse, 5, 8–27, 37–70, 79–89, 102–21, 126–32, 137–90, 196–214, 218–25, 231–73

drive, 6–7, 23–30, 42–79, 86–93, 103–8, 111–21, 137–43, 153, 162–77, 198–241, 255–69

ego, 4, 9, 16–31, 39–42, 51–70, 90–99, 141, 146, 150–53, 159–68, 178–81, 192–203, 208–9, 214–74

ethics, 17, 36, 40, 52–58, 74, 108, 138–49, 206–9, 240–63, 271

Eribon, D., 133

Ferenczi, S., 103, 114, 141

Fitzgerald, F. S., 73

Foucault, M., 131–43

Granoff, W., 124, 197

Granon-Lafont, J., 128

hysteria, 175–96. *See also* neurosis

Hegel, G. W. F., 17–18, 43–45, 180, 202, 206, 264

Huxley, A., 87–88

Imaginary, 16, 26, 37–39, 50, 63–82, 86–94, 98–100, 106, 113, 118, 122, 126–29, 146–53, 165–66, 171, 178, 183, 186–90, 192–94, 200–202, 207–10, 213–20, 226, 240–46, 252–56, 262–66, 271–73, 277n6

Kafka, F., 233, 258–69

Klein, M., 64, 226, 267, 278n6

Law, 4–9, 16–30, 36, 42–44, 50,
57–92, 103–32, 157, 195–209,
225–36, 245–74
Lalangue, 2, 64, 83, 147–48, 158–62,
170, 268, 275n4
love, 29–32, 37–42, 50, 58, 62, 65,
99–119, 130–31, 140–41, 146, 165,
175–81, 187–93, 198–205, 214–18,
230–36, 243–48, 269–74

Miller, J.-A., 6, 43, 52, 79, 261, 275n3,
276n17, 281n24
Mobius strip, 5, 27–28, 77, 126–29,
186

name-of-the-Father, 30, 73–84, 90–92,
99–103, 106–10, 120, 126, 132, 157,
184, 194, 218–30, 243–52, 260–67
neurosis, 21–24, 37, 66–67, 83–84,
99, 147, 161–62, 176–87, 197–208,
218–20, 237–55, 263–71. *See also*
hysteria
Nietzsche, F., 68, 122, 127, 213, 247,
257–58, 264

object *a*, 1–9, 26, 38, 51, 61, 63,
67–108, 119, 121–22, 130, 138–40,
148, 163, 179, 183, 187–192,
196–213, 219, 223–72, 277n6
Oedipus complex, 30, 44, 65–68, 78,
90, 101, 112–14, 118, 226, 246–48,
262–68

perversion, 67, 83, 87–88, 92, 99, 106,
115, 133–38, 179, 183, 188, 193,
197–215, 236, 244, 261–68, 271

Phallus, 6, 29–38, 63, 122, 73–132,
182–232, 246–71
pleasure, 14–72, 85–122, 137–49,
162–68, 184, 193–94, 205–17,
229–44, 257–72
Polanyi, K., 87
Proust, M., 149, 163–71, 248
psychoanalyst, 7, 14–15, 27, 68–69,
84, 103, 122, 124, 133, 135, 142,
148, 175–83, 191, 202, 210, 221,
241, 251, 256, 272
psychosis, 61, 67, 80–83, 109–10, 127,
161–62, 169, 199–201, 206, 217–
67

queer theory, 104, 131–43

Rabinovich, D., 52
real, 4–8, 21–28, 36, 38, 41–59,
60–63, 68–84, 88–98, 109–27,
129, 147, 149–55, 162–63, 165–72,
187–252
Roudinesco, E., 3

savoir, 3–4, 9, 19, 24–26, 66–69,
79–82, 88–92, 112–25, 150–54,
169–72, 190–218, 235–60, 268
sexuality, 21–22, 27–32, 38, 46, 62,
75, 83, 88–89, 98, 101–43, 195–271
sexuation, 6, 75, 124–25, 138, 191,
212, 258
Soler, C., 23, 80–81, 191
symbolic, 4, 8–9, 16, 23, 26–30,
39–41, 45, 50, 55–56, 60–63, 68–94,
99–103, 108–15, 120–26, 148–53,
187, 202, 219–52, 261–72

trauma, 21–24, 40–42, 167, 177, 199

Printed in the USA
CPSIA information can be obtained
at www.ICGtesting.com
CBHW021051100124
3325CB00005B/74